WILD MARY

Patrick Marnham lives in Oxfordshire. His most recent book, *The Death of Jean Moulin: Biography of a Ghost* – about the French Resistance – was described by the *Daily Telegraph* reviewer as 'a brilliant mix of political thriller and wartime history'. He is the biographer of Georges Simenon and Diego Rivera, and has been awarded the Thomas Cook Travel Prize and the Marsh Biography Award. He started his career on *Private Eye* and is a former literary editor of the *Spectator* and Paris correspondent of the *Independent*. He is a Fellow of the Royal Society of Literature.

ALSO BY PATRICK MARNHAM

Fantastic Invasion: Dispatches from Africa
So Far from God: A Journey to Central America
The Man Who Wasn't Maigret: A Portrait of Georges Simenon
Dreaming with His Eyes Open: A Life of Diego Rivera
The Death of Jean Moulin: Biography of a Ghost

PATRICK MARNHAM

Wild Mary

A Life of Mary Wesley

VINTAGE BOOKS
London

Published by Vintage 2007

10

First published in Great Britain in 2006 by
Chatto & Windus
Random House, 20 Vauxhall Bridge Road,
London SW1V 2SA

www.vintage-books.co.uk

Addresses for companies within The Random House Group Limited
can be found at: www.randomhouse.co.uk/offices.htm

The Random House Group Limited Reg. No. 954009

A CIP catalogue record for this book
is available from the British Library

ISBN 9780099498179

Penguin Random House is committed to a sustainable future for
our business, our readers and our planet. This book is made from
Forest Stewardship Council® certified paper.

Typeset in Sabon by Palimpsest Book Production Limited,
Grangemouth, Stirlingshire
Printed and bound in Great Britain by Clays Ltd, St Ives plc

Contents

List of Illustrations

Unless otherwise stated, all the photographs are from Mary Siepmann's albums or from private collections.

The author and the publishers have attempted to trace holders of copyright in both photographs and text quotations. If there have been any inadvertent omissions or errors, these can be corrected in future editions.

'. . . As the years go by the truth becomes more and more agitated; the energies that go into the maintenance of the fortress are herculean; the guns must be manned night and day . . .'

Diana Petre, *The Secret Orchard of Roger Ackerley*

Introduction

Jumping the Queue

In January 1970, a failed writer named Eric Siepmann living in a remote cottage on Dartmoor and suffering from Parkinson's Disease was taken to hospital, unconscious. There, four days later, having contracted pneumonia, he died. The inquest was held in Torquay and the verdict was 'natural causes'.

Eric Siepmann's death left his wife Mary and their teenage son with a widow's pension, £50 a month, no savings and no professional qualifications. Throughout the years of their marriage Siepmann had written plays, poems, novels and short stories, as well as works of criticism and popular philosophy, but very little had been finished and nothing published, with the exception of one forgotten novel and a short memoir of his life as a youthful philanderer. When his life ended, he could look back on twenty-five years of failure. Mary Siepmann had never been to school and was unqualified to teach; she could scarcely cook and so, to make ends meet, she took a series of casual jobs in antique shops. She knitted jerseys and sold them to people she knew, and in summer she rented out her cottage and went to stay with friends. She had a small monthly income from a family legacy, but it often arrived late; and at the end of each month, while waiting for her pension, she frequently lacked the money to buy heating fuel or postage stamps.

All her life she had tried to teach herself to be a writer. Despite many failures she had never given up and a few months before Siepmann's death, two of her children's books had been accepted by different publishers. They were well received but made no money. By 1977 she had finished a third book, about children communicating with the dead, and an adult novel that was about a widow's decision to commit suicide, but she failed to find a publisher for either.

In her handbag Mary Siepmann kept a small engagement diary and in

1978 – eight years after her husband's death – she wrote 'Please do NOT Resuscitate' inside the front cover. This message became an annual habit. At the back of her diary she noted the Samaritans' twenty-four-hour emergency number for people in despair. She had three sons but her youngest had left home and no one had visited her that Christmas. The last time she had seen her second son, Toby, she had said, 'I've worked it out. If you go on coming to see me like this I will see you twice more before I die.' She spent both Christmas Eve and New Year's Eve on duty for Torbay Samaritans, listening to other people's suicidal thoughts.

In 1981 her car, an elderly Mini, failed its annual test and she realised that she could not afford to repair it unless she sold her cottage on the moor and moved into a town. She put her house on the market the following day. A letter arrived from her literary agent saying that both the novel, *Jumping the Queue*, and the children's book, *Haphazard House*, had been rejected by a further six publishers. Just after her house went on the market, Mary fell ill and in her under-heated cottage she developed bronchial pneumonia. In February of that year a retired naval officer seeking a property to buy on Dartmoor was sent to view an isolated cottage above Buckfastleigh, and instructed to let himself in. Having looked around the ground floor he went upstairs where he found the vendor, a woman of sixty-nine, in bed, too ill to speak but able to wave him on to continue his tour. He offered to get her an oxygen cylinder and returned later with his wife, saying that if she had not seen the situation for herself she would never have believed it.

Mary Siepmann had been brought up not to complain by stoics who did not complain, but her diary entries tell the story.

Friday: *ILL*
Saturday: Very *ILL*
Sunday: Very *ILL* raving
Monday: very ill [in handwriting too shaky to read clearly]

By Thursday it was 'Still ill never felt so terrible in my life'. On Sunday she had a diagnosis: 'BANGCOCK [*sic*] FLU is something special'. On Monday the doctor must have called again – 'Double pneumonia'. And sixteen days after first going to bed she wrote, 'Temperature back 104.' It was three weeks before she was up and dressed after an illness that had nearly saved her the trouble of taking an overdose.

If her story had ended there, no one who knew the unhappiness she had experienced since the death of her husband would have been very surprised. But a week after her recovery Cullaford Cottage was sold and she became absorbed in the effort of packing up and moving to a small terrace house in the centre of Totnes, her local market town.

Much as she had been attached to the cottage at Combe, where she had lived for seventeen years, Mary found life in the centre of Totnes a welcome distraction. In a 'very tall house in a narrow street squeezed between a pub and a Gospel Hall', spurred on by morning hymns and evening profanities, she started to paint her shelves, unpack her books and hang pictures. Carpets were fitted, a new bed delivered and her son, Toby, who had been living and working in New York for fourteen years, moved back to London and started to visit her again. He was in need of her help with a High Court case that threatened to ruin him. All this gave her a renewed sense of purpose and the words 'Do NOT Resuscitate' disappeared from the front of her diary.

In July 1981 her literary agent, Tessa Sayle, wrote to her once again about her two unpublished titles, *Jumping the Queue* and *Haphazard House*. 'I don't feel we would have much chance of finding anyone willing to take either of these books. However I shall be very happy to keep the Mss and mention them to publishers as I see them, just in case someone is adventurous enough to give it a try. I cannot undertake to submit them actively until things improve . . .' Stimulated by her new life, Mary decided not to take this semi-dismissal lying down. It was true that the publishers had not been encouraging. Constable returned *Jumping the Queue* with the comment, '[We have been] put off by the general morbidity . . . quite a creepy book . . .' Macdonald, who had published one of her earlier children's novels, wrote that *Jumping the Queue* was 'Not commercial enough'. Eyre Methuen and Michael Joseph were unconvinced. Dent found the characters 'too off beat to believe in'. These criticisms, sweeping and undefined, left little scope for rewriting, but she was confident that her books were good and the novelist Antonia White, a very sharp critic, had admired *Haphazard House*.

In October Mary paid a visit to Washington and New York, paid for by Toby and a friend, Kate Ganz, and while there she tracked down the London-based publisher Anthony Blond who found himself taking her out to lunch. She began a campaign to sell her books herself. The only way she could do this was by personal introduction, the fate of unsolicited manuscripts submitted by complete strangers being too well known. In

May 1982, after a year of self-agenting, Mary wrote to Tessa Sayle saying that she had found two publishers who had agreed to read her Mss. 'I hope you don't mind this?' she wrote, with the hesitance, modesty and good manners of the unpublished writer. 'Would you be so kind as to send the right manuscripts to each of these publishers? I shall be most grateful.' Tessa Sayle duly sent off the books and for two months there was the customary silence. Mrs Siepmann went to Cornwall for two nights to stay with friends and to visit Boskenna, the great stone house standing on the cliffs near Land's End where she had spent so much of her youth. At home she continued to attend Sunday Mass regularly at Buckfast Abbey, where her husband was buried, and wrote to congratulate Father Gabriel Arnold after he had preached an uncompromising sermon against the Falklands War. A month later she noted that the Argentinian forces had surrendered. On 23 June her diary entry reads 'Car accident'. And then, in the space of two weeks, her life was transformed by three events.

On 10 July she received a telephone message that the High Court case that had concerned her so much was settled, she would not face cross-examination and her costs would be paid. On the envelope containing the letter from her solicitors that confirmed this news she wrote 'Black cloud lifted'. Two days later she heard that *Haphazard House* had been accepted by Dent; her third children's book would finally be published. And then, on 27 July, Tessa Sayle telephoned her again to report that Macmillan wanted to take *Jumping the Queue*. After thirty-five years of writing and rejection her first adult novel had been accepted.

When she sold her first novel Mary could not afford to travel to London to meet her publisher. On the back of an envelope that reached her that week she wrote the times of the trains from Totnes to Paddington and beneath, in large letters, '£50', the amount of money advanced to her by Tessa Sayle to enable her to pay for the trip. It was a year almost to the day since Sayle had written saying that it was not worth continuing to submit either book. Mary was seventy years old.

What was truly remarkable about her achievement was not the age at which Mary Wesley started her career as a professional author, but her reaction to success. On the day after she returned from the meeting in London she was at her desk and by the autumn 'Work' had become a settled daily entry in her diary. She was no longer writing in a personal vacuum. By 5 March, seven months after *Jumping the Queue* had been accepted, she had completed her final draft of what she was already calling *The Camomile Lawn*. Macmillan accepted *The Camomile Lawn* on 19 April,

Jumping the Queue was published nine days later and on 12 May, when she received the contract for her second novel, her diary reads 'Work on new Book'. *The Camomile Lawn* was published in March 1984 and the third book, *Harnessing Peacocks*, was put on a train to London on 12 September and accepted three days later. This explosion of energy continued over eight years, with a book being delivered one year and published the next, a speed of production that went a long way to ensuring the author's commercial success.

In some ways Mary Wesley's first novel was untypical of the nine that followed.* *Jumping the Queue* was written from immediate experience and had been completed unhurriedly over a period of three or four years as part of the process of grieving. The heroine is Matilda, a widow in her fifties who is planning to 'jump the queue' – commit suicide. She lives in an isolated country cottage and her four children seldom visit her. Her closest and most dependable friends are her animals, a gander, a cat and a dog. She has worked out the perfect method of suicide; have a party – for one. Take a bottle of good Beaujolais and a ripe Brie to a quiet beach on a summer's evening and, after a last supper, swim out to sea. Following the failure of Matilda's plan, caused by the unexpected arrival on the beach of gatecrashers, a noisy party of young 'hoorays', she returns home but on the way meets a man who is on the run from the police. He is suspected of murdering his mother and he too is about to commit suicide. Matilda gives him shelter and then tells the fugitive the story of her life. Her two daughters are sluts, her favourite son is homosexual and never comes to see her, her other son is a crashing bore, her best friends tell her that her adored husband used to sleep with them, her oldest male friend reminds her that he is the only person who knows that she once committed a murder by pushing ('biffing') her husband's mistress into the frozen Serpentine and watching her slip through the ice. The woman had been called 'Felicity'.

Although *Jumping the Queue* differs from the rest of Mary Wesley's writing, it already contains the mixture of humour and menace that were to become characteristic. Matilda, interrupted in her ideal suicide by the superior young 'hoorays', pees into the hollow of a rock where they are about to lay out their picnic. As she leaves the beach she can hear their

---

* *Jumping the Queue* (1983) was followed by *The Camomile Lawn* (1984), *Harnessing Peacocks* (1985), *The Vacillations of Poppy Carew* (1986), *Not That Sort of Girl* (1987), *Second Fiddle* (1988), *A Sensible Life* (1990), *A Dubious Legacy* (1992), *An Imaginative Experience* (1994) and *Part of the Furniture* (1997).

comments, 'Oh super . . . what a super salad dressing. What did you put in it? I've never tasted anything like it, it's super.' Matilda has an aching sense of loss for her husband, though his death was not recent and despite what she has learned about him since. Her children are bored by her grief. Her background is middle-class and criminal. In her world, middle-class crime frequently goes unsolved; crimes such as rape, smuggling, murder, aiding fugitives from justice and heroin dealing are undetected and attract little official attention. For successful completion these crimes require no more than a certain forbearance with life's setbacks, a little planning, a little luck, a cool head and a plausible manner. To all appearances Matilda remains an inoffensive, law-abiding figure who finds solace for her loneliness and grief in the company of pet animals. She decides to end it all but instead introduces a suspected murderer into her home. She then drinks too much and goes to sleep; the fugitive lies awake and listens to her snoring. During the night Matilda wakes up screaming in fear. She is old enough to be the fugitive's mother and the crime for which he is wanted is the murder of his mother. She starts to think about matricide. Is it such a 'special' crime? She had often longed to kill her own mother and she begins to calculate which of her four children would be capable of killing *her*; three of them certainly, not her beloved homosexual son, no, but only because he could not be bothered.

Mary Wesley always resisted any suggestion of a connection between her fiction and her life, but to anyone who knows about her life the biographical references are there in her novels. The nature of the link that can properly be established between a novelist's work and life was described by Evelyn Waugh, writing after the early success of his second novel *Vile Bodies*:

> There must be a connection of some kind between a writer's work and his life. His knowledge of the world is limited by his experience . . . a writer who has never been seriously in love cannot make his characters seem so . . . But here the connection ends. Nothing is more insulting to a novelist than to assume that he is incapable of anything except the mere transcription of what he observes . . . Novel writing is a highly skilled and laborious trade . . . One has for one's raw material every single thing one has ever seen or heard or felt, and one has to go over that vast, smouldering rubbish-heap of experience . . . until one finds a few discarded valuables. Then one has to assemble these tarnished and dented fragments . . . and try to make a coherent and significant arrangement of them.

In the case of Mary Wesley some of the characters and events she described in the ten novels she wrote between the ages of seventy and eighty-four chime with the events of her biography. But the most interesting links are not to be made with the daily events of her life, but with her subconscious reactions to these events. The imaginary world Wesley created in her last two decades was dark, humorous, complex and high-spirited. During that period she worked for months in succession, living in the company of the characters who came swarming up from the cellars of her imagination after so many years of knocking, demanding to be released. She wrote in a tearing hurry, acutely aware that there was little time left, and so impatient to start the next book that she could barely manage to complete the work in progress. From the start, her characters inhabit a world in turmoil; a world threatened by moral disintegration, whose confident certainties dissolve as its ruling class decays. A senior civil servant awaiting his knighthood is remembered for raping his best friend's wife. The Range Rovers peel off the motorway for a family reunion in Wiltshire, driven by an MP, a chief executive, a diplomat; these men are meeting to impose an abortion on their younger, unmarried sister-in-law. Cousins go off to war, ready to die for their country, having raped the girl who hero-worshipped them.

Mary Wesley's style was uninhibited; it was arsenic without the old lace. Matilda strikes the authentic note when she says, 'I adore fucking.' In *A Dubious Legacy*, her eighth book, with the best still to come, daily life has taken on demonic form. One reviewer wrote, 'There is real malignancy here . . . [Mary Wesley] has a truly nasty bite.' Another said, 'She has a superb eye for the little deceptions and secrets which cement families together.'

The 'little deceptions' in this plot include the seduction of two young wives by a much older family friend, so that when he is on his deathbed both the goddaughters nursing him with such touching devotion are, unknown to their legal 'fathers', his own natural daughters. The family life Wesley described so expertly was not just based on deception and secrecy, it was dysfunctional. But to an Italian journalist who asked her to explain the 'ambiguous and nightmare atmosphere' of her work she said, 'I write about life as it could easily be, and very often *is*.'

If the families were dysfunctional their individual members, particularly Mary Wesley's heroines, were disconnected, by choice or circumstance, from all family affection or support. The disconnecting circumstances included early bereavement, war, impossible parental pressure to conform or parental abandonment – or sometimes a combination of these trials. The solutions her characters found included suicide or flight, domestic service or a career of seduction.

Mary Wesley's novels began to appear twenty years after the Youth culture of the Sixties had replaced the more respectful society of the post-war period. Time had put her on the wrong side of this generation gap, so she was well placed to break the taboo of her respectable generation's silence by informing the children of the Sixties and Seventies, and the grandchildren of the Eighties and Nineties, that their parents and grand-parents had led lives at least as interesting as their own. Women readers were attracted to her heroines, who defied convention to live life on their own terms, and paid the price if they had to.

As time passed she became a celebrity and dominated her countless publicity interviews, teasing each new inquisitor with the best of all diver-sions, a slightly different story. The stories were intriguing and broadly correct, but they were designed to distract attention from a far more remark-able story that she was careful not to reveal, and one that helps to explain the violence and darkness of her books. Asked why she had stopped writing fiction at the age of eighty-four, Wesley gave a characteristically clipped response: 'If you haven't got anything to say, don't say it.' In fact, she did have more to say and she set out to write an autobiography. But she gave up when she reached the point where she was aged forty-one. In what was to be her final year she decided instead to talk to a biographer and describe how one woman of her time and class chose to live her life.

PART ONE

1912–1939

CHAPTER ONE

Snobbery and Poverty

'Habit and long success made the British look at the twentieth century through nineteenth-century eyes.'

James Morris, *Farewell the Trumpets*

Mary Wesley's early life was by her own account as dramatic as a novel and the narrative circled a number of fixed points. She had been a mutinous child who was rejected by her unaffectionate mother. Her mother had told her that she had been an unwanted child and that if she had to be born it would have been better if she had been a boy. Her mother also told her that she and Mary's father both loved Susan, Mary's older sister, more. In this situation she was comforted by her nanny, who became a near-mythical figure in the writer's memory. 'I had a wonderful Nanny . . . her name was Hilda Scott and she was marvellous but she was only with us until I was three . . . I once asked her what time was I born, and she said, "You were born when we were dressing for breakfast, darling, and your mother handed you to me and said, 'Here take the baby'." She was the be-all and end-all for me. She was much more to me than my mother, she took me on from the moment of birth until the day my mother dismissed her.' Her earliest memory of her father was when he sent a message up to the bathroom to ask her to stop screaming. She was screaming because she had just been told that Nanny was going and was to be replaced by a governess . . . '[When she left] I was standing at the top of the stairs in my grandmother's house . . . and I remember what I was wearing, and what Nanny was wearing, and that she was weeping . . . and I couldn't understand it. I can remember the pictures on the walls and where we stood . . . It made me very insecure; I've never felt secure again. I never got any security from my mother.'

All the warmth of Mary's childhood memories* was bestowed on either her nanny or her grandparents. 'I have a theory about my nanny, that she started me off writing. She used to tell us fairy stories. She'd say there was a Queen of the Fairies and a King of the Dwarves, and we used to write letters to them from a very early age, and then we'd get an answer, of course written by Nanny, which was absolutely lovely . . . When she left my sister and I continued to write these letters and my mother was very disgruntled because she had to answer them . . . Nanny always kept in touch with me . . . She was always loyal and whatever I did later in life, if I behaved badly and everybody was on top of me – because I was divorcing or something like that, she'd stand by me and she never criticised . . .'

Mary Wesley was born Mary Farmar at Red Lodge, Englefield Green, near Windsor, the home of her grandparents, on 24 June 1912. She was the third child of Harold Mynors Farmar, an officer in the Lancashire Fusiliers. In 1914, when Mary was two, her father went off to war and her mother, Violet, moved the family to London to live with her own mother, Hyacinthe Dalby, at 14 Montagu Place, off Bryanston Square, halfway between Harley Street and Hyde Park Corner. Mary, her mother and her older brother and sister, Hugh and Susan, lived in that house with its bottle-green front door throughout the Great War.

As a young surgeon Mary's grandfather, William Dalby, had kept polo ponies and bred pugs. Later he became a celebrated consultant, Sir William, 'the great ear, nose and throat man of his day'. He was knighted for pioneering work on lip-reading and the operations for mastoid and tonsillectomy. But by the time Mary knew him he had retired from St George's Hospital, Hyde Park Corner, and she remembered her grandfather in his wheelchair with a nurse and 'a terrifying Turkish bath in his dressing room. First there was a fierce old man with a white moustache shouting at the dachshunds and then there was an old man with a white beard quarrelling with his nurse.'

Mary could remember the first air raids on London in 1915, which caused great excitement among the children. Sir William declined to take cover, 'Why should I get out of bed to please the Germans?' he said and slept through the bombs. But the children were scooped up, wrapped in eiderdowns and taken down to the basement, where, beneath a print of Field Marshal Lord Roberts, they would wait for the boy on a bicycle

---

* Repeatedly published in newspaper interviews.

ringing his bell which was the signal for the All Clear. On one occasion Hugh, aged seven, 'always a disobedient boy', was in the hall when a Zeppelin in flames passed over the house on its way to crash in the park. Ignoring all warnings, Hugh rushed out into the night and the bombing with his mother shouting, 'Come in at once. You'll catch your death of cold.' On most nights, when she was small, Nanny carried Mary upstairs to bed. As they passed the white marble bust of the Duke of Wellington she was lifted up to kiss him goodnight. Lady Dalby did not reproach Mary when she grew tall enough to chalk the Iron Duke's mouth pink and to black-in a moustache.

The Dalby household included a cook, Mrs White, a parlourmaid called 'Brown' and four other maids, and there were also a number of animals. In the dining room there was a caged canary that was covered with a green baize cloth during meals to stop it trying to drown the conversation with its song. There was a dormouse and there were guinea pigs, various pugs, a Pekinese and a dachshund called Bingo. All her life, until she was too old to look after them, Mary kept animals, particularly dogs, and counted them among her friends. When the organ grinder came by, Lady Dalby went out to give him money with an orange for the monkey; Mary was made to stay on the steps and watch until the monkey had finished the orange. Her grandmother distrusted the organ grinder and suspected that he might eat the orange himself. On the outbreak of war, Bingo, the dachshund, was verbally abused in Hyde Park as 'a dirty Hun'. This did not dissuade the Dalbys from keeping another dog called Bismarck that had to be destroyed because it bit people, nor did it discourage Mary's mother and grandmother from speaking in German in front of the children.

Despite the war this was, for a child of four, a certain world. London was the capital of the Empire and Hyde Park was at its centre. The Duke of Wellington was not just a bust on the staircase; he was a naked warrior in the park, bronze and twice life size, with a luxuriant fig leaf struggling to cover his manhood. And he stood just outside the hospital where grandfather's fame had been won. For Mary it was all of a piece; Sir William seated in his bath chair, the Duke erect on his plinth and the King reigning on his throne, all formed a hierarchy in which she too had her place.

Apart from the Zeppelin bombing, Mary's clearest memory of the Great War was of seeing her father seated on a horse beside the King. In 1916 Mynors Farmar was appointed liaison officer to the 3rd Australian Division, commanded by General John Monash. On 27 September this division completed its training and, prior to departure for France, was inspected by King George V on Salisbury Plain. The 3rd Australian Division was twice as large as most divisions and it took two hours for its 27,000 men to march past. Mary, aged four, remembered the three horses in line, the King in the middle on a black horse, Monash on a chestnut and her father on a bay. She remembered that the King was the smallest of the three distant figures, and that when the parade was over she lost her favourite white teddy bear in a cabbage field. Mary also recalled how her father appeared to be 'sadder, thinner and grimmer' each time he returned home on leave from the front, with his head shaved because of the lice.

The war ended in November 1918, Sir William died one month later and Hyacinthe Dalby took over as head of the family. In an unpublished memoir Mary Wesley wrote, 'My grandmother was lovely. She had snow white hair, enormous brown eyes and black eyebrows and she was always calm. She wasn't really calm, she bubbled inside like I do, like a kettle, but calm she seemed. She became my adored one. She had a tremendously dominating personality under that velvet exterior and she never lost control except sometimes when she laughed, when the tears would stream down her cheeks as they do mine . . .' When Violet complained that she found her youngest child 'difficult', Mary's grandmother disagreed. And fierce Sir William, seated in his bath chair, once pointed at Mary with his stick and said, 'That child will have brains.' Looking back on her childhood Mary Farmar saw herself as the daughter of 'a wounded soldier'.

Mynors Farmar's military career spanned the death of the Empire he had been trained to serve. As a young officer in 1898 with Lord Kitchener's Nile Expedition he had been present at the Battle of Omdurman. This engagement came one year after Kipling, foreseeing imperial decline, published his prophetic 'Recessional'.

God of our fathers, known of old
Lord of our far-flung battle-line . . .

Omdurman was a classic instance of that far-flung battle line, an awesome demonstration of imperial power, mounted to avenge the death of General Gordon. Mynors Farmar, aged twenty, had held his commission for only four months when he found himself in the front line, facing a massed attack by 50,000 to 60,000 dervishes, but protected by modern artillery and the Maxim gun. Through field glasses he watched the Khalifa's Host as it approached. He remembered the chiefs riding into battle on caparisoned chargers, clad in chain mail and steel casques, some of which had been taken during the Crusades. By the end of the day forty-eight British lives had been exchanged for those of 11,000 dervishes.

Mynors saw no more action until the 25 April 1915, when he landed on the beach at Tekke Burnu on the first day of Gallipoli. As the men of the 1st Battalion, the Lancashire Fusiliers disembarked on to the submerged barbed wire, the sea turned red with their blood. They suffered a fifty per cent casualty rate within minutes of landing and six VCs were awarded 'before breakfast'. Mynors Farmar, who started the day as a captain and was twice wounded, ended it in command of the 86th Brigade, every officer senior to him having been killed. He was five times mentioned in dispatches, recommended for the VC and awarded an immediate DSO. Two years later, in 1917 in Flanders, as a major with the 35th Division, he was wounded again and awarded the CBE after the Battle of Passchendaele.

The Farmars were a military family. The social registers record a line of soldiers and sailors going back to 1599, when a younger son of Sir George Fermore of Easton Neston went to Ireland as a lieutenant and was granted large holdings of land. The Fermores became Farmars, served with Cromwell in Ireland, helped to found Pennsylvania and then resettled in Youghal in County Tipperary. By Mary's account the Farmars were hidebound, unimaginative and obedient to convention. But the progress of the family, as it racketed across the world and down the years in a wild chase after glory and plunder, could have inspired Fielding or Smollett. The Farmar baronetcy received in 1780 became extinct in 1916; the vast estates they purchased in Virginia were forfeit at American Independence. Captain George Farmar RN promoted Horatio Nelson to midshipman on HMS *Seahorse*, recaptured the Falkland Islands in 1770 and nine years later went down with his ship, HMS *Quebec*, guns blazing, after engaging a superior French force in the English Channel. Farmars governed Singapore and Malassa, then gambled away much of their wealth in the society of the Prince Regent. Mynors Farmar's father was Major-General William Farmar of the 50th Regiment (The Queen's Own) who was severely wounded in the Sikh Wars and who later served in the Crimea. Mynors's brother was Major-General George Farmar CMG, also of the Lancashire Fusiliers; he too served on the Nile and he was mentioned in dispatches ten times during the First World War. George Farmar married Bertha Paget, a descendant of the Earl of Uxbridge who had commanded the cavalry at Waterloo. Lord Uxbridge's leg was shot off while he was seated on his horse beside the Duke of Wellington. 'By God, I've lost my leg,' remarked Uxbridge. 'By God, and so you have,' Wellington replied.

The social registers that trace the connections of the old English ruling class make relatively few references to money, but without a clear picture of family fortunes it is impossible to understand how the class system of the eighteenth and nineteenth centuries worked. In contrast to other countries, such as France or Spain where the class system was inclusive, and where inheritance was divided again and again, the English followed a system of primogeniture in which the right of succession was restricted to the oldest son. This tended, over the generations, to make the rich richer and more powerful. It also meant that successive waves of younger sons had to learn to live by their wits and that society had to be flexible enough to allow them some reward. Where no reward was available, they had to look elsewhere; primogeniture may partly account for the rise of the British Empire. In social terms primogeniture meant that privilege and status were intimately linked with wealth. The wealthy were always welcome within the British aristocracy, however lowly their origins; while the impoverished were eventually expelled, however grand their descent. But despite the risks they took and the gallantry they displayed the Farmars never converted their plunder into a position of solid respectability; they were more successful as privateers than they were as placemen. In some ways Mary Farmar, headstrong and unruly, was a throwback to that age. And by the time she was born the Farmars had both feet on the slippery slope.

The family's financial decline had been caused by three considerable blows. First, the United Irishmen in the rebellion of 1798 burned out Mynors's great-grandfather's house at Fergus in County Cork. Disenchanted with Ireland, this Farmar decided to invest his fortune in Canada; so he liquidated his remaining wealth, bought gold bullion and chartered an American sloop to carry it out to the New World. Unfortunately the captain of the sloop was in collusion with a French privateer and the cargo was captured and taken to Bordeaux, where it was declared forfeit. As a result Mynors's grandfather was so impoverished that he could afford to send only one of his sons to Eton; the other boys were not given the same opportunity of consolidating contacts at school. The third blow came many years later. A trusted family solicitor (who would eventually receive seven years for embezzlement) absconded with grandfather William Farmar's entire fortune. His wife, who had some money of her own, had to pay William Farmar's debts. In his memoir Mynors wrote, 'A large family is a difficult thing to manage in the caste into which we were born, when means are small. There were some periods, especially just after the crash, when there were bad cooks and poor quality nurses . . .' And he told Mary that he could remember, at the age of eight, watching 'the horses and carriages diminish down the drive', and with them all chance of Eton or a smart regiment. For his six sisters it was worse. With no hopes of a dowry it was their future husbands who disappeared with the horses; only one of the six married, the rest died spinsters.

In this situation the support of William Farmar's second wife, Ellenor Girardot, who was of Huguenot stock, was decisive. Ellenor 'kept up with all her friends and relations', and kept their house in Southampton going. She died in her sleep in 1929, aged ninety-four, after giving herself her bath and putting herself to bed. Major-General William Farmar was eventually awarded £150 a year as a 'Good Service Reward' for his conduct during the Indian Mutiny. He devoted this money to his eldest son Hugh, getting him through Eton and Sandhurst, and into a good 'social' regiment, the 60th, the King's Royal Rifle Corps. George, the next in line, was clever and won open scholarships to a less expensive school and to Sandhurst.

So it came to the turn of Mynors, the youngest. His father died in July 1896, just before Mynors passed into Sandhurst, which meant that there was even less money around than before. But influence was mobilised. William Farmar had been a friend of the Duke of Cambridge whose retirement as commander-in-chief of the British Army, at the age of seventy-seven, had finally been accomplished one year earlier. If Mynors was to afford Sandhurst it would have to be with an honorary Queen's Cadetship. Fortunately his maternal uncle had married one of the Princess of Wales's ladies-in-waiting and there were friends at court. Mynors, aged seventeen, was introduced to Queen Victoria at a bazaar held at Carisbrooke in the Isle of Wight and on the Queen's personal recommendation he went to Sandhurst free of all expense. Limited means had prevented him from joining the influential old Etonian network, but at Sandhurst, and through his brother Hugh, he made many Etonian friends. 'My way was paved for me by my brothers' and my Father's friends,' he wrote in his memoirs. With the Lancashire Fusiliers in 1898 that way in theory lay bright ahead, to dominion and glory; in the event to Colenso, the Curragh Mutiny and the Amritsar Massacre, to Gallipoli and Passchendaele.

When he retired Mary's father wrote a memoir for his children that he entitled *Some Notes and Experiences of Harold Mynors Farmar*. It is a work of exemplary modesty – Gallipoli is dealt with in one page – but in some respects it might have been subtitled 'The Silences of Colonel Farmar'. Mynors's father, the Major-General, had sired thirteen children by two

wives over a period of twenty-six years. But Mynors makes no mention of
his father's first family at all, and writes as though he had two brothers
whereas in fact he had three.[*]

Another omission was rather closer to home. By his own account Mynors
married the younger sister of a beautiful woman with whom he had been
in love. Rose Dalby's portrait had been painted by Millais, but when Mynors
first met Rose in 1901 she was already married to a naval officer called
Charles Worsley. Worsley was frequently at sea, and Rose was living at
Wei-Hai-Wei, the leased British port and base in north China. Mynors,
who had become friendly with Rose's brother from weekends spent playing
country house cricket in England, now became infatuated with the flirtatious and highly attractive sister. To escape from inquisitive eyes on the
naval base, Rose engineered a trip to Peking, then 'the Forbidden City' and
a restricted area since the previous year's Boxer Rising. 'Somehow it was
arranged', wrote Mynors, 'that I should be escort.' Rose was to stay with
Dr Morrison, the celebrated *Times* correspondent and secret agent, 'in his
house in the Tartar City . . . [and] I was to take my chance . . .' Quite quickly
Mynors was invited by Dr Morrison to be a fellow guest. 'This was
delightful for me, but no one told me that the paper wall which separated
my room from that occupied by Rose provided a shadow show for her of
all that happened on my side. She was careful where she placed her own
lamp.' When Rose returned to Hong Kong she sent Mynors a present and
when they both returned to England she asked him to stay with her at
Devonport; by now their friendship had lasted for five years and Mynors
realised that it could be taken no further. Rose introduced him to her
parents and he began to call on Sir William and Lady Dalby in London.
It was 'during the third visit, in rather a crowded drawing-room, I began
my engagement to marry her sister Violet', and that is the first mention
in his memoirs of his wife. Mynors's affection for Violet was apparently
transferred from her older married sister.

Mary Farmar had military connections on both sides of her family. Her
maternal grandmother, Hyacinthe – who had married William Dalby – was
the daughter of Major Edward Wellesley of the 73rd Regiment (The Black
Watch). This officer had died of cholera at the age of thirty-one in the
Crimea, where he had been sent to join the staff of Lord Raglan, the

---

[*] The invisible man is his half-brother Richard, born twenty-five years before him,
who changed his name to Cotgrave to secure an inheritance.

commander-in-chief. After Edward Wellesley's death his widow was granted a grace-and-favour apartment in Hampton Court Palace in recognition of the fact that her late husband had been the great-nephew of the Duke of Wellington. In consequence Hyacinthe grew up beside the haunted gallery of the Palace.

Hyacinthe Wellesley, who lost her father in infancy, was descended from the 'unlucky' branch of the Wellesley family. In 1728 Richard Colley, a wealthy landowner of County Meath, succeeded to the estates of a cousin by marriage, Garrett Wesley, on condition that he change his name to Wesley, which he did. With this double fortune the Colleys, now 'Wesleys', acquired public office and titles. Within two generations the head of the family was made 1st Earl of Mornington and 'Viscount Wellesley' of Dangan Castle, all in County Meath.

The 1st Earl of Mornington had two remarkable sons. The younger was Arthur Wesley, a military genius who later became the 1st Duke of Wellington. Mary was descended from the 'Iron Duke's' older brother, Richard Colley Wesley who, by ending French rule in India, defeating Sultan Tippoo and destroying the empire of Mysore, brought southern India within the British Empire. Richard became Governor-General of India and when, in 1797, he was given an English barony he chose the title of 'Baron Wellesley of Wellesley in Somerset', so effectively changing the family name; his younger brother Arthur necessarily followed suit.* Richard Wesley, later Wellesley, who was Mary's great-great-great-grandfather, seems to have been a more complicated character than his more celebrated younger brother. In 1786, while visiting Paris as a young man, Richard had met a beautiful young actress called Hyacinthe Rolland. He took Hyacinthe back to London with him as his mistress and they had five children. In 1794, after the birth of their fifth child, Richard married her, but under the law of the day the existing children remained illegitimate. This was unfortunate for them, in view of their father's illustrious career. He was twice Lord-Lieutenant of Ireland, 1st Marquess Wellesley, a Knight of the Garter and 2nd Earl of Mornington, but despite all his influence and energy he never succeeded in getting a special bill through Parliament to legitimise his children. When he died his titles passed to a younger brother and there was little fortune to leave. In the end his adored elder son, also called Richard, who should have been the second Marquess, became an

---

* The Wesleys, whose name the Colleys had assumed in 1728, claimed descent from an Englishman called 'de Wellesley' who was alive in Ireland in 1261.

undistinguished member of the House of Commons, quarrelled with his
father over the way his mother had been treated and – having made two
attempts at suicide – died at the age of fifty-four, leaving an eight-year-old
son, Edward, the great-grandfather of Mary Wesley. 'My family', she once
said, 'was descended from the Iron Duke's older brother – but on the
wrong side of the blanket.'

The wrong side of the blanket was an uncomfortable situation without
the pillow provided by financial means. Hyacinthe Rolland was never
accepted either by Richard's mother or by London society; even Byron's
notorious mistress, Lady Caroline Lamb, was warned against attending
Lady Wellesley's parties. In *The Young Melbourne* David Cecil wrote that
Hyacinthe Rolland cannot 'have been very attractive in herself' since 'she
was a Frenchwoman of very shady reputation', in other words, a tart. David
Cecil produced no evidence to support this description and in any event
the Dowager Lady Melbourne, who issued the warning against Hyacinthe
Rolland, was herself thought to have borne three of her six children to
men other than her husband. Hyacinthe, in other words, was suspected of
low connections rather than low morals. When Richard eventually died,
having lavished a great deal of money on many women (the Iron Duke
thought that his brother should have been 'castrated'), he left his family
with little fortune and none of his titles.

The Marquess's oldest son had died in debt with his mind wandering.
His daughter, Anne, had very wisely married a wealthy young baronet, Sir
William Abdy. Anne Wellesley, like her mother, was a considerable beauty
and very spoilt, and she was, according to her mother, 'terribly hard to
control'. When she was sixteen her mother noted that, 'For all her pretty
smile and big languorous eyes she is far from gentle . . . She is a fine strap-
ping wench who promises to be precocious and to have violent passions.
I'm afraid when this girl falls in love, she will be untameable, impossible.'
This prophecy was fulfilled. When Anne did eventually fall in love it was
not with her wealthy husband. Sir William Abdy turned out to be not very
bright and more or less impotent.

There were no children of the marriage, Lady Abdy had numerous
admirers and in September 1815, three months after the Battle of Waterloo,
she eloped with one of them, Lord Charles Bentinck. The elopement took
place quite publicly from the Abdys' town house in Hill Street, Mayfair,
by gig, and caused a great scandal. Sir William, who was in love with his
wife, made a fool of himself by signalling his distress. He first agreed to
Anne's request, made under pressure, to take her back, and then when she

changed her mind he sued Lord Charles Bentinck for £30,000. The Duke of Wellington had to force a Bill of Divorce through Parliament in order for Anne to be married to Lord Charles before the arrival of their first child. Sir William never received his £30,000.*

The similarity in the fortunes of these two families, the Farmars and the Colley-Wesleys, is striking. Both were Anglo-Irish gentry, both at one point changed their name for money, both jockeyed for influence at court, in both cases financial imprudence led to ruin. The Wesleys eventually produced two men of genius, the Farmars were the more reckless and dashing, and prospered under the less formal rules of engagement of the eighteenth century. And both lived by the same code; if you could not afford the subscription you were thrown out of the club.

Mary Farmar was six years old in November 1918 when the Great War ended. Over the next fifty years her parents' assumptions, and those of 'the caste into which she had been born', steadily unravelled. Britain's far-flung but rather brief period of world rule had ended; the day of the nobility and the gentry ended with it, and their values became increasingly irrelevant. Unlike many, including her older brother and sister, Mary seems to have realised this. When she left childhood she was aware that she faced a choice as to who she would become. In making that choice she was no doubt influenced by the family baggage: the reduced expectations of the Farmars, the small crowd of skeletons in the Wellesley cupboard, illegitimacy, suicide, elopement, ruin, none of them highlighted in the reference books, but none of them entirely forgotten. And, somewhere in the background, the memory of Anne, a girl who had been 'untameable, impossible', who had married a suitably rich man, who had grown bored and bolted in a gig, and who had displayed a high-spirited enjoyment of sex.†

---

* Today's equivalent would be over £20 million in equivalent earning power.
† In the course of time Anne Wellesley was accorded a handsome posthumous rehabilitation when one of her children became the grandfather of the late Queen Mother and great-grandfather of the present Queen.

CHAPTER TWO

A Formidably Obstructive Child

'The very fact that a person is a relation can be irritating.'

Part of the Furniture

'I always felt a rush of pleasure when I saw my mother after parting,' Mary wrote in an unpublished memoir, 'but I do not believe the feeling was mutual.' Away from her mother, Mary could remember her courage and admire her, and forget about the rejection and constant disapproval, the distance that caused the gulf between them. Violet was conventional, not particularly clever and utterly without imagination; in addition she was highly possessive. 'She did not like me, but I was a possession . . .' Violet taught her children to love God and honour the King, and she taught them how to behave, but she never gave her youngest child the sense that she was loved. 'My mother was incapable of hiding her feelings,' Mary said, 'and I was just a boring appendage.' Many years later, in a confidential moment, Violet disclosed to Mary that because Mynors loved Susan best, she had to love Susan best as well, to stay closer to Mynors. Mary described this explanation as 'wonderfully tactless'.

Following the departure of Nanny, Violet started the system of governesses that would provide almost all the schooling Mary received. She had a series of sixteen French, Swiss, Italian and Danish governesses who taught her French, some Italian and long passages from Shakespeare and the Bible. She once asked her mother why there had been so many governesses and was told, 'None of them liked you, darling.' In later life Mary complained that she thought this must have been unfair, but at other times she admitted that she had been 'a formidably obstructive child'. She was eight before she agreed to learn to tell the time or read by herself, and even then she had to be bribed by her father with a box of chocolates which, as she always remembered, he eventually forgot to give her. Her first book was *Harry and Lucy* by John Ruskin. Her family nickname became 'Wild Mary'.

Mary was taught the piano, although she naturally declined to play it, and she read Scott, Dickens, Victor Hugo, Charles Kingsley, Charlotte M. Yonge, Grimm's *Fairy Tales*, *Alice in Wonderland*, Edward Lear and *Treasure Island*. Her mother first read *Treasure Island* to the children while they were on holiday in Devon, but she thought that Mary was too young and sent her out of the room. Violet had a very penetrating voice. Sitting in the dark on the stairs outside, alone, excluded for being too young, Mary could hear every word and was struck by how like the cove near their holiday house was Black Hill Cove in the book. For years afterwards she had nightmares about Blind Pew.

In November 1918 the family were staying in a cottage near Salcombe, in Devon, when the milkman told Violet about the Armistice; Mary remembered that her mother burst into tears. Her father came home for Christmas, her grandfather died on 29 December and they moved out of Montagu Place to start the gypsy life of an army family. In the first twenty-five years of married life, Mynors and Violet moved house twenty-seven times. They lived at Seaford, Woolwich, Nuneaton, Camberley and on Salisbury Plain. Mary hated this. 'We had no stability,' she said, 'and I grew up knowing no one of my generation because we were always moving. It became a habit with my mother. "I think your father would be happier in the country," she would say. And so we moved when there was no need to.' Mary responded with misbehaviour. At the age of seven she committed what she described as her 'first' theft, lifting some peanuts from a street vendor's stall in Portsmouth. She was marched back by her mother and made to apologise. Rebuked by a gentle old schoolmaster for inattention, she threw his silver-topped cane out of the window and then climbed on to the roof of the house, causing havoc while her parents were giving a dinner party. She practised 'the ready lie, the candid glance, the juggling with time' that were essential for successful deception. This behaviour helped to impair her scrappy education. To good French and some Italian was added a smattering of German, but nothing was ever done thoroughly and all her life she counted on her fingers. Susan and Mary were brought up in a Victorian way – sacrificed on the altar of male advantage. Mynors, who had been excluded from the magic circle by his own father's poverty, was determined to reinstate the family connections. So, while Hugh went to a regular prep school, followed by Eton and Balliol, and exhausted all the available money, the girls were left to fend for themselves with a governess and whatever books were to be found in the schoolroom library.

In the early winter of 1920 Mynors Farmar, now a lieutenant-colonel, was sent to Constantinople to join the staff of the Allied commander-in-chief. Violet joined him in the following April. Mary, whose 'splendid pigtails' were the envy of her circle, was left with Susan in the care of her grandmother and a Danish governess. It was the first of a long succession of years when her father was usually absent, in either the Levant or India. Four letters written by Mynors to Mary during her childhood were among her papers when she died. For her seventh birthday his letter came with 'this little gold pin . . . for your present, to keep all the days of your life . . . All love to you, dear little one.' Two years later he wrote to her from Constantinople, 'My dearest Mary, May your midsummer birthday be lovely . . . Bless your heart . . . I sat on the hill this morning and thought of you all . . . Your Daddy who loves you.' His Christmas letter of 1921 said, '. . . It is a year today since I said goodbye to you in the early frosty morning at 14 Montagu Place. It has seemed a long year to me away from you . . .' And in February 1923 he wrote to her from India, where he was in command of a battalion of the Lancashire Fusiliers, '. . . I soon shall come to you in my chimney corner and all loneliness will vanish too . . .' If Mary's relations with her mother were never loving or easy, she felt less rejected by her father, even though he spent so much of the time away. Mary who blamed her mother for many things, never blamed her father for his absence or neglect.

In 1924 Mary's mother sold their house in Camberley and took the children to Italy, in order to perfect their Italian. They went to Portofino, then a little-known fishing village, and stayed in a *pensione* which had marble stairs but no bath. The visit took place during the 'Mussolini election' in April, which was influenced by violence and intimidation, and she remembered the Fascists in Portofino with dog whips stalking up and down the piazza. In Portofino the popular response seemed to be not to vote at all. Violet and the girls next moved to Tuscany, where they were joined by a mysterious companion, 'Major Barnes', who was deaf but very erudite. He knew the whole of Dante by heart and – appalled by the 'villainous' Genoese accents they had acquired – taught them a pure Italian. Major Barnes was separated from his Italian wife, who lived in Milan, and he was in love with their mother. Violet, now with her *cavaliere servente*, took the children to Florence, Sienna and Assisi, where Mary fell in love with St Francis, appropriately enough since like many English children she regarded dogs as more or less human. They attended church frequently, and Mary was struck by the frescoes depicting hell in the Campo Santo, the burial ground in Pisa, after which other frescoes depicting heaven generally seemed 'rather wishy-washy'. It was in the city churches of Tuscany that Mary acquired a lifelong love of the theatre of the old Roman Catholic Mass. When she was sure that her mother was not looking she would disobey her instructions, dip her fingers into the holy water font and cross herself. In Florence they went to Mass at Santa Maria Novella, to hear the sermon of a Monsignore who had travelled up from Rome. The church was packed for the famous preacher. He chose to tell them the story of a saint who died in the odour of sanctity; her corpse smelt so delicious that people came from miles around just for the experi- ence. Mary remembered the story and how the church was in darkness, with only the pulpit lit up as the fiery sermon bucketed on. Her mother, who did not understand Italian but could identify a good accent, said that it all seemed a bit melodramatic but that the architecture had been interesting.

Violet Farmar was a good-looking woman whose hair went white when she was still young and who had 'strange grey eyes with thick lashes, eyes without any green or blue in them, just grey as granite, but not cold'. Violet was without fear. During a visit to Perugia, Mary saw two youths beating a mule and forcing it to haul an overloaded cart up a hill. Horrified, Mary shouted at them to stop and then, when she was ignored, attacked them. Just at that moment her mother emerged from a nearby shop to find her nine-year-old daughter struggling in the gutter with one of the youths. Violet promptly set about the second youth with her umbrella and as a crowd gathered she instructed the onlookers to wedge the wheels of the cart and release the mule; then, using Mary as her translator, she summoned the local *Fascisti* to unload the cart. Mary always remembered this inci- dent not for the role she herself had played but for the courage her mother had shown. It reminded her of an earlier incident, in 1918, when they were living near Salcombe in a cottage on the shore and one night, with an autumn gale and a spring tide, their precious dinghy was washed off the beach into a tremendous sea. Roused from sleep, Mary watched as her mother rushed into the great breakers in her dressing gown and nightdress to catch the boat and drag it to safety. Courage was taken for granted in Mary's family. In the same rowing dinghy her brother Hugh, playing truant, aged ten, had been swept out to sea one evening and had kept his head, waiting all night for the tide to carry him back into the bay. No one had missed him because he was thought to be in bed. Mary's sister Susan, an outstanding horsewoman, also possessed considerable courage; beside her Mary as a child was more timid and thoughtful.

Mary remembered one other incident that exemplified her relationship with her mother. They were walking together on the high cliffs at Bolt Head and Violet, standing on the edge, told Mary to come closer so that she could look down on to the waves crashing over the rocks below. But Mary refused. Her mother said, 'Don't be so stupid. I'll hold you.' But Mary refused again and would not approach the edge. Mary was not frightened of heights, she was frightened of her mother. 'I didn't trust her. Not one inch.'

Violet's limitations as a mother may have been a consequence of her own upbringing. Her mother, Hyacinthe, had been a very strong character with striking good looks and, like earlier Wellesleys, highly sexed. She had three daughters. The oldest girl, Dulcie, was conceived too soon after her first-born son, so Hyacinthe mounted her horse and jumped it at higher and higher fences, a reckless attempt at abortion that failed to work; Aunt Dulcie was born on time and lived to hear the tale, which in due course she related to Mary. Dulcie, according to Mary, was 'sharp, clever [and] jealous'. She was jealous of her second sister Rose, who had not been jumped over the poles before birth and who was beautiful. But she was also jealous of her youngest sister, Violet. When Sir William Dalby, their father, died he left more money to Violet than he left to either Dulcie or Rose. He did this because Dulcie and Rose had both married husbands with private means, whereas Violet's husband, Mynors, only had his army pay and – due to ill health, a legacy of the war – his path to promotion was blocked. The result of Sir William's forethought was 'feeling' between the sisters 'which lasted for years and soured relations'. For Violet, jealousy among siblings formed the routine background to family life.

On returning with the children from Italy, Violet set off again, this time for India, leaving the girls in the care of Hyacinthe Dalby. In the absence of her parents Mary grew even closer to her grandmother Hyacinthe. 'She was the only person in my life for many years I would have died for . . . I loved her jealously and possessively, indeed I daydreamed of my mother and sister dying so that I would have her to myself.' In old age Mary kept a silver-framed photograph of her grandmother by her bed. No photographs of her mother were displayed in the house. Hyacinthe had taught Mary her prayers, and she gave her favourite granddaughter her own prayer book inscribed 'To dear little Cynthy from her affect. Cousin Dicky Wellesley. Brighton 1856'. And Mary kept this book by her bed until it disappeared shortly before she herself died. She also kept three letters written to her by Lady Dalby in 1922, commiserating with Mary for the loss of a dead goldfish and signed 'Fond love, ever your most affectionate Grandmum'. One has a postscript: 'I often think of my dear little girls'. The letters are careful to show no favouritism to either Mary or Susan, which seems to confirm the jealous rivalry between the two.

Hyacinthe in 1924 was quite ill; she had suffered a stroke and was beginning to fade at the age of seventy-three, but she was still happy to play with the children. '[She] took us to Lyme Regis with an Italian governess who smelt under the arms. Half-paralysed my grandmother hired a pony bath chair and we seized the reins, and the pony bolted up and down the steep hills with my sister and me running behind and my grandmother weeping with laughter and helpless inside. What lunatic grown-up people allowed us to treat our invalid grandmother so?? . . . I loved that wild laughter she had, quite out of control with it even when she was half-paralysed, and six months later dead.' Mary was inconsolable when Hyacinthe died and her father sent her to stay with Cara Bell, one of her grandmother's oldest friends, while the funeral took place.

The loss of her grandmother when Mary was thirteen, in the autumn of 1925, also meant the loss of the house in Montagu Place. Mynors wrote, 'We felt the death of Lady Dalby acutely. Up to the end she was always a Strength and a Standby. The loss of her personality and of her home, was a very grievous one.' For many years Montagu Place had been the Farmars' only regular family home and Mary for years afterwards lulled herself to sleep 'by walking up the steps to the bottle-green front door, into the hall and up through the house, recollecting every bit of furniture in the dining-room, the drawing-room, grandfather's study, the stairs, the bedrooms, remembering . . . the rocking horse in the telephone room, the bust of Wellington outside the drawing-room door that Nanny always held me up to kiss goodnight . . . The last time I stopped in the street [in 1997] to look up and remember . . . there were fourteen doorbells but I still regard it as home.'

Mynors returned to India after his mother-in-law's death, and in April 1926 Violet took Mary to Brittany for a lengthy visit, at the end of which she left her alone for three months in a hotel in Dinard. Mary was just fourteen.* The most enjoyable part of this time was being alone in the hotel.

---

* The visit included the period of the General Strike and inspired the first part of *A Sensible Life*: 'In the spring of 1926 middle-class English families took their young to Brittany for the Easter holidays. It was thought good for them to catch a glimpse of foreign soil, see some sights, learn a few words of French.'

It was in Dinard that Mary was taken to St Malo by an older English boy, who was still at Harrow, to buy a revolver in order to deal with the strikers when he returned to England. Mary was allowed to run wild with the hotel manager's Alsatian puppy, and one day near St Briac she came on a Breton man beating a dog. She ran up and kicked the man's shins, making him drop the dog. Her mother had always told her, 'If a strange man stops and talks to you, darling, whip up your pony and canter on' and she had always wondered what would happen if she wasn't on a pony. There was no pony in St Briac so, having kicked the man, she ran as fast as she could and since he was drunk she got away. She also took exception to a smaller boy who was playing on the beach and half drowned him in front of his father, who turned out to be the exiled heir to the Russian throne. None of the English mothers who had agreed to keep an eye on Mary bothered to do so, but she made friends with some of their husbands. A general called Dorien-Smith taught her to play tennis and the husband of a pregnant guest took her up and down the coast on expeditions looking for a parrot. She also fell in love with a White Russian called Alexander Smirnoff, who nicknamed her 'Masha' and flirted with her. These men, the age of her father, who treated a skinny girl as a young woman, intrigued Mary, at the same time making her feel vulnerable.

Then her mother arrived and put a stop to these irregularities, and took her back to London to buy her a brown school uniform with felt hat. Violet and Susan were to set sail for India while Hugh, who had by now left Eton, also went abroad before going up to Balliol. Mary was therefore left alone in England and put in a 'home school', effectively a boarding school where the children stayed on through the school holidays. Mary said goodbye to her mother at Waterloo Station; she then took the train to St Leonards-on-Sea. She had never set eyes on the school before her arrival and was not to see her parents or her sister again until their return from India two years later in 1928. This experience was not uncommon for 'children of the Raj', but Mary resented it bitterly. In one way it was worse than being orphaned since her parents, though still alive, had chosen to leave her. Occasionally photographs arrived in the post from Mhow in India showing Susan in a smart riding habit on her polo pony, Morning Star, or Susan on an elephant with turbanned attendants. Mary stuck these tormenting reminders of her sister's good fortune into her album and carefully identified them opposite a page on which her own solitary portrait appeared. This picture, labelled 'Self', shows a sturdy child with a square chin and a determined expression framed by dark pigtails falling to her elbows, and a tendency to glare at the world from beneath knitted brows.

During her parents' two-year absence Mary's chief consolation at 'home school' was a pet bullfinch that took seed from her mouth. She recalled that everyone at the school was obsessed with sex but no one knew anything about it, and that there was a lesbian teacher there who made her life hell. She was also surprised to find that other children cried for their parents since she never did although she 'tried jolly hard'.

When her mother eventually returned it was to find that Mary weighed nine and a half stone instead of her usual seven and she was taken away and sent for two terms to Queens College in Harley Street, which provided her with her single brief acquaintance with formal education. No sooner had she settled happily in Queens College than her restless mother removed her and sent her to a finishing school at Poissy, outside Paris, from which she was duly removed after three months when Violet discovered that the girls were badly chaperoned. There followed a short course at a domestic science college, Evendine, near Malvern, in the spring of 1930, which was designed to train her in the supervision of servants, and that completed Mary Farmar's schooling. By the time she arrived in London she had seen three plays, five films and had heard no concerts in her life; she 'knew nothing' of classical music and apart from the Uffizi she had only once visited an art gallery, the Wallace Collection. Looking back on her youthful ignorance she wrote, 'I . . . marvel that I did not make an even greater mess [of life] than I have.'

Beneath the reticence and bravado of Mary's own account of her childhood there are clear signs of trouble ahead. The wild little girl who tormented sixteen governesses, refused to learn to read or tell the time, 'bubbled inside . . . like a kettle', screamed like a siren, ran out on to the roof of the house, bolted over the hills with a paralysed grandmother, stole toffee in the street and narrowly failed to drown the heir to the imperial Russian throne, was finally dumped like excess baggage in an institution where she developed a deep sense of resentment. It had not perhaps been a good idea to leave such an intelligent and sensitive child with no formal education. Trapped in an existence where she did not trust those who should have protected her – her mother on the cliff at Bolt Head, her father often in danger and so far away for years at a time – and naturally impulsive, she awaited an opportunity to express her anger in some mutinous act.

A clue presented itself almost as soon as family life was resumed in

1928. Her brother Hugh had made friends at Balliol with a tall, good-looking Rhodes Scholar from New Zealand called John Platts-Mills who came to stay with Hugh for weeks on end during the long summer vacation. Mary, aged sixteen, fell in love with Platts-Mills and washed his socks. She was delighted by him because he laughed at her family and kept a notebook of how often she was asked to clean the car, do the shopping, exercise the horses, plant out the Canterbury Bells or simply 'Be an angel'. Platts-Mills was the first of Mary's friends to point out how badly she had been educated; he introduced her to William Blake and, noting how she was treated by her domineering sister, won her heart by remarking that 'Susan would make the perfect mounted policewoman'.

CHAPTER THREE

Having a Field Day

'You are such a sidelong girl . . .'
Claud to Laura, *Second Fiddle*

In November 1932 Colonel Farmar – his health broken – retired from the army and moved to London, where he started to work as a volunteer for his old friend Tubby Clayton at Toc H, the welfare centre for ex-servicemen. At the same time his daughter, Susan, announced her engagement to an army officer, Lieutenant–Colonel Archibald McLaren of The Cameronians who was stationed in India and was almost as old as her father. So Mary, aged twenty, found herself living in a flat in Queen's Gate, 40 Alexandra Court, with a bossy mother and a silent father who was downhearted at the imminent departure of his beloved elder daughter. In the circumstances she had little option but to embark on a brief period of good behaviour.

Violet decided that the time had come for Mary to be presented at court, an elaborate ritual that was observed several times a year at Buckingham Palace. According to Patricia Arbuthnot – who later married the Communist journalist Claud Cockburn, and who had been presented in 1931 – it was all that remained of the ceremonial surrounding 'the court of Imperial Britain'. A girl had to be presented by a sponsor who had herself been presented; since the sponsor was in most cases a close relative the rigmarole was an effective way of marking out a social inner circle. Both Violet and Mary wore 'court dress'. This was full evening dress with the addition of a train, hanging from the shoulders to the ground, a headdress decorated with three white ostrich feathers and white kid gloves that extended above the elbow. Colonel Farmar, also present, wore the dress uniform of the Lancashire Fusiliers, with decorations. The ceremony was quite testing. The debutante had to walk five steps forward, make a deep curtsey to the King, take two more steps, make a deep curtsey to Queen Mary, take another two steps and curtsey to any other member of the Royal Family present and then take five steps in reverse in order to avoid turning her back on royalty. 'To do this manoeuvre gracefully,' recalled Patricia Arbuthnot, 'wearing very high-heeled evening shoes and a ground-length dress, requires the suppleness and balancing ability of a circus performer.' If a debutante fell over her train while walking backwards, the nastier debs sitting in rows on either side giggled. Mary was eventually presented three times: to King George V in 1932, to King Edward VIII in 1936, and to Queen Elizabeth in 1937.

The rest of the social season consisted of attending debutantes' balls, dancing the charleston, the foxtrot and Viennese waltzes, and talking about 'servants and hounds and hocks and copses and foxes and birds', the pre-occupations of a world to which Mary could never happily belong.

At the domestic science college in Malvern she had for the first time made friends of her own age, girls who, unlike her, had received a formal education at schools such as Sherborne or St Paul's School for Girls. With these friends, Angela Russell, Eve Bray and Christian Davidson, Mary now turned the season into a high-spirited quest to 'discover the facts'. 'Have you discovered any facts, yet' became the group's battle-cry. In the interests of research Angela Russell introduced Mary to the Holland-Martins at Overbury. The Holland-Martins had six sons. Ruby, the oldest, watched one of his horses bucking Mary and shouted, 'Hold on to the saddle back and front, darling. I always do.' This unorthodox instruction ran against everything Susan had ever told her; on the other hand, Ruby Holland-Martin had ridden in the Grand National. So Mary followed his advice from then on and found it helpful. Christian Davidson next took her to stay with the Baden-Powells at Pax Hill. Lord Baden-Powell, the founder of Scouting, forbade all lipstick and nail varnish, so the girls cleaned their nails with a hairpin as the chauffeur drove them up from the station in the Rolls. Lady Baden-Powell's mother was often present. She loathed the Scout movement and loathed her son-in-law, and whenever she saw her daughter attired as a Guide 'she would let out a shriek worthy of Melba' and run to the end of the drive where she would lie down in the main road until she was carried home bodily. Mary noticed that the old lady enjoyed this performance very much. All went well until Mary was discovered in bed with one of the younger Baden-Powell boys, keeping warm, after which she left Pax Hill under a small cloud.

It was not until her parents sent her grouse shooting in Argyllshire that

Mary met her first serious admirer, an army officer named Alec Knox. Violet was delighted as Knox was entirely 'suitable'. He had passed out top from Woolwich, played serious rugby and was obviously in love with Mary. He was young, clever, sensitive, handsome and rich. He let Mary drive his car and kissed her 'with tremendous respect', perhaps too much since, although she liked him a lot, she was not in love. But she was nonetheless very upset when a telegram arrived from the War Office while she was staying with Mrs Knox announcing that Alec had died suddenly of pneumonia, in India. Mary told her mother, but Violet did not really notice as she was distracted by Susan's wedding plans and 'Oh dear, darling, was he in love with you?' was all Mary got by way of comfort. Fortunately, shortly after this sadness she was introduced to Peter Hope.

Mary met this tall young man at a dance in the autumn of 1932, while staying with Eve Bray. He had no money, no prospects of inheriting any, was the same age as Mary and worst of all 'a Roman Catholic', which put him some way beyond the pale for Violet – who remained stubbornly loyal to her husband's Huguenot ancestors. His father worked in the Admiralty, for MI6. Peter Hope was brilliant, short-sighted and funny, and about to take a good degree at Imperial College, which was just round the corner from Mary's parents' flat. He would drive up in his car and toot the horn, and she would hurry down; for the first time in her life she was seriously in love. The main thing she remembered about the day she was first presented at court was of escaping from Buckingham Palace in time to dine and dance with Peter Hope at the Berkeley Hotel. At Imperial College the porter pinned notes to the board reading, 'Mr Hope, sir, do you realise you only have four weeks left till Finals?' Meanwhile, at Alexander Court Violet was muttering, 'Are you thinking of marrying that young man? You know he's a Catholic?' Hope was shocked by Mary's ignorance and gave her a copy of Russell's *History of Western Philosophy*, which she read.*

---

* Many years later Mary remembered that Hope joined the Foreign Office, which is what he may have told her, but his eventual entry in *Who's Who* showed that he actually went to Cambridge to take a doctorate in science after Imperial College and that he joined the War Office in 1938. In between his university degrees, in 1933 he had a posting with the British Embassy in Dublin, possibly work experience with MI6, who may have thought that a Catholic would be useful in that country. He was working for military intelligence in London in 1940. He transferred to the Foreign Office in 1946 and ended his career as Sir Peter Hope KCMG, ambassador to Mexico in 1972.

Mary's affection for Peter Hope became such an 'obsession' that after a few months even her mother noticed. Deciding to separate them, Violet sent her daughter first to Scotland for August and September, then to India to spend the winter with Susan and her new husband. The plan did not work because Hope wrote to Mary from Dublin, insisting on a meeting before her departure. Joining in the conspiracy, Mary took the train down from Scotland early, telegramming her mother, 'Expect me on Monday,' knowing that her parents never used the telephone except in emergencies. At Crewe, a day ahead of schedule, she diverted to Holyhead; Hope, 'very tall, very young, very ignorant', was waiting for her sitting on a railway truck as her train drew in, she 'full of terror and determination'. They had an afternoon and evening and one night in the station hotel, where the staff spoke Welsh. They walked on the cliffs and found a cove where they could take off their clothes and swim. 'I went to one end and he the other. I rushed into the sea which was extremely cold, and looking up, saw him naked and infinitely larger' than the Donatellos and Michelangelos she remembered from Tuscany. With the facts within sight at last Mary, like Rose in *Not That Sort of Girl*, was 'aghast at the size of his sex'. That night they went to bed for the inevitable fiasco. Next morning, swearing eternal love, Hope caught the six o'clock boat back to Dun Laoghaire. Mary, 'crippled' with the fear of pregnancy, returned to London and three weeks later sailed for India by P&O from Tilbury. In a letter to her sister, written before she sailed, Mary said that she had told 'a suitor' that she was 'going to India for six months to join the fishing fleet'. 'The fishing fleet' was the name given to girls who went out to India looking for a husband.

Violet, anxious as usual to be rid of Mary so that she could concentrate on Mynors, took no trouble over Mary's chaperone and chose a general's wife who was sailing in first class. Mary's cabin was in second class and they were supposed to share meals in the dining room, but the chaperone took no further interest in her activities. On the first night, entering the Bay of Biscay, Mary left the porthole open and the cabin she shared with another girl filled with water. They were rescued by two brothers sharing an adjoining cabin and spent the rest of the three-week voyage drinking, dancing, flirting and swimming. 'For the first time in my life I was really free.' There were escapades ashore in Marseilles and Port Said, and the photographs she kept in her album show a healthy-looking girl in a bathing costume surrounded by muscular young men.

Her new reputation disembarked with her at the Gate of India in Bombay, where her brother-in-law's Sikh bearer took her luggage and saw her on to the train to Peshawar on the North-West Frontier. 'As all the young men I had collected on the ship were going the same way the journey was far from tedious,' she later wrote. One by one the officers left the train to join their regiments, with happy memories of a free-spirited girl who had been very badly chaperoned.

Many years later Mary told her granddaughter, Katherine Davies, that in India she had 'had a field day'. Susan put it differently, saying that her younger sister's behaviour in India had been so wild that she had to be sent home. Mary remembered a succession of dances, several every week at the club, dinner parties, tennis and squash, and riding polo ponies across the plain or mountain ponies through the hills. Since young ladies were not expected to sleep with their admirers they were invited instead to marry them. 'Will you marry me?' meant 'Can we make love?' Susan's efforts to restore order were not a success. On one occasion five young men turned up at the Colonel's house, all expecting to take Miss Farmar to the ball. Asked for an explanation, Miss Farmar said that she had 'felt too shy to say "No"'. On another occasion Mary was invited to a fancy dress party at Government House. She chose 'a large gentleman in the Tank Corps' as her partner and made the costumes herself; they appeared as two Victorian children in blue-and-white check dresses with little round hats and pantalets; he carried a hoop and she a monkey on a string. Her partner, who sported a thick moustache, was not pleased when he changed into his costume to find that the décolletage showed the hair on his chest. When they arrived the Governor welcomed them with a smile and ushered them into the ballroom, where they discovered that it was not a fancy dress party after all.

The only young officer who had any real success with Mary was John Hudson, an ADC to the Governor, who was unusual in that he had taken the trouble to learn a native language. Unfortunately he was already engaged to the daughter of the Governor of Bengal. His fiancée, whom he later married, was absent in England and Mary decided that it would be wrong to 'poach', but was shocked to find that she was tempted to do so.

Other officers, whose energetic flirting got them nowhere, had less fond memories. Bill Bailey, a gunner who had been on the boat, misread the signals and in his letter accepting defeat wrote, 'I was shooting in the hills and met a wild bear and got hugged. I thought it was you.' Earlier, angered by yet another last minute 'No', he had taken Mary riding in the mountainous Kuram Valley and lent her his steeplechaser, which soon bolted.

Alan Johnson, also a gunner, rescued her and explained, 'He was trying to kill you.' The horse was notoriously dangerous.

A success on the dance floor with Brigadier Auchinleck of the 62nd Punjabis* proved to be one too many and Susan arranged for her passage home. Back in England, in the spring of 1934, Peter Hope was waiting. For days she avoided his messages until Violet became exasperated and told Mary that she had to speak to him. They had supper at the Dorchester and both 'cried into the soup'. Hope did not realise that India had turned his sweet young thing into a reincarnation of Becky Sharp. He told her that she had broken his heart, but within six months Mary read in *The Times* of his engagement to a fellow Catholic.

In the summer of 1934 Mary developed an inflamed appendix that had to be removed in an emergency operation in St Thomas's Hospital. She was sent to convalesce with her father's first love, Aunt Rose, who remained a beauty into old age and who had married her second handsome sailor in 1924. 'Uncle Charley', Rose's first husband, had died of war wounds in 1921 and Rose had then decided to make herself useful by finding a husband for a spinster cousin. The pair set off for Malta and returned after a short visit with the cousin still a spinster but Rose engaged to another naval officer, 'Uncle Humphrey'. Uncle Humphrey had a house in Suffolk called Lowood. From there Mary was taken on a fishing expedition to the Faeroe Islands by her brother Hugh; and it was in the Faeroes, surrounded by thousands of miles of stormy ocean, that she had her first carefree experience of sex.

John Montagu-Pollock was an old Etonian student of architecture who, in the opinion of Mary's mother, was 'practically family'. Their grandmothers had been best friends, their mothers were best friends and John's great-uncle had married Mary's great-aunt. At the last moment, as Hugh's and Mary's train was pulling out of Euston, Montagu-Pollock leaped into the carriage to join them. He had been pursuing Mary for some weeks, shedding his girl-friend for the weekend that Mary came to stay with him in East Worldham House, Alton, in Hampshire, and chiding her not to spell Montagu with a final 'e' 'in that vulgar fashion'. In the absence of his girlfriend he described his feelings as 'curiously un-brokenhearted'. Unlike Hugh, Montagu-Pollock

---

* Later Field Marshal Sir Claude Auchinleck GCB, Supreme Commander, India and Pakistan (1947); architect in 1941 and 1942 of Rommel's defeat in the Libyan Desert.

was not interested in fishing and as there was nothing to do in the Faeroes except fishing or making love, 'John began my initiation'. He did this 'with much laughter and friendship in a spirit of joint and relaxed discovery which was good for both of us'. Hugh remained 'blissfully oblivious', boating from island to island in pursuit of the sea trout. Montagu-Pollock and Mary, all fear of pregnancy forgotten,* spent the days in bed, teaching each other as much as they could in the three weeks available.

In September Mary, still with John, went with older friends to Spain, to Cadaques and Barcelona, and what would much later be called the Costa Brava. They spent the days sunbathing and swimming, eating figs and drinking sherry, and the nights making love, since Mary's chaperone, a painter called Trix McCartney, believed that young people should be left together. Spain was in political turmoil, and in Barcelona shots were already being exchanged in the streets.

Mary liked Pollock but refused to take him seriously, and there were several other admirers around. One was Rory McLeod, whose mother was a portrait painter, and who aspired to be a singer. He lived in a flat underneath Noël Coward, and Coward, who was appearing in his own play in the West End, could not bear it and paid him money not to sing. Then there was Alexander Bethune, known as 'Derry', who was in love both with her and with a girl called Clodagh who worked at Elizabeth Arden. Derry could never make up his mind between Mary and Clodagh, neither of whom was in love with him. He eventually married somebody completely different in 1955. Derry Bethune's mother had a brother called 'Chico' Maitland-Heriot, a stylish bigamist who had a large house at Timsbury, near Romsey in Hampshire, and Derry frequently took Mary to stay for the weekend at his uncle's house. There she met Chico's legal wife who, on discovering her husband's bigamy, had taken to her bed in protest, although she was in the pink of health. Mary and Clodagh would visit Mrs Maitland-Heriot in her bedroom where Clodagh would give her Elizabeth Arden facials.†

* * *

* In *The Camomile Lawn* an unmarried girl, aged nineteen, who is newly launched on an adventurous sex life, is fitted with a female contraceptive by a sympathetic lady doctor. The scene rings true to life.

† *A Dubious Legacy* reproduces the atmosphere of Timsbury, the wife in bed, the girls calling on her, the discussions about how you accept a proposal of marriage from somebody 'suitable' who isn't suitable at all because you are actually thinking of somebody else.

From Mary's point of view the chief advantage of all these young men, after India, was that not one of them was in the army. Mary's father was a soldier, as were most of her uncles and cousins, and her sister had married an army officer. For that reason alone she was determined to marry a civilian and on returning from India – between Peter Hope and John Montagu-Pollock – she started to see an old friend who was a different sort of civilian, John Platts-Mills. By this time Platts-Mills, having been crammed for the All Souls fellowship, which he failed,* had been called to the Bar, joined the Labour Party and was sharing a flat at the top of Bedford Street, in a house that eventually became the Communist Party's headquarters. Also in the flat was an Old Etonian pro-Communist banker called Lewis Clive whom Mary described as 'a serious and enormous young man'.

Lewis Clive and John Platts-Mills exerted a great influence on Mary. They sailed together in John's decked-in lifeboat, moored on the river at Christchurch, and would take Mary with them, giving her an intensive course in twentieth-century politics and a stiff reading list. Lewis and John were 'muscular Marxists'; what they had in common were Leander and the Party line. They were big, athletic, clever and energetic, and Mary found them rather attractive. Lewis was an outstanding oarsman; he had been captain of boats at Eton, had stroked the Oxford boat and later won a Gold Medal at the 1932 Olympics. He took Mary to the Eton and Harrow Ball and then, wearing his pink socks and cap, he took her to Henley. Later he took her to meet his former housemaster at Eton and then to Balliol to meet F. F. 'Sligger' Urquhart – the don who had also been her brother's tutor.† Lewis Clive fell in love with Mary and – used to getting his own way – assumed that she would marry him, when he got round to mentioning it. In the interim he invited her to go to bed, which Mary, still rather in love with Platts-Mills,‡ declined to do.

Responding to the influence of John Platts-Mills and Lewis Clive, Mary started to work as a volunteer at a canteen for the destitute that had been set up underneath the arches near Waterloo Station. There she handed out

---

* John Platts-Mills, *Muck, Silk and Socialism* (2001), p. 54.
† Dean of Balliol and influential tutor, held popular summer reading parties for undergraduates in his Alpine chalet.
‡ Mary was attracted to Lewis and John as a pair. In *A Sensible Life*, Flora, still a schoolgirl, the age of Mary when she first met John Platts-Mills, swims in the river with two young men who are close friends. They hold her and kiss her at the same time. Young men in pairs became a recurring feature of her fiction.

plates of 'saveloy sausages and mashed potatoes and mugs of weak tea' to unemployed coal miners from the North. The experience made her aware for the first time of the political problems and social misery of the day. Another of the volunteers, a miner from the Midlands, was a passionate Shakespearean who spent as much time as he could in the nearby Old Vic Theatre. He told her that as a Communist he disapproved of kings, but that he made an exception for King Lear 'because he was mad, poor sod'. To the canteen customers Mary was 'an oddity' and she thought that they probably disapproved of her, but they took care to protect her from any violence in the street and she continued to work there, unknown to her parents.

After a while, Mary grew tired of being teased by John and Lewis and complained to her father about her lack of education, so Mynors, partly in jest, suggested that she should sign up at the London School of Economics. He had studied there after the war. Mary took this suggestion seriously and discovered that it was possible to enrol as an extramural student for a course in International Politics, which she did. This opened a new world for her since most of her fellow students were 'angry young men from Mitteleuropa', socialists or radicals, who had been born Austrian but now found themselves Czech or Yugoslav. For these men and women politics was not just an academic discipline and the lectures were frequently interrupted by violent disputes. The best-looking student was the son of Axel Munthe, the celebrated physician and author of *The Story of San Michele*, who founded an LSE branch of the Conservative Party that Mary supported – partly to tease Lewis Clive who had very little sense of humour.

And then one weekend she was taken to stay with a family who were to have a completely different influence on her life: the Paynters of Boskenna, in West Cornwall.

Betty Paynter was the only child of Lieutenant-Colonel Camborne Paynter of Boskenna. Boskenna was an old stone house on the cliffs near Land's End, surrounded by gardens, woods and farms, and with a private seashore, and the Paynter family had owned it for over 250 years. When Mary first went there it was 1935 and the house was still at the centre of what seemed to be a lost world, a world that had its own rules and customs and mysteries. She described it as the house 'that was to become my home and steal my heart'. The Colonel was the last of the Paynters in the male line to own Boskenna and his long reign was a period of colourful decline. He had inherited the estate in 1885, when he was twenty-one. At that time he was a cavalry officer so his mother, a widow, ran the place for him. She installed as head gardener a Devon man, John Collins, who had worked for her for years and had clouted the Colonel as a boy when old Mrs Paynter so requested. Colonel Paynter retired from the army in 1902, after the Boer War, and came to live at Boskenna and farm. At that time Boskenna extended over 2,000 acres and included ten farms as well as several flower farms and a long piece of coastland that stretched as far as Lamorna Cove. The estate employed many in the nearby village of St Buryan. Paynter was not only a considerable landowner and employer, he was also a Justice of the Peace, a member of the county council, chairman of the district council, chairman of the Newlyn Harbour commission, a High Sheriff of Cornwall and honorary colonel of the local militia. If a coroner's inquest had to be held, it was no surprise to find that Colonel Paynter was the foreman of the jury. With all this patronage at his disposal he reigned over the district as an eccentric and benevolent despot.

After restoring the house and gardens at Boskenna, Colonel Paynter set about the estate. He installed electricity and the telephone, imported the first motor car, built a new school in St Buryan, installed mechanical water pumps for his tenants, built and opened shops and a garage, and regularly organised parties at the house for the children of St Buryan.

Although the Colonel could be authoritative, he was also generous. Alice Grenfell who worked at Boskenna for twenty-six years, and who died in 2005 aged 102, remembered that when she first went there as an under-housemaid her wages doubled from her previous position in Penzance, where she had worked for the town clerk. The rise was welcome since she was trying to save £5 to pay a dentist to repair her teeth. When she had asked her father to pay he had said, 'You shouldn't have teeth. I've brought you up not to ask for what you can't pay for.' He was referring to the fact that in St Buryan it was the custom for girls to have a total extraction before marriage to save their husbands from having to pay the dentist; the local soft water rotted people's teeth. In west Cornwall in the Twenties and Thirties, with tin mining and agriculture both in decline, a landowner like the Colonel, who not only paid good wages but also gave his workers extra time off, inspired loyalty.

In 1904 Colonel Paynter had married Ethel Venning, daughter of a London surgeon who had once operated on King Edward VII. Their only child, Betty, was born in 1907 and there is a photograph of the little girl with her mother and father and the estate manager seated outside the house surrounded by six female servants and seventeen male servants, including Collins the head gardener and the butler, George Aukett. The photograph is undated but from Betty's appearance one can see that it must have been taken shortly before the First World War. Seated on the ground near the Colonel's feet is a boy, Jim Grenfell, older brother of Alice, who also worked on the estate. When the war came the Colonel served in the Devon Yeomanry and on being posted to France as a Town Major (administering recaptured towns) he took Jim Grenfell with him as his batman. Both returned safely, but the bell had tolled for the privileged world of Boskenna. Over the next forty years, until it was sold and broken up, the estate and the great house, and the safe privileged world it once enclosed, were living on borrowed time.

West Cornwall in the 1930s was a long way from London, and people still had their own way of doing things. At Boskenna the tenants paid their rents to the Colonel once a year and in person, after which he entertained them to a raucous dinner. As time passed, his leases became more whimsical. They might be granted on condition that the tenant *had* served in the army, or was *not* a Roman Catholic (Camborne Paynter had no time for 'Popery') or *could* play bridge. Some of the most singular leases were granted to the colony of artists the Colonel encouraged to settle on his land at Lamorna Cove, which became a centre favoured by painters such as Laura Knight and Alfred Munnings, and was well known to Stanley Spencer, Russell Flint, Ruskin Spear, Rodrigo Moynihan, Henry Lamb and others.

Colonel Paynter's daughter Betty was once reported to be engaged to Guglielmo Marconi, who had become one of her admirers while working in West Cornwall on his celebrated radio transmitter. For some reason the Colonel was irritated by this story and horsewhipped the pack of newspaper reporters who gathered at Boskenna for the next meet of the Western Hunt. He was an enthusiastic motorist but had little time for the Highway Code. In the 1930s Betty also had a motor car, they were the only two drivers in the neighbourhood, and they once met and collided at Boskenna Cross. The Colonel alighted, instructed Betty to stay with the cars, walked home and telephoned the police, telling them to arrest his daughter and charge her with dangerous driving. He heard the case himself and imposed a driving ban of several months. His own driving habits were notorious in the parish of St Buryan and beyond. Once, as he sped down the lane, a terrified delivery boy leaped off his bicycle and jumped into the ditch. 'Foolish boy, foolish boy,' said the Colonel as he flashed past. 'I've nearly run him over once already this morning.'

Boskenna was said to be full of ghosts. Mary's friend Pat Morris, who

stayed in the house in the 1940s, remembers it as being 'very haunted' but
not unpleasantly so. 'You just knew that everyone who had been there was
walking about.' The Colonel took the ghosts for granted. Once, when a
guest complained that there was a strange man sitting in a chair in the
library, the Colonel said, 'Get Aukett to offer him a drink. That usually
gets rid of him.' Aukett was George Aukett, the butler, who had originally
worked for the Colonel's grandfather. Aukett played the violin at private
recitals and 'rendered popular ditties with great sense of humour' according
to *The Cornishman*. Mary always called him 'Orchid' and took his picture
standing outside the house the year before his retirement.

Mary described Colonel Paynter as 'an eccentric, hospitable and incredibly tolerant father'. He in turn adored Mary and it was largely due
to him that Boskenna became her ideal house. The imaginary ideal house,
or 'great house in the West', that appears repeatedly in her fiction, notably
in *The Camomile Lawn*, *Not That Sort of Girl*, *A Dubious Legacy* and *Part
of the Furniture*, was clearly inspired by Boskenna. It is typically a house
from which the sea can be heard breaking on the rocks at the foot of the
cliff, where an owl patrols the cliff path and where you lie in bed and hear
the cawing of rooks or the clatter of horses' hooves in the early morning,
or watch the firelight flickering on the bedroom ceiling late at night. The
fictional Henry, master of Cotteshaw in *A Dubious Legacy*, whose father
had enjoyed *droit de seigneur* in the neighbourhood, bears some resemblance
to the real-life Paynters of Boskenna, whose distinctive features were said
to crop up regularly among the children of St Buryan. In extreme old age
Alice Grenfell happily recalled the time when as a young girl she had
received her first wages from the Colonel and he had smiled at her and
said, 'You belong to me now, Alice.'

The Colonel's tolerance was partly due to the fact that Betty's mother
had died in February 1933, after which the house lacked any conventional
governing influence. The extra-legal funeral arrangements made for Mrs
Paynter were very much in character. She was said to have died after a
short illness. In any event, as one friend of the family put it, 'They didn't
get on.' No undertaker was involved since the Colonel had his wife's body
taken to St Buryan church on the back of the estate lorry. The coffin was
plain oak with iron handles. After the funeral service the coffin was taken
back to the Boskenna estate and Mrs Paynter was supposedly buried with
her dog at her feet in a private grave on the cliffs between her Japanese
garden and a flower farm. Others remember a service on the rocks below
the cliff, where the Colonel scattered his wife's ashes into the sea and then

turned to the mourners, rubbed his hands and said, 'Well, that's that. Now who's for a game of bridge?' There was no inquest.

His wife gone, the Colonel, whether through grief or high spirits, dedicated himself to a second youth. He spoke French, Italian, German and several other languages, and his daughter Betty was encouraged to make Boskenna the centre of a cosmopolitan circle of friends, young people from London who were looked on unfavourably by those who were trying to keep the estate going. Mary described it as 'an entirely new set of people, sophisticated demi-monde'. A new neighbour, Wylmay Le Grice, was taken by her husband to visit the Paynters and donned twin-set and pearls for the occasion. They rang the doorbell of Boskenna and after a long wait the door was flung open by a statuesque and naked young lady who said, 'How do you do? I'm Paula.' The Colonel had brought her down for the weekend, from the Windmill Theatre in London.

Mary became one of this circle and was a close friend of Betty's before and during the war, and for a time their lives followed a similar course. Both women eventually converted to Catholicism, both knew wealth and extreme poverty, both were to marry slightly marginal men who were haunted by suicide. Betty's husband eventually shot one of her lovers and was tried for murder. But despite these similar destinies and their many shared adventures, the friendship remained, on Mary's side at least, a guarded one. She quickly noticed that Betty had been brought up to hunt for a wealthy husband; her first question when a possible new man was under discussion was always 'Is he rich, darling?' rather than is he beautiful, or clever, or good in bed? Betty was not beautiful but she had a fine slim figure, huge dark eyes, thick black hair and a large nose that she had broken while out fox hunting. She also possessed an inexhaustible sexual energy that made her very attractive to men.

Mary never drew a full portrait of Betty, probably because she was so fond of Betty's daughter, Sonya, but in *A Sensible Life* there is a minor character called Joyce who sounds familiar. Joyce was 'a very agile girl'. She flitted from flower to flower and brightened people's lives, or, to put it another way, fucked with 'all and sundry'. 'Joyce was fun; there was no lasting malice in Joyce. She thought of Joyce rather in terms of a necessary sexual assault course to be surmounted by young men such as Hubert and Cosmo, just as, when boys, they had manoeuvred through the scholarship or common entrance to their school.' Betty's father, their house and her boyfriends were to appear repeatedly in the world created by Mary Wesley fifty years on.

CHAPTER FOUR

Two More Old Etonians

'God, when I think of the time I've wasted going to bed with Old Etonians.'

Mary Wesley

It was during the three years that followed her return from India in early 1934 that Mary first started to lead her life on parallel tracks and to divide her friends into separate compartments. She could restrict herself to Queen's Gate and the conventional circle of her family and her brother's friends that was a continuation of her London season. Or she could escape to the singular and unaccountable world of Boskenna, where she soon made a particular friend of a fellow guest, an Armenian refugee and Communist called Boris Melikof. As a child, Boris had escaped from persecution in Romania by walking beneath his mother's skirts, clutching the family jewels. He had found it hard to take British society seriously since the day he found his first wife in bed with his mother – a lady who eventually became editor of Paris *Vogue*. A third circle was formed by Mary's intellectual and politically committed friends in London, the world of the Waterloo soup kitchen, the LSE and Communist Party meetings, of John Platts-Mills and Lewis Clive. It was at this time that Lewis Clive made a determined attempt to win Mary.

He showed his hand in May 1935, when she was with a party of her brother's friends who had taken a villa in the Basses Pyrénées. Lewis was not invited, nor did he have her address in France; Mary's mother had to forward his first letter from Queen's Gate.

My Darling Mary
    You were sweet this evening and have been many another evening as well. I find quite thrilling those rare occasions when you seem to disclose

that you like me a little bit too. I'm afraid that that is a terrible admission of youthfulness, right from the start, but there it is, and it is no use trying to conceal it . . . I know that the drawback of loving anybody is that one may necessarily get hurt later but . . . I have the advantage of being particularly insensitive and I feel quite sure that there will be no suicide talk whatever should occur. My few admirers (old women mostly) I think have always thought of me rather as 'a nice boy': not very exciting of course – but *so* sensible! Sober-mindedness being one of the few good qualities that really are commonly attributed to me, let me urge you not to overlook it and not to worry too much for me . . .

I love you very much because you cut your hair short and make your own clothes and are nice to your family and sweet to me and care nothing for great possessions and occasionally feel as I do, glad to be alive . . . Tell Roger I did remember to post his letter . . .

With all my love, Dear Mary, Lewis

Roger was Roger Barnett, a darkly good-looking member of the house party who, according to his cousin Rachel Fenwick, was also close to Mary.

Rachel Fenwick, another member of the house party at Lannes Puyes, remembers Mary at the age of twenty-three.

Her general behaviour and language were what made her attractive. She certainly was not shy. In fact she never cared what she said. At the same time she was tremendously interested in the Labour Camps I had visited in Germany, which were training camps for the Hitler Youth and reputedly full of very good-looking young men. Mary always remembered that I had attended Hitler Youth rallies out of curiosity, and could explain what was actually going on.

One of the pleasures of the house party in Lannes Puyes was that the young women were able to escape from their parents. 'We all had a battle to get away from home,' Rachel Fenwick recalled. Like Mary, she had no qualifications and had taken a £3-a-week job at the Selfridges' Information Desk.

Mary was away for three weeks and Lewis Clive wrote to her three more times. He mentioned plans to go skiing and to learn German with her. Then, when he heard that she had fallen ill with jaundice, he offered to travel out and accompany her home, only to learn that another young man had already driven out in his Bentley to do precisely that. Never mind; Lewis battled on. He told her about the 4th of June at Eton and how he wished she had been there. 'I can imagine nothing pleasanter than watching fireworks in the dark with you.' With each of these letters Lewis Clive dug himself in deeper, and from the rising misery in his tone it is clear that he knew what was happening. Violet, oblivious of details like Communist politics as long as Clive was not Roman Catholic, thought he was wonderful. 'Are you going to marry that nice young man?' she would ask her daughter. As the letters diminished in ardour, 'My darling Mary' to 'Dear Mary', Clive's schemes became more fantastic. By letter number three he was hoping to take her for a week 'on a small boat . . . on the West coast of Scotland sometime in August', unless 'a rather questionable excursion' she had been planning on the Continent would 'get in the way'. In his last letter he set out a programme for her return stretching from Thursday evening to Monday morning. 'Peggy' had asked him to join her party at the Guards Boat Club Ball at Maidenhead, 'and you please are to come along too . . . It is always a quite first-class binge and a bit of a blind withal; just what you want to set you up after jaundice.' Clive had gone 'so far as to read up Jaundice in the Enclypaedia [*sic*] B.' and 'gathered it was a nasty business', but had failed to gather that the usual convalescent regime involved lengthy rest and no alcohol.

Lewis Clive's last letter sent to Lannes Puyes was two pages shorter than the first three and ended, 'There seems to be mention in your letter of a great many more Swinfens than I had heard of. I should hate to think that several extra had been allowed to hurry to your bedside, what time I was being sternly repressed.' It concluded, 'herewith much love for what it may be worth.'

Sadly for Lewis Clive there was to be no German study trip, no skiing, no West coast sailing expedition. The jaundice had been serious, made worse by Hugh's attempts to cure Mary with a diet of raw eggs beaten into brandy; the 'doctor' who rescued her, and who was actually the local vet at Lannes Puyes, accused Hugh of trying to poison his sister. The Bentley that brought her home belonged to a wealthy young peer, Carol Swinfen, who had gone to collect Mary with his mother, the Dowager Lady Swinfen, widow of a senior judge.

Carol Swinfen was richer than Lewis Clive, not as clever but more amusing, much less bossy and much more patient. He had first met Mary in 1932 when Cara Bell, a close friend of Mary's grandmother Hyacinthe as well as John Montagu-Pollock's grandmother, introduced them. Cara Bell gave a dinner party to which she invited both Carol Swinfen and his mother.

Lady Swinfen took an immediate liking to Mary and her son seemed to concur. After leaving Eton, Swinfen had gone to Christ Church, Oxford, which he left without taking a degree; his unusual explanation for this setback was that he had been crossed in love. His father having been Master of the Rolls, Carol from a sense of duty felt that he too should go to the Bar, although he was not called until he was aged twenty-eight. He lived with his mother and his older sister in a large house in Ovington Square; he was not an ambitious man but he was generous and he knew how to enjoy himself. He crept up on Mary unobtrusively. Their initial meeting was in 1932 and he first asked her out two years later, having been crossed in love for a second time in the interim.

Carol did not make friends easily. Rachel Fenwick said, 'None of us liked him much, and I'm not sure she did really. I think he was an escape route.' The 'rather questionable' excursion on the Continent that Lewis Clive had been fearing took place in the autumn of 1935 when Mary, having recovered from jaundice, obtained permission to climb back into Carol's Bentley and with two other friends, a cheerful-looking girl called Molly Tute and a tall, thin, dark young man called Eric Cuddon, set out on a two-month tour of Europe, across Germany and as far as Bulgaria, returning home via the Gross-Glockner Pass and the battlefields of Flanders. They drove through Nuremberg just before the Nuremberg laws prohibiting marriage and sexual relations between German nationals and Jews were passed, and Mary took a photograph of civilian women giving the Nazi salute as they walked by a Nazi street shrine. Carol's excellent European contacts led them on through Vienna, Budapest and Sofia to Sarajevo, and on the way back Mary took more photographs, this time of anti-Jewish notices by Lake Constance on the road to Friedrichshafen.

When Mary got home, she found Lewis Clive as attentive as ever. He stopped taking her to smart parties, realising that he was unlikely to rival Swinfen's invitations to events such as the State Opening of Parliament. Instead, he took her to his own preferred world of Communist Party meetings near King's Cross, which Mary, too young for total commitment, found earnest and boring. She preferred to go dancing. Mary was not very kind to Lewis Clive and might have spent less time with him if it had not been for the affection they shared for John Platts-Mills. She once arrived at their flat in Bedford Street to be told by Lewis in his habitually forceful way, 'Mary, you have to go and see Janet and tell her John doesn't want to marry.' Janet Cree was a painter and Platts-Mills had fallen for her. She had then given him an ultimatum – marriage or farewell. Mary replied, 'No fear, Janet is bigger than me and might hit me, apart from which I think John should stop messing about.' Platts-Mills's next ploy was to put a notice in *The Times* announcing Janet's engagement to somebody else, while telling all his friends that he was broken-hearted. The messages of congratulation flooded in, Janet paid no attention at all and in 1936 Platts-Mills, having started to earn some money at the Bar, submitted to his fate and married her.* Perhaps inspired by John's brutal tactics, Clive once said to Mary 'We will get married in March', an act of desperation from a man who hated the idea of marriage, but Mary corrected him by pointing out that his statement did not amount to a proposal.

For her birthday present in 1935 Lewis Clive gave Mary a copy of *Seven Plays* by Ernst Toller, the exiled anti-Nazi author of *I Was a German*. In his introduction to Mary's edition, Toller referred to the fact that Hitler had burned his works in public, and wrote,

> But even the power of dictators is limited. They can kill the mind for a time and they can kill it in any one land. But across the border they are impotent; across the border the power of the word can save itself . . . the word, which in the long run is stronger and greater than any dictator, and which will outlast them all. Thus these plays come to be published in the land of Shakespeare and Shelley, the scene of the author's . . . exile, the land which has become a second home to him.

Like several other anti-Nazi exiles Toller committed suicide, in New York in 1939. In offering his friendship Lewis Clive was also offering Mary the chance to become part of his political world, to respond to the work of Ernst Toller and engage with the politics of the Popular Front and the Campaign for Peace. She was attracted by this invitation to join the progressive vanguard of the day. But she turned it down.

Swinfen continued to creep up on Mary even as his rival was losing hope. His mother, old Lady Swinfen, had been a friend of Betty Paynter's mother, who had died in the previous year. The long game of cat-and-mouse that Carol had started when Mary was in hospital in 1934, and continued in 1935, was resumed in 1936. He gave her a ticket for the trial of Lord de

---

* In due course they had six sons and remained together until her death, fifty-six years later. When their first son was born Lewis Clive insisted that he be put down for Eton.

Clifford in the House of Lords and took her to the peers' stand in Horse Guards Parade to watch the funeral of King George V in January 1936. At Easter they went to Boskenna, where she photographed 'Orchid' standing by the car with a tray of drinks in his hand. At Whitsun they made a return visit to Lannes Puyes with Rachel Fenwick and Evie Rich, no wistful letters this time from Lewis Clive. By now Clive had resigned from the family bank and started a political career as a London County Councillor. That summer Susan came back from India with her son Robin, aged nineteen months, and Mary played with her nephew on the beach at Westward Ho. Violet was there too. Then she and Susan went to stay with their Aunt Rose in Lowood in August, they played tennis and Mary bought a very glamorous two-piece sunsuit, not, at that time, called a bikini. Carol invited her to stay with his mother at Edenbridge and the two-piece sunsuit went too. In September they went back to Boskenna together. By this time they were invited everywhere as a couple. It was a cosmopolitan house party that included many European guests, among them Germaine and Willi Halot, who lived in Brussels, and Boris Melikof.

This was the year when the warnings of the Comintern and the Anti-Fascist movement began to come true. In May, 1936, Italy had occupied Addis Ababa in the first of 'Fascism's aggressive wars'. In July the Spanish Civil War had broken out and the Comintern had announced the formation of the International Brigade. In August Hitler had turned the Berlin Olympics into a showcase for Nazi ideology. It was not a time to abandon the cause, if the cause meant anything to you at all. But in London, as Franco's Nationalist army advanced on Madrid, and Britain and France refused to intervene in defence of democracy, the talk was all of Mrs Simpson. Through her friendship with Carol Swinfen, who of course was a member of the House of Lords, Mary became more closely involved in what London considered to be 'a national crisis'. In May 1935, Mary and Carol had celebrated King George V's Silver Jubilee by 'dancing through the night', as had the Prince of Wales and Mrs Simpson. In the summer of 1936 Mrs Simpson began divorce proceedings against her second husband, Ernest, a former officer in the Grenadier Guards who knew how to take it on the chin and was prepared to swear that he had committed adultery by spending the night, albeit fully dressed, in a Brighton hotel bedroom with a lady named 'Buttercup Kennedy'. In July the Prince, by now the uncrowned King Edward VIII, entertained at St James's Palace, with Mrs Simpson present for the first time without her husband. In this world, in Carol Swinfen's company, Mary was an insider. She dined in the same restaurants, went to the same nightclubs and 'danced with men who danced with girls who had danced with the Prince of Wales'.

Mary liked Carol because he was always good-tempered, reliable and kind. He did not 'dither like Derry or fly into a rage like Lewis'. He was not jealous and he did not mind when she teased. He was a shy man with deformed hands, which made him self-conscious if people asked about them, but he got on well with children, who accepted his deformity without judgement once it was explained. As a child Carol had been determined to do everything normally despite his missing fingers and one day a footman, watching him trying to tie his shoelaces, said, 'Master Carol, you can do anything other people do, but it will always take you a little longer.' He never forgot this advice and it gave him a lifelong habit of patience.

Carol's mother thought that patience could be overdone and remarked that if Carol did not hurry Mary would not be able to go to the Coronation. Betty Paynter invited Mary to join her in Brussels with the Halots; Boris Melikof, by now also in hot pursuit of Mary, went with them but on their return Carol was at Victoria Station to meet Mary's train. He told her that he had just bought a Lagonda for £400. Two nights later he took her to dine at Quaglino's and at the end of the evening, sitting in the library of his mother's house in Ovington Square, he proposed. She heard herself saying 'Yes'. Their engagement was announced on 25 October 1936. The immediate consequences were predictable. Following the announcement in *The Times* a formal portrait appeared in the social columns and *The Tatler* published a picture taken at Boskenna of Mary holding a huge bunch of hydrangeas. There was a splendid ring and a wardrobe of beautiful clothes. In *A Dubious Legacy* Wesley described that sort of engagement.

> 'Did you mean what you said this afternoon?' Barbara flinched closer to James as a hunting bat whispered and dived after moths.
> 'When I suggested that we get married?' James did not look at her. 'Yes I did.'
> 'If you still mean it I'd like to.'
> . . . 'Sealed with a kiss?' he suggested . . .
> Returning the kiss, Barbara was surprised by an incomprehensible sense of loss and disillusion, which she quickly dismissed.

Lewis Clive and Mary had broken up that summer off the Devon coast while sailing in John's boat. They were becalmed in Bigbury Bay, Mary and Lewis having a heated argument in the bows, the three other crew members remaining tactfully in the stern. Lewis announced that he was late for an appointment in Scotland, so John decided to put him off the boat there and then. He and Mary rowed Lewis ashore to a deserted beach 'and watched him climb the cliff with his pack on his back'. Following this farcical incident, Mary never saw him again except once when he was walking fast, by the Natural History Museum, on the opposite side of the Cromwell Road. But she kept three other letters from Lewis Clive, written to her after she announced her engagement in October. In the first he offered his congratulations and added, 'Tell [Carol] . . . that had I myself been a marrying man he would have met with the most strenuous opposition . . . dear Mary, all my blessings on you both . . . I am still a bit inclined to wish that I was to be the other party.' The second letter was written in reply to her distinctly mischievous invitation to him to be an usher. ' . . . It is sweet of you to ask me and much as I shall dislike seeing you handed to the care of another, I am very much tempted to do anything you say. BUT – I can make no attempt to assume a proper frame of mind. I consider church weddings a foul and monstrous sham and I hate the clothes both you and I will be required to wear. But if you will have me on those terms, I will come – always d.v. of course.' The thought of this long face in a prominent position on such an occasion may have dissuaded the bride; in any event Lewis Clive did not act as an usher at Mary's wedding. He accepted the invitation but on the eve of the wedding she heard from him for the last time. It was a card from his new address, a flat he shared with Norman Pearson in Queen's Gate, close to Mary's flat, and dropped in by hand. 'Dear Little M, All sorts of love and good wishes for tomorrow though I can't come myself . . . May I make this small contribution to furnishing your house . . . By this means I feel sure every penny will go to its right destination – like the C.P. collecting for the Spanish Govt. I hope you have a lovely day and a lovely time afterwards. Lewis.' He botched his signature and had to sign his name again.

One year later Lewis Clive left a note on the mantelpiece of the flat in Queen's Gate: 'Gone to Spain.' He was killed in action with the International Brigade, shot in the head on 4 August 1938, at the age of twenty-seven, fighting with conspicuous gallantry on the Ebro. Mary opened the *Evening Standard* one day and read of his death.

She always denied that he had gone to Spain because of her – and he had many more serious reasons for going. But he would never have volunteered if Mary had agreed to marry him, and the comment in his last letter about 'the C.P.' collecting money for Spain was a bitter crack at her expense that found its target. In 1997, hunting through some old papers, Mary found a packet of letters from Lewis Clive and 'felt a terrible pang – I have barely thought of him for years but seeing that writing brought him back. How have those letters survived? I have destroyed all the others . . . If I had married Lewis my life would have been very different. But he was too young for me, too bossy and I was not in love with him, he lacked humour.' Lewis Clive was a schoolboy and Oxford hero, he was highly intelligent, but with Mary he made a fatal mistake. He assumed that because he knew more than she did, Mary would happily take direction.

Mary Wesley commemorated Lewis in *The Camomile Lawn*. The character of Oliver does not die on the Ebro, but he has the same idealism, lack of emotional finesse, impatience and bad luck. Oliver, like Lewis Clive, takes himself very seriously, and he too is driven distracted – by the flirtatious Calypso. The fact that Mary kept the bundle of seven love letters suggests that Lewis had once mattered to her 'a little bit too' and may for a time have been a rival to Carol Swinfen.

Summarising her relationship with Carol before their engagement Mary wrote, '. . . He lent me his car when I needed it, he was always around, always agreeable, he became as well as a friend, a habit.' She also said that Carol Swinfen had been a very nice man but that she should never have married him. 'My generation very often had parents like I did who wanted their daughters to marry a certain kind of person and live in a certain kind of way. I tried very hard but I found it very boring.' On another occasion she said that she got married to get away from her mother. The fact was that marriage gave a young woman status and freedom. Living at home with her parents, with no money, no job and no qualifications, she had nothing to do except what she was told. Her main weekly occupation was her social life, which essentially consisted in meeting a procession of young men in the hope that one day she would receive a proposal she was prepared to accept.

But there was more to her decision than settling for a comfortable habit. In choosing to marry Carol Swinfen, and ending the hopes of Lewis Clive, Mary was closing down one side of her dual existence and embedding herself in the little world of England and the priorities of the parish pump.

One week after the announcement of her engagement Mary again attended the State Opening of Parliament to watch Edward VIII read the King's Speech for the only time in his life, seated on the throne which he would never occupy again. Mary and Mrs Simpson sat near each other in the same gallery and looked down on the peers and peeresses in their coronets and robes. The King abdicated one month later. Marriage, the institution that would take Mary to a coronet, robes and a seat in the chamber below the gallery, was about to take Mrs Simpson out of the House of Lords for ever. The Abdication Crisis boiled over and boiled away during the first six weeks of Mary's engagement. The Duke of Norfolk ('Bernard') continued imperturbably to organise the Coronation, magnificently indifferent as to which of the Royal Dukes would in due course wear the crown. On 11 November, Armistice Day, Norfolk organised an exhibition in his town house of correct dress for peers and peeresses. It was time for Mary to be fitted for her robes.

In retrospect Mary was quite clear that in marrying Carol she had not been tempted by the Swinfen money, since she had never cared about money or possessions – Lewis Clive had got that right at least. Nor, she said, was it the title; her father considered it 'a rather unimportant peerage' and regarded his own family as much more distinguished. Had she wanted a title, 'Derry's*' would have been older, prettier and more chic' – although the wife of a baronet was not awarded a ringside seat at the Coronation. In Mary's opinion Carol's mother had been largely influential in the proposal and had waged a long campaign of pressure on her son, at the original suggestion of Cara Bell, John Pollock's grandmother. With the matter settled old Lady Swinfen made plans. The wedding reception would be held in Carol's sister's town house, the honeymoon would be in America, because that was what Carol had always wanted. Carol chose a house in South Kensington, 25 South Street (now South Terrace), off Thurloe Square, and bought it. Carol's mother and Mary's parents made long lists of wedding guests, mostly relations who were hardly known to Mary so that she was unable to ask many of her own friends.

The marriage took place on 23 January 1937, at the church of All Hallows, on Tower Hill. The service, conducted by Mynors's friend, the Rev. P. B. 'Tubby' Clayton, founder of Toc H, was attended by a large gathering and must have cost Colonel Farmar, who was not a rich man, a packet. The bride wore a shimmering white gown and train, and her veil of Honiton lace was crowned with orange blossom and white camellias sent up from Boskenna by Camborne Paynter. The congregation included eight generals and three admirals, at least four of the bride's disappointed admirers, and numerous Old Etonians including the bridegroom and the best man who

* Sir Alexander Bethune, 10th Baronet.

was the bride's brother, Hugh. The wedding followed an unusually short three-month engagement, which ensured that the 2nd Baron Swinfen's new wife would be back from her honeymoon in time to take her seat in Westminster Abbey for the forthcoming coronation of King George VI. *The Times* reported that the bride's veil had belonged to her great-grandmother, Hannah, the wife of Major Edward Wellesley, which reminded those able to read between the lines that the bride's mother was third cousin to the Duchess of York who was shortly to be crowned Queen.

Lord and Lady Swinfen spent the first night of their honeymoon in a suite at the Berkeley Hotel and, on the following day, took the train to Southampton, where they stayed in the South Western Railway Hotel. On 25 January 1937 they sailed for New York in the SS *Pennland*, which Mary described as 'a horrible German ship with a Nazi crew'. It was a Red Star liner whose owner, Arnold Bernstein, had been arrested in Hamburg in 1936. Most of their fellow passengers were German Jews seeking refuge in the United States from a similar fate. In America, Mary and Carol visited Washington, Charlestown, New Orleans and Florida, and came home by first class on the *Queen Mary* but, as Mary remembered later, 'there was, puzzlingly, no sex'.

On hearing of Mary's engagement in November 1936, the bohemian John Montagu–Pollock wrote her a rather barbed letter of congratulation.

> Mary darling, I am very glad to hear your news . . . I suppose we shall all have to settle down and be respectable some day . . . but I trust Trixie is wrong when she says that marriage is the end of all good things like fried kidneys and that only those who live in sin are allowed to drink hot *chianti* out of enamelled mugs . . .

But he need not have worried; the conventional period of Mary's marriage did not last long. For less than two years she relished being free of her mother's daily control and became instead the spoilt bride of a rich* and devoted husband though, unusually among the men of her acquaintance, he showed little interest in sleeping with her. The new Lady Swinfen had a cook and a maid, a black pug puppy and a kitten, a leopard-skin coat and the keys to her husband's Lagonda. Her father had recently started

---

* When Carol Swinfen's father died in 1919 he left £192,000 (the equivalent today would be £25.7 million). This fortune was placed in two family trusts for the benefit of his widow, and the 'heirs of his body', his only son Carol and his two daughters.

researching his family's history and had decided that his older brother, George, was the rightful claimant to the extinct earldom of Pomfret. Mary's response was to register her pug puppy with the Kennel Club as 'the Earl of Pomfret'. The registration was refused. After the Coronation Mary's photograph was taken standing in the taxi queue outside Westminster Abbey, looking wonderfully glamorous in her robes and tiara, and already holding a cigarette. On the facing page *The Tatler* printed the photograph of the German representative, General-Major Stumpff, with Iron Cross, jackboots and steel-grey coal-scuttle helmet.

Mary stopped seeing John Platts-Mills and John Montagu-Pollock, and dropped many of her old friends. Carol, supposedly a busy barrister, went off to his chambers every morning and returned in the evening at the cocktail hour. Mary recreated the atmosphere of the semi-arranged marriage, the feeling of being caught in a luxurious trap, in *Not That Sort of Girl*:

> It was not an entirely fraudulent thing to do, thought Rose . . . part of me wanted to marry Ned. Much of me longed for the security, a house in London, the house in the country; the big wedding was tempting, the clothes I had never been able to afford.

Ned shows Rose around his country house, called Slepe – so that she can see what a lucky girl she is: 'He led Rose about, showing her every room, satisfying himself that she belonged in it, then walking her through his fields, showing her the boundaries of his property, bonding her to his land.'

Later Mary could not think of 'one single reputable excuse' for having married Carol Swinfen: it was true that she was tired of the weight of other people's expectations, tired of saying 'No' to men who only wanted to sleep with her, and very tired of living with her mother. The only escape for girls in her position was marriage. Evelyn Waugh's first wife, Evelyn Gardiner, married him to get away from home and in that case too the way to marital catastrophe lay straight ahead. When Mary agreed to marry Carol she was strongly attracted to two other men, Boris Melikof and a new friend she had met at Boskenna, Pip Holman. Boris at first refused to respond to Mary's considerable interest, somewhat to her frustration, as, following her marriage, he was 'busy behaving like a gentleman about me', which had certainly not been his habit before. But other friends of Carol's flirted with her under his nose and he made no comment. Apart from Pip Holman they included Gage Williams, who lived in Cornwall, Dennis Bradley and Eric Cuddon who had travelled with them to Sarajevo in the

Bentley. Dennis Bradley invited Mary for a week of 'advanced riding' on
Exmoor and she accepted, only to be told by her father that the idea was
'quite improper'. Later she realised that Carol had been too timid to raise
an objection himself and had sent her father round on his behalf.

Some of Carol's diffidence may have been due to his crippled hands; he
may even have doubted that Mary found him attractive, because he could
not caress her. But if they had little physical understanding, she did at least
find his family history much more interesting than her father had supposed.
The brother of the Master of the Rolls, Carol's uncle, had been bailed out
of prison in Naples and then murdered in Mexico. There was an un-
mentionable person who was kept by a paid companion secretly in the country
and was 'the result of the Master of the Rolls' sister being raped or some
such event'. And in the middle of the night the police would occasionally
ring Carol to say, 'Lord Swinfen, could you come down and bail out your
sister, milord. She and Mr Allchin* are drunk and disorderly in the station.'

Mary took a strong dislike to a large portrait of Carol's father, Charles
Eady, 1st Baron Swinfen, in judicial robes, full-bottomed wig and monocle,
that was hanging in the hall of her new home, and had it moved. Carol
told Mary that his father's rather brief career as Master of the Rolls, from
May 1918 until shortly before his death in November 1919, had enabled
him to buy his title from David Lloyd-George. Since he had no chance of
winning the distinction that long service would have achieved, Sir Charles
Eady took the short cut provided by the prime minister. The deal went
through as he was in the process of resigning (he was dying of cancer) and
the barony was announced barely two weeks before his demise. It was an
accepted convention of such deals that the recipient of a hereditary title
should be well enough to enjoy it for some time; it was not supposed to
be passed directly to a nondescript heir. But Sir Charles decided to press
on; when the man from the Lord Chamberlain's office came round to see
him, he donned a very good suit, had himself propped up behind his
desk with his back to the light and settled government bills to the tune
of £50,000. In June 1919, when he was already too ill to preside over the
Court of Appeal, Eady had written a will that was witnessed by his doctor.
Once he was made a peer he decided to change his will so, on 8 November,
one week before his death and one week after he had become the 1st
Baron Swinfen of Chertsey, he drew up a codicil in which he varied the

---

* Later Sir Geoffrey Allchin KBE., CMG, MC, Ambassador to Luxembourg (1955).
He eventually married Carol's sister.

family trust set up in his first will and bequeathed £40,000 to a separate fund 'for the support of the said barony' which has been lately 'conferred upon me and the heirs male of my body . . .' Once again the will was witnessed by his doctor. Lord Swinfen had made his name and his fortune as a Chancery barrister and drawing up a will should have been well within his powers. But due to ill health he inserted a succession of complications so that many years later his estate was to cause fiendish difficulties for his heirs, for Mary and for her children. His mentor, Lord Cozens-Hardy, had been a more notable judge than Eady but it still took him seven years' service as Master of the Rolls before Asquith authorised his peerage. Presumably it cost Cozens-Hardy rather less than £50,000. When Carol told Mary the story of the Swinfen peerage she was interested to see that he 'actively admired' his father for running rings round the system.

To Mary's disappointment they soon moved from their new house in South Street to her mother-in-law's house, No. 12 Ovington Square. Her bridesmaid, Venice Myers, Carol's niece, used to spy on them wistfully from her barred nursery window in the house opposite. Years later Mary recalled nothing but boredom, but Venice saw their apparent happiness, the fun they had together, the outings in the leopard-skin coat and the Lagonda, the horse-play and high spirits of Carol and Mary when they came to play with her.

Carol remained uninterested in sex until one evening in March 1938 they were invited out to dinner with a Polish film director called Sacha Gulperson. Both Carol and Mary became extremely drunk, so drunk that, as Mary later recalled, she fell down the stairs when she got home, after which she crawled back up to the landing and, all inhibitions forgotten, conceived Carol's son and heir. Roger Swinfen Eady was born at home in Ovington Square on 14 December 1938; a near-miracle, engendered by parents who – according to Mary – had slept together 'eight times in two years'.

The one place where Mary could continue to lead a less conventional life was in Cornwall and in July 1937 there was a great event at Boskenna, the wedding of Betty Paynter, which was attended, according to the local news-paper report, by 'an assembly of notabilities such as has been rarely witnessed in West Cornwall'. The bridegroom was 'Olaf Poulsen de Baerdemaecker, of Chateau Hemelryck, Ghent'. The 300 guests included several members of the Bolitho family, neighbouring landowners. The bride's bouquet, from Constance Spry, was flown down from London by Lord Semphill, the noted aviator, in his private plane. Mary arrived several days early to help with the preparations. The hundreds of wedding presents included a diamond and sapphire ring from Carol and Mary, and a Jean Cocteau drawing. There was also a copy of *The Seven Pillars of Wisdom* and an onyx and leopard-skin cigarette case and powder box from Sir Delves Broughton.* 'Orchid' gave Betty a silver teapot and retired from service at the end of the day. The bride wore a full-length pearl satin dress ('without knickers', in Boris's overheated imagination) and following the ceremony Betty and Olaf left Cornwall to start a new life in Ghent. The Colonel, thinking ahead, sent a trusty man, Donald Jarvis, to act for Betty as her butler. Jarvis stayed with her, learning French, until after the outbreak of war and was eventually evacuated on one of the last boats out of Ostend.

Mary never believed in the marriage of Betty Paynter and Olaf Poulsen. She said, 'They both married under false pretences. Olaf thought he had netted an heiress and she thought she had scooped up the heir to a Ghent shipping dynasty. Unfortunately both their fathers were broke.' This joint misapprehension may have explained the lavishness of the presents. The wedding was a striking example of a mutual 'sting'. Colonel Paynter gave his daughter a silver fox fur coat while Mr and Mrs Poulsen senior responded with a motor car. Centuries of family tradition, Cornish piracy versus Viking brigandage, clashed and fought each other to an honourable draw. The marriage broke up after two years following the outbreak of war in September 1939, by which time Betty was pregnant by another man.†

Mary's disillusion with her own marriage to Carol Swinfen became complete over the same period of time. Married life had started with Manhattan, a suite on the *Queen Mary* and the Coronation – where the real Queen Mary, then Queen Mother, wore jewellery worth £1 million, and which Mary found 'very beautiful, strange and enjoyable'. In July there was Betty's wedding, in August she and Carol stayed with friends in Brussels, then the Halots took them to Italy and they drove over the Simplon Pass to Lake Maggiore, Mary in a black straw, wide-brimmed hat photographing the white oxen pulling their farm carts. In Tuscany, in Montepulciano, they stayed with friends of Carol, the Riccis in Palazzo Ricci. But when they were not travelling they were living in London and

---

* Later to be acquitted in the 'Happy Valley murder case' that followed the shooting in Kenya of the Earl of Erroll.
† Olaf Poulsen died in 1942, in Belgium in unexplained circumstances. In St Buryan there was a rumour that he had been trying to run with the hare and hunt with the hounds of the German occupation.

when they were in London they were close to Carol's mother and Mary's parents. *Vogue* invited Mary to model hats, but Carol, on his mother's advice, refused permission. If Mary's brother, Hugh, on meeting her in the street, no longer asked her to come and help him pack as he was going away for the weekend, her imperious sister, Susan, had not given up. Mary once came home to find that Susan, assisted by the lodger, Derry Bethune, had rearranged all the furniture in her drawing room. 'I asked Susan what she was doing and she said she thought I would prefer it properly arranged. So I just said "Put it all back exactly where it was", and had a bath and went out for dinner with a boyfriend.'

But if Susan could finally be repulsed, parental authority was implacable. Carol, whose father had died when he was fifteen, was not accustomed to defying his mother. Mary could not forgive his timidity. When Carol's mother offered them Ovington Square in place of the much smaller South Street, everything was settled before Mary knew. She was pregnant, she needed a larger house, her mother-in-law, the Dowager, would provide the additional staff (one parlourmaid), and Mary hardly needed to be bothered with the details. She was furious, but outmanoeuvred. They moved. When Carol was alarmed by her flirtatious behaviour he did not confront her – he never had done so – which was why he had won her, and he never would, which was one of the reasons why he was to lose her. Instead, he made the mistake of enlisting her father's aid, not realising that his chief attraction as a husband had been as a shield against her parents. Mary, in bed with flu, was visited by a fulminating Mynors, who was instructing her to cancel her social life, just like the old days. The final straw came after Roger was born, when they were choosing godparents. Carol and Mary decided to ask Boris Melikof to be their son's godfather; Boris was young, affectionate and their friend. They felt close to him and he accepted. The result was an ultimatum from Carol's mother and Mary's parents; Melikof was unsuitable. He was a foreigner and a former boyfriend. If Melikof was a godfather none of the Farmars would attend the christening. Mynors delivered this ultimatum in person, while Mary was still resting in bed after the delivery. Her milk stopped, the baby had to go on a bottle and she attributed this to the anger she felt about the family's interference. Boris, who had the mistaken impression that he might have been responsible for Roger, was hurt. Carol put up no resistance, and Mary was ashamed of her own weakness and of the hurt felt by Boris. One month after the birth, she wrote to a more acceptable candidate, Roger Mynors, a fellow of Balliol, a cousin and a family friend. The eminent Latinist replied to the invitation in his meticulous, scholarly hand from Harvard where he was lecturing, and wrote of 'a wave of pity for the poor child when his prospective name appeared'. It was a mischievous choice. Roger Mynors naturally thought the child had been named after him; Mary later said that she had been thinking of her old flame, Roger Barnett.

With the arrival of her son, Mary decided that she had done her duty by her affectionate but not very exciting husband. She had presented Lord Swinfen with a delightful, outgoing child, who relished physical activities and looked the spitting image of his father. Carol had the heir, now she wanted to get on with her own life. She was an attractive, mischievous, clever, frivolous girl with low self-esteem, a strong sex drive and no sex life. She flirted with her husband's wealthy friends, attended the Falmouth regatta, visited country houses, dropped out of her left-wing circle, fitted in with her mother-in-law's suggestions and grew bored. If marriage was not to be a shield from parental interference, she decided to resume a private life where they could not follow.

She turned back to Boskenna and there made another of her lifelong friends, Paul Ziegler. He was the son of a banker from Bohemia who had been advised by his older brother to leave Prague before the arrival of Hitler. Peter Rodd gave him an introduction to Boskenna and one day he came hurrying up the cliff path in the distinctive Ziegler way, a sort of 'ambling, rapid shuffle'. Betty swooped on him and carried him off to the Red Bull Hotel in Camborne for the afternoon. That autumn war broke out and Mary's life was transformed.

PART TWO

1939–1945

CHAPTER FIVE

Lady Swinfen Goes to War

'If there's a war I'll sleep with you before you get killed. That's what maidens did in books and I am a maiden.'

Calypso to Oliver, *The Camomile Lawn*

Throughout 1939 Mary and Carol began to spend more and more time apart. Roger had a nanny. In the spring Mary went to Paris alone to stay with friends. She also travelled to Denmark. Carol was convinced that there would be no war. Mary, informed by her circle of friends exiled from Mitteleuropa, was convinced that war was inevitable. She trained to be an ambulance driver and made plans to evacuate Roger. Her parents sold their flat in Queen's Gate and moved to Bicknoller, near Exmoor in Somerset. Susan, home on leave from India with her two children, filled the new house and Mary had to turn to Violet's sister, Aunt Rose in Suffolk, to ask if Roger, Nanny and the pug Pomfret might be booked in for evacuation. Mary decided to evacuate Roger when the London hospitals were evacuated. Carol assured her again that there would be no war. The hospitals were evacuated. Roger and Nanny left for Suffolk on 29 July and Mary went to sign on at her ambulance station in the King's Road. Carol, at her suggestion, had joined Air Raid Precautions (the ARP) and offered to set up the local ARP station in the basement of 12 Ovington Square. It was a wonderfully hot August. Aunt Rose stocked Lowood with food, Uncle Humphrey secretly buried dozens of cans of petrol in his orchard and Mary lay in a hayfield, sunbathing, feeling rather frightened and flirting with an attractive young man.

On the outbreak of war, 3 September, everyone expected the German air raids to begin at once and London awaited its first gas attack. When nothing

happened, the tension and fear were forgotten and were succeeded by excitement. '. . . It is only truthful to say we began to enjoy ourselves,' Mary later
wrote. It was a return of the high spirits, the lack of restraint, the liberating
absence of convention that she had first experienced in India; Becky Sharp
could ride again. Mary had had enough of her 'quasi-celibacy' with Carol.
She took a lover, a successor to Boris; he was the young man she had been
flirting with in the Suffolk cornfields. He had followed her up to London
to join his Territorial unit in Perivale. She never identified him, but he was
almost certainly Norman Pearson, Lewis Clive's last flatmate.

She soon found the Ambulance Service, in the complete absence of air
raids, boring; the work was mainly picking up drunks by night and filling
sandbags by day. She started to look for something more interesting to do
and heard from Betty, who was back in London, that a Cornish neighbour,
John Bolitho, was 'looking for girls'. Betty could not discover what he wanted
them for, 'something hush-hush in Whitehall'. All she was certain of was
that he was 'Edward Bolitho's brother'. When Mary telephoned Bolitho he
asked if she could speak any foreign languages and told her to send him her
family details, gave her the address of his club and rang off. Three weeks
later he called her, in the middle of the night, and told her to meet him
immediately outside St James's Park tube station where she had to wait in
the dark. Growing impatient, she called out the code word 'Six foot five'
and was told to move along by a policeman all too ready to believe her explanation that she was 'waiting for a man'. Eventually the excessively tall figure
of John Bolitho, six foot five inches, loomed out of the dark and invited her
to come up to his office in the government building in Broadway, where
they discussed dairy farming (he was a cattle breeder with a herd of prize
Jersey cows). After an hour or so he offered her a job and, when she asked
what she would be doing, told her she would find out on Monday.

John Bolitho* was a well-connected eccentric; Mary said that he did
not hold a a regular appointment in MI5 but had wangled an office and
was allowed to recruit an amateur staff to work on a private project. He
was trying to adapt a Swedish business machine† – that normally stored
information about his Jersey herd on punched cards – to decode German

---

* Captain R.J.B. Bolitho of Rosel Manor, Jersey. Served in the First World War
in the Devon Regiment, the Signals and the Royal Flying Corps. His son was
killed in action in 1942. From 1942 to 1946 he was 'lent' to the Royal Navy.
† The Power Samas data sorting machine used punched cards to sort and retrieve
quantities of complex information.

military radio call signs. He had five girls in addition to Mary. They were all pretty, bright and unqualified.* Bolitho taught them their trade and paid them out of his own pocket. They called him 'Pullthrough' or 'Push me, Pull you', a disrespectful reference to his supposedly awesome proportions. Bolitho, in his late thirties and straight as a ramrod, was a genial corrupter. He would take the female members of staff out by turn. 'Which of my girls is coming with me to the Opera tonight?' he would say and a willing volunteer would step forward. His girls rode to work on bicycles wearing divided skirts, and changed into something more attractive in the office. 'We had these machines to break German Morse code,' Margaret Royds (later Margaret Ricketts) remembered in 2003. 'We were given sheets of signals and wrote them out on cards with punch holes and put them into a machine that tried to find a pattern; 300 ATS did all the dirty work.' One of the ATS in question was called Mary Watkins. She now lives in Sussex and has reached the age of eighty-seven. She remembers Mary Swinfen very well. 'She was a beautiful little piece of enamel, everything about her was tiny and perfect. She was extremely kind I was only nineteen but if I made an error she never pointed it out except casually. She was never snooty. They called us "female computers". The work was secret. We had to sign the Official Secets Act, but not one of us would have breathed a word anyway. In those days it was heroes, not celebrities, that we thought a lot of.'

Mary recalled that they specialised in Russian and German radio call signs. Lists of signs arrived in batches, which they were told had been compiled by underground listening posts.† The call signs were in groups. Every German unit, whether it was a regiment or a tank, had its genuine call sign and a couple of fake ones as well. Bolitho's girls had to collect and classify them, and then track the movements of the units. They all worked in one room on the first floor with a window looking towards St James's Park and if they asked they were told that they were working for MI5. They had to sign the Official Secrets Act. But no one was allowed to know where they worked, or who they worked for, or anything about their work. At a

* They were called 'Iva' Dundas, Barbara Swanwick, Margaret Royds, Judith Corcoran and Elizabeth Roscoe.
† The identification of German military radio call signs by the use of punched cards became the task of the Government Code & Cipher School (GCCS) at Bletchley Park between July 1939 and May 1940; so Bolitho's unit was probably working on Enigma intercepts.

time when you could rent a room in a friend's flat in Gloucester Place for
50 pence a week they were paid £2 to £3 a week. Bolitho's method of selec-
tion had been quite simple: 'Tell me your name and who your parents are.'
In Margaret Royd's case this reduced her to 'father in Scots Guards, mother
a Drummond'. Mary was 'father in Lancashire Fusiliers, mother a
Wellesley'. They got on very well together and laughed a lot. Another girl
called Gladys, thought to be rather obvious and not terribly bright, was
nicknamed 'Glad Eye'. Mary was very fond of John Bolitho, who never
bought one of anything, but always two. He had 'two hats, two bicycles, . . .
two fur coats for his wife, and he set up his office inside MI5 with two
thousand pounds'. With the arrival of Mary he had three brace of girls.

At lunchtime Mary would put on her mink cape and mink hat and 'bike
off to the Ritz for lunch with one of her boyfriends'. As Mary Watkins
remembers, 'She often popped out.' Once she met Peter Hope in the street
and they arranged to lunch at the Ritz. He told her he was a Signals officer
and showed her the loaded revolver he wore in a holster under his arm. It
was raining hard so after lunch he offered her a taxi back to her office. She
declined because no one was allowed to know the address. They took separate taxis and re-met in the lift. He was working on the floor above her.

Within MI5, Bolitho's girls were regarded at first as a bit of a joke: on
6 April 1940 Mary reported that something seemed to be going on as all
'her' Germans had moved from opposite the Maginot Line to Schleswig
Holstein. Her superior officer dismissed this as 'a lot of balls'. That night
the Germans invaded Denmark and Norway. After that people paid them
more attention and later in the summer the entire unit was moved into
Bletchley Park. Mary was offered an army commission if she would go
with them, but she declined. She did not want to be an army officer, did
not need the extra money, was not interested in wearing a uniform and
Bletchley was not at all handy for the Ritz.

Mary never introduced any of her friends in MI5 to Carol but she sometimes mentioned him in the office as someone she was 'fond of', who would
not talk to her when he came home and whom she was bored by. Living
in Ovington Square, she was close to the Brompton Oratory and she told
Margaret Royds that she often went in to the church during evening Mass
because she 'loved the rituals'. On her days off and at the weekend she
would leave London to visit Roger, now one year old and still living in
Suffolk with Aunt Rose, his nanny and Pomfret. They stayed there until
January 1940, much to the distress of Roger's Grandmother Swinfen.

*   *   *

In London Mary discovered that her lover, Norman Pearson, was two-timing her so she told him that she 'wasn't a team player' and looked about for someone else. The collection of agreeable cads who had gathered around her in Boskenna weren't really the answer and Boris Melikof was in France. She started seeing more of Paul Ziegler, and one evening in October she went to a cocktail party he gave at his house in Montpellier Square. Paul was still with Warburg's, where he had been since 1936, but he spent his free time as an air-raid warden. He introduced her to a tall, hunched, hawkish man, standing with his back to a bookcase. This was Paul's older brother, Heinz.

The Zieglers were German-speaking Bohemians, but they had been born in the Habsburg Empire. The Treaty of Versailles had placed Loyovitz, their family estate, and Prague, in the newly created Republic of Czechoslovakia but they regarded this as an unfortunate detail; in spirit they remained Viennese in exile among the Slavs. There were three Ziegler brothers. Hans had left Prague and gone to the United States before the outbreak of war. He became a friend of Mary's when the war was over. Paul, the youngest, came to England first. He worked for Warburg's bank, fell for Betty Paynter, but told Mary that his main goal in life was 'to become a hermit'. Heinz was the oldest. He was not a banker, he was a scholar and a university professor. Like Paul, Heinz proved to be very good company, witty and clever. He had given up his job as a professor of political theory at the Charles University in Prague and left his wife in safe keeping with a trusted Swedish friend in Paris. He was worried about his father, who was Jewish but who had stubbornly refused to leave Prague. He was nine years older than Mary and very attractive to women; according to his younger brother Hans, 'Heinz rarely had his trousers on.' As for Mary, she was by her own account 'ready and ripe for fun, nothing serious, nothing heavy, just some amusing and sexy fun'. He wanted someone who would take his mind off his troubles and make him laugh. As with Paul, it started as a light-hearted affair.

A vivid portrait of Heinz Ziegler was painted by Mary's distant cousin, Patrick Leigh Fermor, in *A Time of Gifts*, his record of pre-war travels. In December 1933, Patrick Leigh Fermor had set out from London to walk to Constantinople. Having crossed Holland, Germany and Austria, he reached Vienna and met a friend, a young banker called Hans Ziegler. Ziegler insisted that Fermor interrupt his march across Hungary and make a diversion north to Prague where the Zieglers lived. Fermor found Prague 'a bewildering and captivating town. The charm and kindness of Hans's parents and his brothers were a marvellous enhancement of it, for an articulate enthusiasm for life stamped them all ... Heinz ... looked more like a poet or a musician than a don and the ideas he showered about him were stamped with inspiration. Paul, the youngest ... was touched by the same grace ...' For Fermor, Prague was a citadel where a spell hung in the air, it was 'the recapitulation and the summing-up of all I had gazed at since stepping ashore in Holland ...' and for a week or so the Zieglers became his guides to this enchantment. Heinz launched 'marvellously abstruse and inventive theories ... about Rilke and Werfel and the interrelation of Kafka's *Castle* ... and the actual citadel that dominated the capital'. Inspired by the library in Heinz Ziegler's flat, Fermor set out to search for links between Bohemia and England. Heinz assisted him. 'He shut his eyes for a few seconds – they were grey with a hazel ring round the pupil – tapped his forehead slowly once or twice with a frowning effort of memory, opened them again and took down a book.' Fermor recalled Heinz's 'eager and cheerful voice'; his younger brother Paul wrote of his 'adored eldest brother's exceptional gifts and vitality'.

In an unpublished memoir Paul Ziegler later recalled the world he had been born into, that had disappeared when he was ten years old. '... In spite of its many imperfections it was civilized, humane and gentle and not yet driven by the ruthless and usually short-sighted demons of large efficiency and small individualism ... We found this was a good and attractive world', in which 'any decent and reasonable human being of any social class could be happy, providing you were in agreement with its guiding values and accepted a hierarchical order which was neither too rigid nor too fluid'. This was a world that died twice, first with the death of the Emperor Franz Josef in 1916 after a reign of sixty-eight years, then in 1918 following the defeat of the Austrian army by the Italians at Vittorio Veneto. Empire was succeeded by nationalism. The Zieglers were henceforward listed as 'Czech', although in imperial Vienna the Czechs had been a people 'viewed as unruly, hard headed and stupid and as the inventors of the very concept of "nation"'. Paul Ziegler remembered that there was a time, in about 1926, when the world seemed briefly to have returned to normal. His father called him in to discuss his future and suddenly said, 'I am sorry for you boys. I can give you a better start than I had, but when I was young I was surrounded by a peace and security in which anybody, unless he was a crook or exceptionally unlucky, could look forward to a happy life. You boys will never see such a time.'

The Zieglers were Lutherans, of Jewish descent.

Religious observance played no noticeable part in our life and we hardly ever went to church ... We were probably deists; a God who had created the universe with man in it seemed the most reasonable answer to the questions why anything existed and where the human mind came from . . . This God was too distant to be worshipped or even referred to . . . If we wanted more personal objects for our worship we erected altars to the great men of the past, to Classical Greece, to Shakespeare and Goethe, to Monteverdi and Bach, Wagner and Verdi, Giotto and Rembrandt, Kepler, Newton and Darwin.

When Paul and Heinz Ziegler left Prague and came to England they felt immediately at home. England seemed to them the only possible replacement for the vanished Habsburg civilisation. Throughout the First World War they had learned English from an Englishman who had been stranded in central Europe in August 1914. They saw England in the 1930s as 'a world of a courteous and gentle grandeur, of a people who courageously but discreetly bore responsibility, of an urbanity which without spoiling it permeated country life, a world convinced that such things as violence, cruelty, ostentation, greed, were bad manners and simply not done'. After a while Paul Ziegler realised why England had made that impression on him, but realised also that he had been looking at a stage set. The similar fates of the Habsburg and British Empires gave him a strong sense of déjà vu. Listening to English conversations in the late 1930s, he was haunted by what he and his friends had discussed in the 1920s: 'Trusted values had proved delusions . . . having been rich we were poor.' Under the Emperors the German-speaking Bohemians had felt secure as 'a sahib class'; they now found themselves a permanent minority. They were no longer protected by the hierarchical order of the old regime and they resented their loss of power.

Mary took to calling in on Paul and Heinz on her way home from work, and their central European culture and politics became part of her life. They became her replacements for John Platts-Mills and Lewis Clive. Both Zieglers were fiercely anti-Nazi without being either nationalistic or left-wing. Heinz was working for Sir Robert Vansittart, the former head of the Foreign Office, who in the days of appeasement had been judged too anti-Hitler and transferred by Neville Chamberlain to the decorative post of 'Chief Diplomatic Adviser'. Among Heinz's first contacts when he arrived in England was Jan Masaryk, the representative of the Czech government in London since 1925. When Hitler occupied Vienna in March 1938, the Zieglers, 'Viennese' in exile, found common cause with Czech nationalists such as Masaryk who opposed Hitler's next project, the annexation of the

Czech Sudetenland. It was Vansittart who, with Winston Churchill, received the emissary of the German army commanders who were plotting to overthrow Hitler at the time of the Munich crisis. At the same time Vansittart kept Eden and the anti-appeasers informed of the Chamberlain government's thinking.

At the time of the Munich negotiations Masaryk went to see his close friend Eden, who had just resigned as Foreign Secretary, to tell him that the Czech government could not accept Hitler's terms. Eden noted his distress. The fate of Czechoslovakia in which Eden, Masaryk, Vansittart and eventually Heinz Ziegler were involved sounded the death knell for appeasement and became the turning point in Britain's and France's belated opposition to Hitler. The Munich Agreement (Hitler's 'last territorial demand') under which the Sudetenland was ceded to Germany and which guaranteed the independence of the rest of Czechoslovakia, signed on 30 September 1938, was torn up within six months when Hitler occupied Prague on 15 March 1939, so making war inevitable. From then on Jan Masaryk was the representative of the 'free' Czech government, the government in Prague being a Nazi puppet regime and Bohemia having become a German protectorate. Paul Ziegler was already in London, Hans was in America. Heinz did everything he could to persuade his parents to leave Prague. But his father, Ernst, felt quite safe at Loyovitz, the great house with its gateways and bell tower, standing in its own walled park. Ernst Ziegler employed too many people to feel himself in danger: if he abandoned his estate and closed the bank they would all lose their jobs. He and Heinz's mother, Alice, had been in England in September 1938 at the time of the Munich crisis and, incredibly, at a period when thousands of Jews were starting to leave Czechoslovakia, had decided to go back. Ernst Ziegler had influence and connections and no fear of Hitler, whose 'vulgar accent', when heard on the radio, did not impress. As Europe slipped into war, Heinz and Paul could only watch. First the border area of Czechoslovakia, the Sudetenland, then Prague (and Loyovitz) came under Nazi control. Ernst and Alice could no longer leave, even had they wanted to. The Ziegler wealth and influence became irrelevant as their country was dismembered, the Hungarians annexing the southern borderlands, the Slovaks breaking away from Prague. Long before the outbreak of war Jan Masaryk and Heinz Ziegler had become citizens of a country that had been wiped off the map.

Masaryk, as Czech ambassador in London, was an eyewitness to the blackmailing pressure Britain and France had put on his government to accept the annexation of the Sudetenland, and the degree to which Chamberlain's government had betrayed the Czech people. On 25 September he had been summoned by Chamberlain to strengthen the presence of Czechoslovakia at an international conference to settle the dispute. Three days later he sat in the diplomatic gallery of the House of Commons, watching the hysterical enthusiasm with which MPs greeted Chamberlain's announcement that Hitler had invited him to Munich. Only his friend Eden, with a small band that included Churchill and Leo Amery, remained seated. Later that day he was informed that there would be no Czech representatives at Munich 'as Hitler would not stand for it'. As William Shirer wrote: 'The Czechs were not even asked to be present at their own death sentence.' Czechoslovakia had been tricked and betrayed by its allies and would shortly be plundered. On 15 March 1939, as German troops marched into Bohemia and Prague, Mr Chamberlain finally understood whom he was dealing with and announced a British guarantee of Polish independence.

With the outbreak of war, Jan Masaryk and Heinz Ziegler could at least feel the first stirrings of hope that Czechoslovakia might one day be brought back to life. But the only British politicians trusted by the Czechs after the bitter experience of Munich were Eden, Churchill and Lord Cranborne, and they remained out of power for the first eight months of the war. The Czech exiles met and intrigued with, and against, each other in Masaryk's flat in Westminster Gardens, Marsham Street, within easy walking distance of Mary's office in Broadway. Their activities were a matter of legitimate interest to MI5. Technically speaking, German-speaking Bohemians such as Heinz and Paul Ziegler were more or less 'enemy aliens', a matter of official suspicion and subject to internment. In Nazi terms, as 'Sudetenland Germans' they were traitors, not Czechs. But the Zieglers were not supporters of the pro-Nazi Sudeten German Party, they were Social Democrats. In those uncertain circumstances Heinz's position as an adviser to the Foreign Secretary's Chief Diplomatic Adviser was of considerable protective importance.

Jan Masaryk was an embarrassment to the British government for quite different reasons; not because he might feel sympathy for the enemy but because he had identified the enemy long before the British government had managed to do so. Mary's circle of friends quickly became known to her superiors at MI5 and she noticed that she was regularly followed in the evening when she left the office. As Mary Watkins remembers, 'We knew she was going with someone, a foreigner. And there were hints that this was not quite the thing.' Since she now had the entrée to the leading Czech émigrés, and since the Czechs had no idea that she worked for British intelligence, it is hard to believe that no attempt was made to use her new contacts to gather information. If Lady Swinfen had happened to start an affair* with one of the key figures in the Free Czech leadership it would have been no inconvenience to MI5.

On her visits to the Ziegler flat, Mary got to know not only Masaryk but Hermann Rauschning, Hitler's Governor of Danzig, who had turned against the Führer and denounced the Nazis in a book. When Mary realised she was being followed she asked her brother's advice and Hugh suggested that she should paint the mudguards of her bicycle with luminous paint. By her own account this move amused her shadows sufficiently to reassure them and the pursuit was called off; she herself never suggested that she had been asked to report on her friends' opinions.

Heinz made Mary laugh and she learned to see his country's tragedy, which he made light of, through his eyes. Later she remembered,

> He talked very little of his career but a lot about his parents who he adored and Loyovitz. He was professor of economics and politics first I rather think in Berlin, then Frankfurt but when the Nazis came on the scene he moved to Prague . . . He was friends with that bunch in Munich, the [Stefan] George set . . . He knew a lot about music and loved it. Taught me much. He must have known a lot of musicians, because he took me to concert rehearsals and he and Paul were haunted by Furtwängler's secretary, a very ugly woman who was a refugee and kept us entertained with lists of Furtwängler's lovers always ending her sagas with 'but he never made a pass at me', which had Paul and Heinz rolling about in helpless laughter. When I first met him in October, 1939, he was working for Lord Vansittart . . .
>
> More Austrian than Czech, Heinz always pretended he could not speak Czech . . . He rather distrusted the Beneš lot and the Czechs in exile though it was through him I met and made friends with Masaryk . . . To look at he was much taller than Paul with fair wavy hair and grey green eyes. His father called his profile Red Indian. He had very beautiful hands. He was bone thin, long legs and walked in the same hasty shuffling way as Paul, always seeming in a hurry. When he used the telephone the cord would get twisted into knots. He danced very well, loved playing bridge, found P. G. Woodhouse irresistible . . .

---

* MI5 planted a mistress on General Eisenhower in 1944, when the Supreme Allied Commander's military driver was an attractive young Englishwoman named Kay Summers.

After a few weeks the romantic friendship turned into something more serious. One day when she met him for lunch he was in a rage. He had received two letters from Paris by the same post; the first was from his wife Babs who had decided to go to Brazil with his trusted Swedish friend, to get a quick divorce. The second contained a bill for a fur coat that Babs had put on his account just before she left. 'He was much angrier about the coat than he was about the Swede,' Mary remembered. Then, as Mary started to laugh Heinz laughed too, and decided quite quickly to divorce his very pretty German wife, who had been married before and had a daughter, but who had omitted to tell him that she could have no more children. He said nothing to Mary but he was in fact very upset by the departure of Babs.

Mary spent Christmas Day 1939 with Carol and Roger – who was just one year old. Then on Boxing Day she left them and went to Boskenna. Heinz and Paul Ziegler were spending Christmas there with Betty and the Colonel.

At Boskenna the inevitable happened. Heinz and I went to bed and it was wonderful. We walked by moonlight under the trees and in the stillness heard a vixen shriek . . . I remember the vixen, Heinz's bony ribs and Paul not wanting to take in what he saw, but not interfering . . . Love, I would discover, can be ruthless and selfish, as well as sublime. Loving Heinz was one of the best, if not the best thing I ever did and to this day I am thankful and glad of it, grateful for what we had.

That was the Christmas when Boskenna caught fire. The Colonel, growing impatient with damp logs, had poured a spot of paraffin on to the fire in the library and the Penzance Fire Brigade had to be summoned, grumbling mightily at being called out during the festivities. John Bolitho, who was staying locally with his brother, offered Mary a lift back to London but she used the fire as an excuse for remaining longer with Heinz. She discovered that his gaiety and social energy – days filled with bridge, parties and jokes – were a cover for his solitude. He was by now very frightened for his parents,* and would talk for hours about his mother and about Loyovitz. He was determined to go back and to reunite his family.

---

* The first restrictions on the free movement of Jews within the city of Prague had been imposed in November 1939.

CHAPTER SIX

Afternoons in the Ritz

'One of the most difficult things you can do in life is to tell your husband
you have left him without telling him one of the children is not his.'

Mary Wesley

The wartime period was the most vivid of Mary's life and provides the key
to the imaginary world of her novels, but while she lived those years there
was no conscious gathering of material, there was just chaos, exhilaration
and loss.

Mary had been in love with Heinz since October, but after Christmas
they spent more time together. Carol meanwhile had fallen for a very pretty
red-headed woman who worked as an air-raid warden in Ovington Square;
she was called Pamela Hull and she was the wife of his stockbroker. Carol
and Mary began to lead increasingly separate lives. They still shared the
same bed in Ovington Square but were rarely in it at the same time. Mary
would meet Heinz for a sandwich lunch in St James's Park. She remembered the tulips, the starlings on St Paul's Church, Covent Garden, in the
moonlight after dining at the Savoy, having supper together in the house
Heinz shared with Paul, the small restaurants they would go to in Soho.
She told her husband that she worked late and although she never spent
the whole night with Heinz she sometimes slipped past Carol in the blackout
on her way home. Heinz bought her flowers and books, and took her to
concert rehearsals and on Sundays they went together to High Mass in
the Brompton Oratory and lit a candle for his mother. He asked Mary to
promise that if anything happened to him she would care for Alice Ziegler.
It was the long, ominous interlude of the Phoney War. There were no
bombs and for six months, once the German and Soviet armies had finished
with Poland, there was little fighting. At the office Mary's unit decoded

desperate signals from Russian units trapped between the Finnish army and their own front line.

Betty, who had returned from Belgium leaving her husband behind, told Mary that she had fallen for a White Russian ski instructor called Serge who had been conscripted into the French army and was stationed near Paris. In January 1940, Mary heard Betty's 'unmistakable voice' raised in Broadway, in the Passport Office on the floor below. She wanted a visa for France and she wanted it *now*. She left after being refused once again and Mary, worried that Betty would discover where she worked, hurried downstairs and intervened to get her a visa. Shortly after Betty returned from Paris in April she told Mary that she was pregnant, although she never saw Serge again. After the Liberation in 1945 his parents in Paris refused to speak about him. Serge was said to have been among the White Russians who had ended up fighting on the same side as the Germans. He became just another of the thousands who disappeared into the fog of war. According to Boris, who knew him, Serge was 'absolutely straight and thick as two short planks – quite unlike Betty'.

One day Heinz told Mary that he was fed up with the politics of exile and that he had decided to use his contacts to get himself into the armed forces. He had 'a *Baronin*'* working with him in his office, an anti-Nazi German, and he said he would 'give the *Baronin* to Bowra'. In due course Maurice Bowra† did indeed receive the *Baronin* at Wadham College, where she assisted him in his war work and seduced him. The *Baronin* settled, Heinz and Mary had lunch at Czardas, a Hungarian restaurant in Soho, which, despite its plate-glass windows, remained open during air raids, and began to talk about the most amusing way they could live their lives. Mary said that perhaps the most amusing thing a woman could do was to have several children by different fathers. Then they walked down Piccadilly and through Hyde Park to the Serpentine, and strolled under the bridge. Mary never forgot this walk and the path beneath the bridge on the north side of the Serpentine became a place of memory for her. It appears repeatedly in her novels, a place where vows are made and broken, a symbol of the transitory nature of passionate relationships and the dangers of giving all the heart, particularly in wartime. As they walked under the bridge on that spring day in 1940 she had a strong premonition that, deeply as she loved

---

* The Baroness von Wangenheim.
† Short but prominent Oxford don; wit, bisexual and classicist, later influential Warden of Wadham. Coined the phrase 'homintern'.

Heinz, their happiness would not last and some half-remembered lines, 'First Pierrot and then Pierrette, then a story to forget', came into her head.

She once wrote, 'War makes drunkards and lovers, and loosens all values.' In April, Germany invaded Denmark and Norway, and one month later the *Wehrmacht* attacked Holland, Belgium and France. Mary's decoding unit became frantically busy. Bolitho's girls were frequently woken at night and ordered back into the office where they would receive news of the successive military disasters before these were announced in the House of Commons. It was at this time that she was infected by the mood of excitement and fear and recklessness that carried her and her friends forward into the war. 'War is very erotic,' she recalled. 'People had love affairs they otherwise wouldn't have had.' Lovemaking with an attractive acquaintance, provided he had a uniform to take off, became a positive contribution to the war effort. It was a sensation as old as war itself; it must have added greatly to the success of the ball given by the Duchess of Richmond on the eve of Waterloo. As the British Expeditionary Force fell back and the Belgian army surrendered, this mood intensified. By 25 May the BEF was on half rations and had insufficient ammunition to counter-attack. Amid chaos and confusion British forces abandoned Arras and headed for the coast, with retreat turning to rout. The desperation of the situation was far more apparent inside Broadway than it was to the general public. One of the first victims of the German attack on France was Neville Chamberlain, who was forced to resign on 10 May. Two weeks later the first 7,000 soldiers were evacuated from Dunkirk and on the following day, 28 May, Winston Churchill told the House of Commons to prepare for 'hard and heavy tidings'.

Heinz had been through all this three times already – over the Sudetenland, then Prague, then Poland – and he was becoming accustomed to the cycle of Allied failure; lack of preparation, insufficient forces and self-deception were the familiar heralds of Nazi triumph. As Churchill started to prepare the country for news of a great defeat, Mary and Heinz, working for MI5 and the Foreign Office, already knew what was happening. With the British army broken in France and evacuated without its weapons and equipment, it was obvious that an invasion was imminent. On 22 June France fell, and in London the poet James Reeves, seeing the newspaper hoardings, wrote that he 'was conscious of living through the worst day of history'. Her brother Hugh ran into a school friend, George Dawnay, who had been an usher at Mary's wedding. Hugh asked after his mother. Viscountess Downe lived in Norfolk and had before the war been surprised while writing 'Heil Hitler!'

in white paint on the local highway. 'My mother', her son replied, 'is singing a different tune these days. My brother has been taken prisoner and my uniform's still wet from queuing in the sea off Dunkirk.' Jan Masaryk and Hermann Rauschning were on Himmler's 'Special Search List', part of Germany's post-invasion plans, together with Noël Coward and Sigmund Freud. As a German-speaking Bohemian working with the enemy, Heinz would have been shot or sent to a concentration camp when the Germans reached London.

Mary asked one of her bosses, a Cambridge don, about the immediate future and supposed the Germans would be in London in about a fortnight. 'Oh no,' he replied, 'more like six weeks. Shall we dine on the 24th?' She thought about Heinz, of his determination to fight, of all he had lost in Prague and of the only thing he wanted that she could give him, and waited her chance. She conceived at a time when the baby could have been her husband's – it was during the Dunkirk evacuation – and only she would have known whose child she carried. Some time in June she told Heinz; he seemed delighted, even amused. He remembered the conversation in Czardas and called her 'a crazy girl'. To Mary he seemed 'farouche', unsociable or untamed.

In August Bolitho's unit was moved to Bletchley, Margaret Royds left Broadway to get married, Betty Paynter – five months pregnant – decided to move to Boskenna and Mary's doctor told her that there was no question of her staying in London; there was a general instruction that all pregnant women should be evacuated. As the country waited for invasion, London, for those still there, became incredibly beautiful. The sun shone, the city – empty of children and with little traffic – was calm; the parks were full of flowers. 'there was an extraordinary feeling of anticipation, almost exhilaration'.

Heinz had used his political contacts to get into a Czech RAF squadron as an interpreter and was expecting to be posted to Cambridge. The logical thing for Mary to do was to take Roger and his nanny and join Betty at Boskenna.

But first there was an illogical episode. Many years later Mary said, 'The best thing about being pregnant in those days was that you could go to bed with whoever you wanted to, without having to worry about getting pregnant.' She was remembering an evening early in July 1940, when she was still in London with invasion imminent. She had tonsillitis, she was four weeks pregnant and she was feeling too ill to go out to dinner when the telephone rang and it was John Hudson. Hudson had been the most attractive and the least persistent of her Indian admirers. When Mary broke away from 'the fishing fleet' and returned to England in 1934, Hudson had continued with his original plan and married the governor's daughter. Early in 1940 he was recalled from India and ordered to join the invasion force that was being assembled to go to the assistance of Finland. This expedition was cancelled before it could set out and Hudson's unit was redeployed to another lost cause, the Norway expedition. Before he embarked in April 1940, Hudson had telephoned Mary and told her that, despite his marriage, his feelings were the same and that 'six years makes no difference'. They had lunch and Mary acknowledged that even though she had fallen in love with Heinz, there was 'unfinished business' between her and John Hudson. It was a repetition of an earlier experience, of loving one man and being attracted to another. While 'in love' with Peter Hope she had fallen for John Hudson. Now, in love with Heinz, she found her frustrated interest in Hudson to be as strong as ever. In India he had invited her to dinner and undressed her in front of the fire, a memory that left them both eager to see each other again. For the rest of her life her recall of their eventual reunion remained clear.

From her bedroom in Ovington Square, Mary could hear a loudspeaker van circulating, asking for pots and pans, 'one of Lord Beaverbrook's[*] bright ideas for winning the war'. Mary jiggled the telephone receiver by her bed until Biddy answered in the kitchen below and she could issue her instructions: 'Don't you dare give them a thing.' Then the bedside telephone rang properly and Hudson, back from Norway, was saying he 'absolutely had to' see her. Somehow, he persuaded her to get up. They dined at the Berkeley and went back to his rooms in Victoria where their lovemaking was interrupted by an air raid. Thinking of this 'calamitous' incident Mary wrote, 'I don't know why I did such a thing.' She had never been in love with Hudson, but she had wanted him nonetheless. She never saw or heard of him again, and their business remained unfinished until she exorcised the memory by using it in both *The Camomile Lawn* and *Not That Sort of Girl*.

Later that summer Mary packed up Ovington Square, sent some of Carol's pictures to her parents in Somerset for safe keeping, and despatched a

[*] Max Aitken, 1st Baron Beaverbrook, newspaper magnate and friend of Churchill, recruited to wartime Cabinet for supposed expertise in propaganda. The appeal for aluminium saucepans was launched on 11 July 1940.

Sheraton desk, a pair of Zoffanys, a gramophone with a collection of Mozart and Beethoven records and her dog Pomfret down to Boskenna. Carol was concentrating on Mrs Hull and as the Blitz started he disappeared into the ARP, 'a curious underworld of rotas and stirrup pumps, wearing a tin helmet'. He welcomed the departure of Roger for the safety of Cornwall. When told of Mary's pregnancy he, like Heinz, had radiated approval and 'never uttered a hint of doubt'. Mary took a taxi to Paddington Station, said goodbye to Heinz on the platform and cried for five hours on the train to Penzance.

The chief advantage of the move to Boskenna was that it enabled Mary to separate from her husband. Three years after it had taken place, the Swinfens' marriage had become a formality. But she did not announce the collapse of the relationship, even to her friends. At a time when divorcées were ostracised, and when a conventional family such as the Farmars regarded divorce as an indelible stigma, it was far easier for Mary to lead an independent life without publicly challenging convention. No one but Mary knew who had fathered her second child, but she always told herself – and later Eric – that Heinz was the father, and Heinz always accepted this. It nonetheless remained the understanding between Carol and Mary that he was the father and for the rest of his life Carol acknowledged Mary's second child as his own. He did not want a divorce and – on the face of it – it was the war that had separated him from his wife. Mary, pregnant, needed to get out of London; Carol, part of the ARP, had to confront the Blitz. But Mary later said that she knew when she left Ovington Square she would never go back to Carol.

By the time the blitzing of London started* on 7 September 1940, Mary was already in Boskenna and this remained her home until 1945. There were many places in the country she might have gone to have her baby, but Betty Paynter had become one of her closest friends; it was a friendship based on high spirits and a common predicament. Quite a few people in St Buryan, on hearing that Betty's baby was due in November, started to calculate on their fingers. At the relevant time her husband Olaf had been at 'Boskenna Deux' near Ghent, while Betty had been in London or Paris. But Mary's ambiguous situation passed unsuspected and her stuck-up nanny was able to continue snubbing St Buryan. When people met Nanny on a walk and peered

---

* The first daytime raid by 1,300 bombers left 2,000 dead or seriously injured and many thousands of Londoners homeless. The attacks continued at this pace, often on a nightly basis, for nine months.

at the pushchair and said, 'Oh, is that Lady Swinfen's little boy? Let's have a look,' Nanny replied, 'Yes, it's the Honourable Roger' and pushed on. Mary realised Nanny was far too grand for West Cornwall and would have to go.

Betty's father was absorbed in his new role as colonel of the Home Guard and Boskenna filled up with evacuee children. Betty, Mary and Alice Grenfell, the cook, combed out the nits. The girls were crammed into dormitories in the attics and the boys were boarded out in estate workers' cottages. In the winter evenings Mary would tell the children ghost stories, and 'Colonel' would supervise their tap-dancing practice around the Ideal Boiler in the long stone-flagged corridor outside the kitchen, the only warm spot in the house. The boys came from the East End and one of them, called Rusty, soon made himself unpopular. Mary told him that nobody wanted him to stay because he stole things. "Course I steal,' he replied. 'I've got to practise. Me dad's a burglar.' Mary said that was perfectly normal in London but 'We don't steal in the country'. After that he agreed to go straight. The house was a happy hunting ground for children. There was a parrot in the kitchen which greeted all and sundry, including the Vicar, with 'I heard you, I heard you, you bugger.' There were two carthorses called Victoria and Albert that the children were allowed to drive, and there was a resident rabbit catcher and a collection of ghosts. Early in the war, Mary's pug Pomfret died and was succeeded by True. True was a stray mongrel who followed Mary home to Boskenna. After several months she was reclaimed by the butcher from St Just who demanded a large sum on the grounds that he had trained the dog to steal poultry from farmyards while he was delivering meat at the front door. Mary was always very proud that True had left the butcher and chosen to live with her.

Boskenna in winter was a cold house. Open fires in the library and drawing room provided the only heating. The maids would lay fires in some of the bedrooms, but these did not last the night. From her bed, Mary could see the Scots pines outside the window and hear the rooks cawing endlessly in the wind. Here she read T.S. Eliot, and at night, with German bombers rumbling in the sky overhead, found comfort in the lines,

> Repeat a prayer also on behalf of
> Women who have seen their sons or husbands
> Setting forth and not returning:
> Figlia del tuo Figlio
> Queen of Heaven . . .

which 'seemed so apt when it was not possible to exist without anxiety.' She rediscovered her childish delight in the poetry of Shakespeare, Tennyson, Coleridge and Milton that her mother had taught her to recite 'by the yard', even before she could read, and she recited it again before she fell asleep. Her bedroom was haunted by an invisible visitor who entered by a door on one side of the bed and left by a door on the other – always leaving both doors open. One night, fed up with having to get out of bed yet again, Mary said politely, 'Please close the door.' The ghost obliged and did not call again. Mary was frequently bored, and boredom is 'when you start inventing'. Often she would spend the afternoon and evening in bed with a hot-water bottle, reading, writing poetry and trying to keep warm. Paul Ziegler gave her *Grey Eminence* by Aldous Huxley and Rilke's *The Notebook of Malt Laurids Brigge*, Heinz gave her Eliot's *Choice of Kipling's Verse*. She finished *War and Peace*, discovered *The Bible to be Read as Literature* and played Bach, Beethoven and Brahms on the gramophone to her unborn baby. Seeing the war through the eyes of anti-Nazi Bohemians, she could never regard it as an anti-German war. She noticed and remembered the details that complicate the oversimplifications of patriotism. There was her love for a man who hated Hitler but had been born, like him, in the Habsburg Empire. There was the fact that those who loved Beethoven would tune in to a German wireless station in the evening to hear the best performance, possibly conducted by Furtwängler. And there was the way the boys playing war games on the beach at Westward Ho just after Dunkirk would shout 'Bags I be German', the winning side. She once watched 'an enormous bomber' flying low over undefended Cornish cliffs on its way to bomb the radio station at the Lizard in daylight: the evacuee children from London shouted 'That's a Junkers 88!' and waved to the pilot – who waved back. Even in West Cornwall, Mary experienced the war as a cosmopolitan struggle that had nothing to do with her mother's visceral hatred of 'the Hun'.

That autumn, before Betty's baby was born in a nursing home in Penzance, Heinz came to stay. Trying to join in the horseplay of the young men in the officers' mess, he had tripped over a waste-paper basket and succeeded in breaking his leg. He was awarded six weeks' convalescence. Maurice Bowra, alerted by the *Baronin*, rescued him from an RAF hospital and installed him in the Radcliffe Infirmary in Oxford. By the time he reached Boskenna he was well enough to make love. He and Mary had been writing to each other several times a week; sometimes they telephoned, but wartime calls were restricted to three minutes, after which the operator chipped in with 'Time's up' and cut you off. In October Mary had travelled to Cambridge for the weekend; they had walked along the Backs and listened to the organ in King's College Chapel. At the end of her life, Mary remembered those moments as 'imprinted'. Even though he was in the RAF, Heinz seemed to be quite safe. He was almost past military age and as an interpreter he was grounded. But he was not enjoying his time with the Czech squadron. For one thing, he had always pretended that he could not speak Czech. In London Jan Masaryk was battling on, demanding official recognition for the Free Czech government. In December the Foreign Secretary, his friend Anthony Eden, announced that Masaryk's government had 'provisional recognition'. Masaryk was furious and wrote to ask whether 'the Czech airmen are provisionally dead? Yours provisionally, Jan.' Full recognition took another seven months of struggle and incredibly the Munich Agreement that had ceded the Sudetenland to the Nazis was not repudiated until 1942.

But Heinz was losing interest in the shadow-boxing of a government-in-exile. There were rumours that his parents had been arrested and he managed to arrange a transfer to a British squadron, still with a ground job.

Mary's son was delivered on the last day of February in the same nursing home in Penzance where Betty's daughter, christened Sonya, had been born. Growing impatient, she had gone down to the rocks below Boskenna and jumped up and down to hurry things up. Both Mary and her baby were ill after the birth. Carol came down from London to visit Mary in the nursing home and he placed the usual announcement – 'A second son to Lady Swinfen' – in the Court Circular. Heinz, who by this time had been posted to Scotland, could not visit her but a trusted neighbour, Mrs Grant – who had become a confidante of Mary's – agreed to pass on the news.

In June, the Honourable Hugh Toby Swinfen Eady was christened at the parish church of St Buryan. Two photographs of this event have survived. The first shows a conventional family group: Lady Swinfen and her baby, her brother Hugh and John Bolitho, the godfather, in uniform, Mrs Grant and Mrs Bolitho and Betty. This photograph was circulated by Mary to some of her friends. John Montagu-Pollock, the absent godfather, wrote to Mary from Denver, Colorado, thanking her and adding, 'from the benign expression on [the baby's] face it is a little hard to believe that "he has a voice like Hitler broadcasting".' In a postscript he wrote, 'I was delighted to see how well you and Hugh looked in your photos; sorry that Carol was not there too.' In other words the photograph of Toby's christening that Mary kept and circulated did not include her husband. In fact, Carol was there and a second photograph, taken in front of the porch, shows Lord and Lady Swinfen with their two children. Mary stands holding the baby. Carol is crouched down, apart from her and restraining a mischievous-looking Roger. The picture of Carol and Roger is unremarkable; a father gently encouraging his small son to stand still and look at the camera. Beside him Mary is not looking at the camera but through it; she has a strikingly intense expression and she is holding the baby forward, almost as though offering it to someone who is not in the picture. It is a study of a woman with a separate agenda. It was at about this time that one of Mary's friends said to her, 'Do you have to make it so obvious?' When Mary asked what she meant her friend replied, 'Every time Carol walks into the room, you get up and leave it.'

In the published descriptions that Mary left of wartime life in West Cornwall she tended to dwell on the landscape, the flower farms and the odd military incident turning to farce; a German bomber scoring a direct hit on the cellars of the only wine merchant in Penzance, or her neighbour Mrs Favell watching from the cliffs and urging on an RAF bomber that was trying to sink a German submarine – only to be told that evening by her naval officer son that the bomber had been German and the submarine his. These dramatic incidents took place against a background dominated by more practical problems. At Boskenna, Mary made the butter and kept hens, ducks, geese and turkeys, the poultry having the run of the lawns and park surrounding the house. 'A lively black market in petrol and food', masterminded by the Colonel, with the assistance of a local solicitor, Paul Hill, was soon in place. The evacuees kept coming. After the original foursome from the East End a party arrived from Perivale, then more from Plymouth as the German attack switched from London to England's western ports.

These evacuees joined a household that already contained a nursery of four children. The nursery was run by Alice Grenfell, Colonel Paynter's cook, the sister of his First World War batman. Alice had started by looking after Sonya, the Colonel's granddaughter; before long Sonya was joined by Roger and then by Nicky Blackwood, the daughter of a fighter pilot, Bill Blackwood, who had been shot down in 1940 and badly burned. One day Alice Grenfell came into Mary's bedroom while Toby's nappy was being

changed and said, 'Lady Swinfen, you cannot look after that baby. Give
him to me.' And Mary was free.

Lady Swinfen joined the WVS and put her excellent French to use by
helping the Belgian fishermen who had installed themselves with their boats,
families, pets and priest at Newlyn harbour. Mary's work for the WVS was
a mixed success. Following an incident when the Lady Mayor of Penzance
asked her to leave the hall for making 'unsuitable jokes', she and Betty were
redirected to organise the entertainment of any officers or men who wanted
to come to their neighbourhood on leave. This resulted in a long-drawn-out
house party at Boskenna that lasted until the end of the war.

When, forty years after the war, Mary Wesley began to draw on her
memories for novels such as *The Camomile Lawn* the wild girls were unmarried and it was their middle-aged aunt who left her husband. The real-
life wild girls of Boskenna – Mary and Betty – were both married, in the
legal sense at least. They were joined by Diana Blackwood, mother of Nicky,
who had also left her husband and who was determined to take up a social
life that became even more hectic than Mary's. Boskenna's fame spread by
word of mouth, Betty's social energy making her a natural catalyst for any
servicemen on leave. Colonel Paynter, with the Home Guard organised to
his satisfaction, and the Black Market running smoothly, took to wearing
an ancient green bowler hat and continued his war work as master of the
revels. And Mary found that as a young woman separated from her husband
she was considered fair game and required to do 'a lot of fending off'.
Later she wrote,

> I was 'wild' if that is the right word for it, for about four years, but I was
> not happy. I was unhappy at what I did to Heinz, I was unhappy at what
> I was doing to Carol, but being unhappy does not stop you doing what-
> ever is causing the unhappiness. I was to feel guilty and unhappy for
> several years with a variety of lovers, each of them transient . . . If I had
> been a man people would have said, 'He's sowing his wild oats.' I sowed
> mine and must admit that on the whole it was a lot of fun. I was doing
> what girls do nowadays before they marry and if I found it enjoyable so
> did my lovers.

The first of these lovers was Robert d'Alsace. He was a friend of Mary's
admirer, Boris Melikof. On the outbreak of war Melikof had enlisted in
the French army. His last telephone call from somewhere in France had
been cut off in June 1940. After the French surrender, Boris had escaped

capture as a prisoner of war and managed to cross the Pyrénées. In Spain he was arrested and sent to Miranda, the Spanish internment camp; from there he could write to England. He demanded assistance. 'Get me out of here,' he wrote. 'Vouch for me.' The Colonel, who was no leftie, seemed to think that Boris was better off in the camp but eventually wrote the necessary reference. While Boris was waiting he met a fellow internee, Robert d'Alsace, a Parisian barrister who was Jewish and who had escaped from Dunkirk in a dinghy and rowed across the Channel. He had gone back to France to rejoin the French army and then, following the Armistice, managed to make a second escape, this time across the Pyrénées. In Miranda Robert d'Alsace spent a lot of time playing bridge with Boris until both were rescued by the British military attaché in Madrid and sent to England. They arrived together but Boris was detained for months in Patriotic School*, this time by Colonel Passy, head of the Gaullist Intelligence Service in London and even less of a socialist than Colonel Paynter. Robert, on the other hand, was released almost at once and came to Boskenna bearing Boris's letter of introduction.

Mary said that she had no excuse for Robert, other than the fact that he was funny, attractive and a good lover. 'He used to make me laugh, much to Heinz's annoyance. We had a brief affair. I was always rather impressed by his walk over the Pyrénées. Eventually the French sent him to New Caledonia. When he returned he wanted to start again but it was nothing doing.' After the war, Robert d'Alsace returned to Paris, made a lot of money out of insurance and married a rich wife. Mary used to go and stay with them.

John Hudson, and their doomed arrangements, had made little impression on Mary's conscience, but she became very upset, perhaps because it was so enjoyable, about her brief, high-spirited relationship with Robert d'Alsace. Having succumbed, she was appalled and felt that she must tell Heinz what she had done. He was by then stationed in North Wales, so she set out to make her confession, feeling that she had destroyed everything. When she told Heinz what had happened he laughed. He said that she had destroyed nothing, that it was just something that had occurred, that it meant nothing, that it made no difference to him. 'He was very . . . *worldly* about such things,' she said. 'I was quite often unfaithful to Heinz,

---

* Former girls' school in south London used as a holding centre for unknown individuals, including resisters, newly arrived from the Continent. A legendary place in Free French memory.

I couldn't resist it. But he never made scenes. He was always amused and forgiving.' She knew that she would continue seeing Robert d'Alsace and that there would in due course be others. 'It was a flighty generation,' said Mary. 'We had been brought up so repressed. War freed us. We felt if we didn't do it now, we might never get another chance.' This was Calypso's war, as portrayed in *The Camomile Lawn*, the lover on the sofa, the husband on the stairs and the Lagonda abandoned some way from the kerb.

At Boskenna Mary's life alternated between periods of calm – when Betty was in London and Mary was alone with the old Colonel, Alice and the children – and more hectic episodes in the company of her lovers, French, English or Czech, and at least one American. She also spent an increasing amount of time in London, a favourite meeting place being the Ritz Hotel, with its eighty-eight bedrooms and steel-girdered construction. Nicky Blackwood remembers Mary and her mother, Diana, making 'rare appearances' at Boskenna, 'looking mysteriously gay and glamorous, usually swathed in mink and in a hurry.' This period started in 1941 and went on for over three years. For Mary there was a direct connection between her fear of the raids, the whistling shriek made by a stick of bombs falling nearby, and the release offered by sex. She was afraid of sleeping underground. At Boskenna she remembered 'three curious nights with a huge Free French pilot with unusually large feet who left his pants in my bed to be found next morning by the daily housemaid'.* There was another Free French Spitfire pilot known as Chris Martell. He arrived at Boskenna equipped with a pair of black silk pyjamas with his initials embroidered on the pocket. The pyjamas in particular were a great success. Shortly afterwards he was killed when he flew his plane straight into the ground. Then there were 'one or two skirmishes with Mr Jones', undertaken to annoy his girlfriend, 'who wore one red lantern and one green in her ears'. She spent a night with an old admirer, Gage Williams, who had been badly wounded in the First War, on the grounds that he had 'wanted it so long it seemed cruel to deny him'. This followed a day spent riding on Dartmoor when Gage, who drank freely, decided he had just seen a herd of llamas and must have the DTs. Mary was able to calm him by declaring that she too had seen the llamas; they had been released on to the moor by Paignton Zoo.

---

* Because Boskenna was so cold the usual practice was to get into bed before getting undressed. This added to the excitement of the occasion and may also have explained how the underpants went missing.

Above left) The actress Hyacinthe Rolland, great-great-great grandmother of Mary Wesley and of H.M. the Queen, and mistress of Richard Wesley, later Lord Wellesley. He made an honest woman of her by marrying her after the birth of their fifth child.
(*Above right*) Mary's maternal grandfather, 'the great ear, nose and throat man of his day', Sir William Dalby. 'Taken May 2nd 1911.'

(*Right*) Mary's adored grandmother, Hyacinthe Dalby, née Wellesley. Mary kept this photograph in a silver frame by her bedside.

(*Above left*) Mary's father, Mynors Farmar, aged thirty-six, photographed in 1915 shortly before setting off for Gallipoli with the Lancashire Fusiliers. (*Above right*) Mary's mother, Violet Farmar. 'My mother was incapable of hiding her feelings, and I was just a boring appendage.'

(*Above*) April 1914: Mary aged nearly two, at Englefield Green, where she was born. With Hugh.

(*Right*) Mary's beloved Nanny, Hilda Scott. 'She'd stand by me and she never criticised.'

(*Above*) Mary eating seaweed on the beach in Cornwall, June 1913, flanked by her sister Susan and her brother Hugh.

(*Right*) 1917: Hugh, Susan and Mary.

(*Above*) September 1927:
Self. Mary at 'home school'.
All the other members of her
family were abroad, and she
was left behind for two years
by herself.

(*Above right*) October 1933:
Mary fooling around with
two gunners on board ship
on the way to India.
'For the first time in my
life I was really free.'

(*Right*) 1934: Mary paddling in
Suffolk with flighty Aunt Rose
and a dog called Dink.

(*Above*) On the way to the Faeroes with
John Montagu-Pollock who 'began my initiation …
with much laughter and friendship in a spirit of joint
and relaxed discovery'.

Sailing off the coast of Devon: Lewis Clive (*below*,
with an unidentified friend) and John Platts-Mills
(*right*) gave Mary an intensive course in politics and
her first experience of being attracted to two men
at the same time. Lewis, who had hoped to marry
Mary, died in the Spanish Civil War.

(*Left*) A more suitable life: on holiday in the Basses - Pyrénées. Boyfriend Roger Barnett, Mary, Evie Bray.

(*Above*) 1935: Another of many hats. Mary feeding grapes to Carol Swinfen: picnic in Eastern Europe.

(*Left*) Mary in her two-piece bathing costume.

(*Below*) Charles Eady, 1st Baron Swinfen of Chertsey, Master of the Rolls.

(*Above*) Easter 1936: House party at Boskenna. Pat Buckley, Mary, Carol Swinfen, Betty Paynter, Brian Berletson. 'Mary and Betty hunted in pairs. They were deadly.'

(*Left*) September 1936: House party at Boskenna. From the top left: Colonel Paynter, Nina Boulasse, unidentified, Mary, Carol Swinfen, Germaine Halot (almost hidden), Betty Paynter, unidentified, Boris Melikof, Willi Halot. Mary was half in love with Boris Melikof.

(*Below*) Mary's photograph of 'Orchid', aka George Aukett, the long-serving butler at Boskenna.

(*Above*) Mary Farmar and Carol Swinfen married in January 1937.
Mary's brother, Hugh, was best man, and Carol's nephew and niece, Peter and Venice Myers,
were page and one of the bridesmaids (far right). 'My parents… wanted their daughters to
marry a certain kind of person.'

(*Above*) Mary and Carol on honeymoon in
New York. 'There was, puzzlingly, no sex.'
(*Right*) Cigarette in hand, glamorous in her
peeress's robes and tiara, Mary waits in the
taxi queue after the Coronation of George
VI. Next in the line is Viscount Elibank, one-
time acting governor of the Windward
Islands. Carol, on her other side, was cut out
of the picture that she stuck in her album.

Gage Williams died in a motor accident shortly after his unexpected success with Mary.

She spent 'two vague nights' with a Spitfire pilot who flew unarmed missions on photographic reconnaissance. Shortly afterwards he was shot down and killed. Then there were ten days with 'an exquisitely beautiful' young Czech in the Paratroops. She eventually dismissed him because he had 'a cruel mind'. One of her longest affairs was with a fighter pilot called Paddy Green.* This officer had been badly wounded during the Battle of Britain when he was shot down into the sea, but he carried on until the end of the war, flying and fighting, 'winning DFCs and DSOs'. He never told Mary he loved her or wanted to commit himself but he was 'insanely' jealous. 'I love fucking you,' was the nearest he got to a romantic reflection. Mary said that he was 'very beautiful, very reticent and an extremely bad lover, a positive stockbroker of a lover'. He kept a case of whisky under Betty Paynter's bed. At night he would have nightmares and would bail out of bed 'screaming, with arms and legs flailing the air', and she would have to bail out of bed on the other side to avoid getting a black eye. He told her he was terrified, but he was also exceptionally brave. Neither was faithful to the other but Green warned her that if he ever found out she had deceived him he would murder her. 'Of course I haven't been unfaithful,' she would lie and for over a year they would 'rush together' whenever they got the chance.† In 1943 Paddy Green was posted to North Africa, where he told people that Lady Swinfen had promised to marry him, which was untrue, and she never saw him again, although she heard after the war that he had married a Canadian military nurse.

On one occasion General de Gaulle came to Newlyn to visit the French fishermen who were still based there. In his entourage was the head of his intelligence service, André Dewavrin, known as 'Colonel Passy'. Dewavrin was a tall, slim, fair-haired man in his early thirties with blue eyes and a baby face who had the reputation of being brutal and fiercely anti-Communist. He was said to be a member of the extreme-right terrorist group known as 'la Cagoule' (the cowl).†† Colonel Passy was an important figure in the history of the Free French and had a major influence on Resistance

---

* Squadron-leader C. P. Green DSO, DFC, commanding officer of 600 Squadron.
† His previous girlfriend had been Beaverbrook's daughter, Janet. She sent 'blackmailing letters' to Carol, who showed them to Mary and asked her what he should do with them.
†† The anti-Gaullist resister, and Soviet agent, André Labarthe, probably started this rumour.

operations in France. In *Not That Sort of Girl* Mary alluded to the vicious
political rivalry within the French Resistance and the suspicion within
British Intelligence that Colonel Passy was capable of arranging for the
betrayal and murder of Communist resisters. For some reason Passy ended
his visit to Newlyn at Boskenna where, since all the bedrooms were in
use, he was allocated the billiard table. Finding that too uncomfortable he
managed to negotiate the entrée to Mary's room. She described what
followed as 'an odd night'. Passy was apparently on twenty-four-hour duty
and would interrogate her while making love. He seemed mainly interested in asking her questions about her left-wing friends such as Melikof
and Raymond Lee. But the connection with both Raymond Lee and
Colonel Passy raises the possibility that Mary may still have been working
for MI5.

Raymond Lee was another graduate of the Miranda Camp. He never
used his real name and travelled to and from France regularly throughout
the war. He was famously indiscreet and would call Mary at Boskenna over
an open telephone line to say he was just off to Paris and did she want
anything? He had been told by Boris and Robert that she wouldn't touch
him with a bargepole so she gave him a big surprise because she thought
he was bound to die. He was delighted and told everyone, but nobody
believed him because he was a known liar. One Battle of Britain pilot who
knew Mary in those days remembered 'a very, very pretty girl with raven
black hair and a deep laugh. She and Betty used to hunt in pairs. They
were deadly.'

Apart from the changing cast of officers on leave there were other visitors
to Boskenna. Parties of commandos trained on the cliffs using explosives, and
two men from the Special Boat Service (SBS) were taken out across the
Channel night after night, thought to be measuring depths. They used to
come into the house in the early morning for a bath. Two sisters arrived called
the Emmanuels, described in the neighbourhood as 'two Hungarian tarts'.
One was already married, to a very rich man, and the other had her sights
set on a Duke. (She eventually bagged the Duke of Sutherland.) They set
themselves up with two other sisters in the stables where drunken, raffish
behaviour was reputed to take place. Mary did not like any of them much
and felt nothing in common with them, but she could see that from an
onlooker's point of view 'we were *all* a lot of tarts'. Jenifer Murray, who
later became a friend of Mary's, and who was in the WRNS during the war,
does not agree with this description. 'Promiscuity was not the word for
her behaviour during the war,' she says. 'We were all of us in a constant

state of . . . turmoil. Because they were all going to be killed. But Mary once said to me; 'It got to the state where one woke up in the morning, reached across the pillow and thought, "Let's see. Who is it this time?"'

Whereas in the First War the soldiers did not talk about their fear when they were on leave, in the Second War they would open up. Mary's father never told her mother of his fear and exhaustion, as he confessed many years later to Mary. But the pilots who came to Boskenna were quite frank about their feelings. They'd say, 'I'm sorry I'm being so bloody and so rude, but I'm scared witless, and I've got to go back on Ops tomorrow.' And they'd start to talk about it. In these circumstances the impulsive response of women like Mary Swinfen was a precious gift. One of Mary's Wellesley cousins was enjoying herself so much being generous to numerous Polish boyfriends that she used her influence to delay her husband's return to England from his hazardous overseas posting.

'War is very erotic,' as Mary had said. War is erotic because the constant presence of death provokes the need for an intense affirmation of life. Britain under attack, with death threatening every city street and two million men under arms, was subject to that intense need. 'In ordinary life people try to suppress the evil in themselves, or at least I do. But in the war we thought, why the hell shouldn't I do what I want?' Mary said on another occasion. Life, if you were still there to enjoy it, became a party and moral values were inverted. The accepted peacetime rules of both decency and fidelity seemed to have been suspended for the duration. Sometimes, when she was in Boskenna, Mary felt so safe that she was ashamed. In London she could share in the danger. In March 1941, on the night that over one thousand people attended Queen Charlotte's Ball at Grosvenor House, the basement dancing floor at the fashionable Café de Paris received a direct hit, leaving eighty-four 'party-goers' dead. Mary eventually used this incident in *Part of the Furniture*.

Several of her friends, including June Sempill and Elizabeth Pollock, were killed in the Blitz and Grizel Wolfe Murray died at sea in an open boat after her ship was sunk by a submarine. On the other hand, when Mary heard that Carol had nearly been killed by a German bomb she felt disappointed about his survival; the guilt induced by their relationship meant that his life had become an inconvenience. In the dance of the night-time corridors Boskenna echoed to what Mary called 'a death rattle of life'. It was a dance in which conventional standards played little part. While Paddy Green slept beside her, or cried out in fear, Mary could hear Heinz's impatient tramping up and down the passage outside. She once had to lock Boris Melikof in a wardrobe where he spent the rest of the night, to make room for a more importunate lover. Meanwhile the rheumy eye of the master of the revels saw more than it revealed. On the morning after Colonel Passy had disappeared from the billiard room into some unidentified part of a very full house, Colonel Paynter asked his daughter, 'Is your friend Lady Swinfen sleeping with our guest?' At the end of it all Mary was unrepentant. 'There's a lot to be said for looking back on one's sins with enjoyment,' she wrote, 'and on the whole I do.' In old age the memories came in useful on sleepless nights, when Mary said that she counted lovers as others counted sheep.

The habit of loving more than one person at the same time, repeatedly described in her fiction, supposedly started in Brittany when she was thirteen years old and undoubtedly developed in the extreme conditions of wartime, may help to explain Mary's carefree attitude to Heinz Ziegler. At some point towards the end of 1942, or early in 1943, while Mary was distracting herself with her hectic social life, Heinz managed to get himself transferred into an air-training unit stationed in Scotland. He started on Wellington bombers and was selected at the age of thirty-nine as air gunner. She travelled to see him.

> I went up to Scotland, a long tedious journey to see Heinz. He was frightened and thrilled, flying in Wellington bombers, edging his way into operational flying, . . . I found him under a superficial gay exterior a deeply hurt man, mortally wounded ready to die. Gay. All his letters are gay, he rarely admitted defeat nor was he ever defeated even though at one time I thought he was. In truth he soared above a lot of shabby people he admired – me especially.

Jan Masaryk was very angry when he heard that Heinz had switched to 'Ops'. He sometimes invited Mary to supper in his London flat and once asked her to intervene and get Heinz grounded. She would sit watching Jan cook while she ate a whole pot of caviar given to him by Mr Maiesky, the Soviet ambassador. Masaryk said he did not like caviar and as she sampled it she would listen to him telling her how the Russians spied on everyone and of how clever they were at spying. Masaryk would attend a top-secret meeting and later that day Ambassador Maiesky, who had not been present at the meeting but whose 'agents' were there, would be able to tell him what had been discussed. Masaryk was still presumably unaware of Mary's connection with MI5. She liked Masaryk very much. They made each other laugh, but they never had an affair.

By May 1943 Heinz had been assigned to a training squadron, flying Avro Lancaster bombers, and he was given embarkation leave as his crew was preparing to depart for North Africa. He came down to Boskenna to spend some time with Mary and Toby, and they invited Jan Masaryk for a weekend. A week later, on 17 May, Masaryk wrote to Heinz, who was still in Cornwall, in English, the common language of these two Czech politicians: 'Dear friend – delayed action in saying thank you – forgive – been away all week. I loved my visit with you and will not forget it and am resolved to gate crash soon . . . Sincere greetings to Colonel – love to Mary and yourself. Socks will follow soon. Yours Jan.'

When they were alone on that visit, Heinz told Mary for the first time that he wanted to marry her and that after the war he counted on taking her back with him to Loyovitz. Somehow Mary remained unconvinced. She saw a flaw in their relationship: whereas she had discovered him, he had invented her. 'He told the world I was a beauty so suddenly everybody noticed me and I became a beauty. He told them I was funny and gay so I was noticed for that too.' But by this time Heinz knew something of his parents' fate, and Mary sensed that there was something missing in him, too . . . that 'he was ready to die'. She thought that though he loved her and spoilt her he never saw her 'with a clear eye'.

In the summer of 1943 Mary went up to London to have a minor operation and convalesced in a Kensington nursing home which remained open despite the regular air raids. For some time she had been trying to persuade Carol to give her a divorce. He came to visit Mary in the nursing home, looking lugubrious in a bowler hat, to tell her that he was living outside London, at Theale, near Reading, close to Pamela Hull. He had left the ARP after the near miss with the bomb and since June 1942 had been working in the Ministry of Information as a Press Censor, at a salary of £610 per annum.

Towards the end of her life Mary said that Carol had always wanted to marry Mrs Hull. In earlier accounts she said that Carol had made it very difficult for her to persuade him to divorce. She did not want to hurt his feelings by saying that their marriage had become a sham. As she later recalled, 'One of the most difficult things you can do in life is to tell your husband you have left him without telling him one of the children is not his.' She could not say 'Divorce me for adultery', or she might have lost Roger. And yet she and Carol had nothing in common. Throughout their marriage, if she swam, rode, played tennis or climbed cliffs, she never did it with him, and they very rarely touched each other. She said that he 'held forth' but never 'discussed' and if he disagreed with her he just said, 'I hear what you say.' Carol in fact wanted them to stay married while leading separate lives. 'Lots of people have stayed married,' he said, 'and have lovers round the corner.' But that was not at all what Mary wanted. She regarded this 'worldly suggestion' as dishonest and thought that it would prevent her from ever enjoying a normal relationship with somebody she truly loved. Friends of hers such as Betty and the local MP, Alec Beechman, an admirer of Betty's, were appalled at the idea of a divorce and asked her what she would do for money, since she had none of her own. In her last memoir Mary maintained that she had suggested that Carol should have custody of the children. But according to a letter written to Carol by his mother on 15 November 1942, on the anniversary of her husband's death twenty-three years earlier, Mary had asked Carol to grant *her* custody. 'My dear Carol,' his mother wrote.

> This is the anniversary of Swinfen's death in 1919. I wish you could have had his counsel. I feel you are being rushed. Please don't sign anything before we have had a further talk . . . There is no justification in the custodian [i.e. custody] request . . . I may not be here many more years, I should not go hence with peace of mind if you subjected yourself to the inexcusable and rather impudent suggestion to forgo your full paternal rights. You are giving up all that makes life precious – your home, wife and children, and this request is going too far and could be made only by one who puts her own troubles first and other people's second. It is important that your sons should know in future years that you were absolutely blameless, and deserved a better fate . . . All my love Mother.

Carol Swinfen's mother had always liked Mary and had played an active role in encouraging the marriage. But, in November 1942, she clearly knew little about the real reasons for the failure of her son's marriage.

Swinfen was adamant that adultery would not be the grounds for their divorce. He was not prepared to make himself the guilty party by going through the usual sham with the hotel chambermaid and he did not want to divorce Mary for her adultery although, unknown to her, he had ample proof. They had a joint bank account at Coutts and the cheque stubs and statements were always sent to him, so he was able to plot her progress round Cambridge, London, Wales and Scotland month by month. He never mentioned this and it was many years before Mary realised that he had known so much about her affair with Heinz. The only alternative ground for divorce was desertion, which had to be for a period of three years. Carol Swinfen was persuaded by his mother's advice and declined to give Mary custody, but she continued in her determination to be free. On 9 July 1943 she sent him a letter from Boskenna that reads like a classic plea for divorce on the grounds of desertion and may have been written on legal advice.

My dear Carol, I have delayed answering your letter as I wanted to give myself time to think out the whole situation again and not let you think there has been any impetuosity in my reply. Since you wrote I have seen you again when you came down to see the children and have told you again that I have quite made up my mind not to live with you ever again. The fault I know is mainly on my side but I am absolutely certain it's an impossible thing for me and will have a very bad effect on the children. I think you realise how I love the children, and I know you do too. I do not want to take them away from you, and want to share them with you, but I am absolutely certain that the worst thing for them is to live with parents who do not get on, and see and feel irritability and nervous tension going on all round them as they grow up. A home should be in accord, and if we lived together I cannot see this happening – whereas apart I think we can work on a very friendly basis and save the children from any strain. The mistake was made when I married you and I am deeply sorry to have caused you so much unhappiness but I want, as I have repeatedly told you, to make a clean cut while we and the children are still young, and give us both a chance of re-organising our lives. I think the children will eventually be grateful for amicable parents even though they lived apart. As you know I have not been hasty in my decision, nor influenced by people or circumstances. Ever since I left you two-and-a-half years ago I have become increasingly certain that I shall never come back, Mary.

By this time Carol and Mary were known by all their friends to be more or less separated. When she came to London she avoided him at all costs, and when he went down to Boskenna to see the boys she was usually absent. If she was there she insisted that he be given a separate room. But determined to save his marriage if he could, Swinfen continued to procrastinate, an art at which he was a practised master, and Mary realised that she would need her family's support. In September 1943 she took a decisive step and went down to Somerset to tell Violet and Mynors that she had decided not to return to Carol because she no longer loved him and could not bear to live with him. Her parents, she said, put up 'much more fight' than Carol had shown. On the night Mary broke the news she retreated to her room and then, hearing her mother crying, she went downstairs again and 'told them some details of my married life'. These won her father's support and she returned to Boskenna feeling relieved. But Mynors's change of heart did not last and before long there began a bombardment of letters urging her not to do anything so shameful as divorce, and to think of Carol and the children. Not only was she black-listed by her family but they went out of their way to side with Carol, to the extent that Carol telephoned her and asked her to stop her relations coming round to tell him how awful she was.

The family network was extensive. When Mary's determination to divorce was announced Mynors had four sisters and one half-sister still alive, as well as his brother George. The youngest of the females, the spinster Aunt Violet, wrote Mary 'virulent and hurtful' letters while the oldest, the spinster Aunt Bee, who had given 'Lady Swinfen' all the family lace, now, less impressed, demanded it all back. Both these aunts joined in 'the reaching for pens and scratching out from wills in the name of respectability'. Even her friend Betty still opposed the divorce – on the grounds that Mary would have no money. And Heinz was worried at the thought of her losing custody of the children and being left alone while he was away at the war. But Mary pressed on, undeterred.

In the autumn of 1943 she dined in London with Heinz and they made plans for the end of the war; he wanted to take her and Toby back to Prague. He told her that he was expecting to be posted abroad and that he had named her as his next of kin, despite the presence in London of his brother Paul. She promised that if anything happened to him she would look for his mother after the war. They went back to the rooms in Cheval Place, near Harrods, where she was staying and spent the night together, and in the morning he returned to his unit. He had been given a *nom de guerre* to disguise his nationality; Heinz Otto Ziegler was now '87294 Flying-Officer Henry Osbert Zetland'. By the time he and his crew flew out to join their new squadron in October 1943 he had become a rear gunner, often described as the most dangerous position on the plane. 'It was as good as committing suicide,' Mary said. His crew were all half his age and his nickname had changed from 'Ziggy' to 'Uncle'.

CHAPTER SEVEN

Missing, Believed Killed

'I have never been to bed with anyone I didn't love – or at least didn't find attractive.'

Mary Wesley

After Heinz left for North Africa he started to write to Mary more frequently. The letters were full of affection, in her words, 'all his letters were gay.' She kept them for many years, but they have not survived – unlike eighteen of the letters he wrote to Paul Ziegler over the same period. The letters to Paul, written in English, their second or third language,* by one Austrian Bohemian to his Bohemian Austrian brother as they fought against Germany and Nazism, portray something of the reality of life for Mary's lovers when they were not recuperating at Boskenna.

On 14 November 1943 – shortly after arriving in Tunisia – Heinz gave Paul his first impressions. 'The change from the . . . comfortable life of an English aerodrome to the open-air . . . life out here is most exciting. This tastes more like war . . . Whereas my crew is rather inclined to miss the cups of tea I simply revel in odd drinks, flowers and colours . . . What beautiful emptiness. Everything seems reduced to its essentials. No wonder that the human birthplace of monotheistic religion had to be in the desert.' He asked Paul to send him a hundred of Marcovitch's Black and White Medium cigarettes and added, 'We are by now members of the not quite unknown 104 Squadron. Fully operational indeed.' A week later he wrote again: 'I am already quite proficient in making my corner of the tent . . . into something like a home, photographs helping . . . I have become fond of bullied

---

* RAF censors would have delayed or rejected letters in German.

beef and spam . . . By the way [there are] no shops filled with silk stockings or cosmetics. I am afraid I won't be able to send war parcels to all our
lovelies . . . Don't forget to write regularly and make all the lovelies write
as well.'

His next letter contained the news that he had met one of Mary's RAF
boyfriends. 'Last night I ran into Billy Armstrong . . . We had a long talk
and got on very well indeed. He is a nice type . . . Exchanged Boskenna
news and opinion – one could write another Proust series about the
Boskenna world . . .' All he could find to send home were food parcels and
he sent 'one to Gelda, one to Pam and one to Mary *pour les enfants*'. In
Tunis there was 'quite decent food and a drinkable Algerian wine . . .
sinfully expensive – the French robbing us with great mastery'. Occasionally
the university professor emerges from behind the gaunt shape of the rear
gunner; Heinz was a diligent student of correct RAF form. 'By the way –
to be "clued up" or "clueless" is partly replacing "gen". "Wizo" [*sic*] has
taken the place of the completely obsolete "wizard". "Piss-poor" is another
extremely popular expression.' And despite the elegance of his handmade
Marcovitch cigarettes, Heinz was careful to look 'incredibly scruffy and
thus operational', in the approved RAF manner.

The shadow that lay over this correspondence was eventually mentioned
by Heinz in a letter dated 6 December, when he abandoned the 'carefree
warrior' stance and wrote about what was truly in his heart. Until 1935,
when the Nazis began to meddle in Czech politics, the Zieglers had been
an assured and happy family, regretting the Treaty of Versailles and the
loss of Vienna, but confident in their identity, their place in their world,
and the security afforded by their love for each other. Ernst, their father,
was a reflective and generous-hearted man who ran a successful private
bank in Prague. Alice, their mother, was the centre of a very close-knit
family. The three boys were companions as well as brothers, surrounded
by a large circle of friends. Influential people in a prosperous country at
the heart of a thousand-year-old civilisation, the Zieglers had thought they
knew more or less what lay ahead. And then their world unravelled. Alarmed
by the threat of German nationalism, Ernst sent his sons, one by one, away
from Loyovitz to settle abroad. Certainty was replaced by bewilderment.
Ernst refused to follow them, their mother stayed by their father until it
was too late. In September 1938, by international agreement, the powerful
Czech army withdrew from its well-defended mountainous frontier posi-
tions without firing a shot, and Hitler's forces overran Bohemia, placing
Ernst and Alice at the mercy of Nazi policy.

The persecution of the Czech Jews proceeded by stages. Bohemia was absorbed into the Reich Protectorate, ruled by Reinhardt Heydrich, 'Protector of Bohemia and Moravia', Head of the German Security Police and deputy-chief of the Gestapo. Those Jews who, like the Zieglers, were in mixed marriages where the wife was regarded as 'German', and where the children had not been raised as Jews, were at first placed in a special category. By the Goering Directive of 28 December 1938 they were classified as 'Mischlinge of the First Degree', and were not subject to 're-housing' or deportation. In September 1939, Czech Jews in the general category were banned from walking in the street after 8 p.m. In July 1941, they were banned from entering the Prague woods, which surrounded Loyovitz, and which had become a refuge for fugitives. Then the Wannsee Conference, held in Berlin in January 1942, established the camp of Theresienstadt, on the eastern border of Czechoslovakia, as a ghetto for older Jews and for Jews who had been decorated during the Great War. From the start it was conceived as a holding camp on the road to deportation.

On 29 May 1942, Czech resisters, armed and organised from London, assassinated Heydrich as he drove to work in his office in Prague. In reprisal, 1,331 Czechs were immediately executed, the mining village of Lidice, near Prague, with all its inhabitants, was destroyed and 3,000 Jews were deported from Theresienstadt to the death camps in the east. Ernst and Alice Ziegler were arrested and sent to Theresienstadt six weeks later, on 20 July 1942, their 'privileged' status terminated. Loyovitz was seized and plundered to pay for the costs of re-settlement. The everlasting house with the great park, protected by its high iron gates, had become a symbol of the old European order that the Nazis destroyed.

On 2 January 1943, Ernst Ziegler, aged seventy-two, died in Theresienstadt. Heinz and Paul heard of their parents' arrest and of their father's death later that year, and before Heinz left for North Africa. Of their mother they knew only that she too had been sent to Theresienstadt and that she had not been reported dead. The fate of his parents made Heinz angry, and more determined to fight, whereas Paul seems to have gone into a state of shock. When Mary asked him for news of Alice Ziegler, Paul told her that his mother was 'in a nursing home'. Paul had been taking instruction at the Brompton Oratory, his local Catholic church, since early in the war, and went there to light candles for his parents every week.

In his letter of 6 December Heinz wrote, 'Father's birthday. Would he be, is he, pleased with what I am doing? How is mother feeling today? Paul, my dear, if only we could make her feel how close she is every minute of the day, how ever-present love makes her. It's the same with father. Mustn't get morbid today. Must think and feel of them in a happy way.' A month later he wrote, 'Went to a Church, one of the few buildings left – a pleasant Jesuit effort. It's a year that father died . . . I am praying that the three sons may be re-united with darling mother . . . If only we could have that reunion party soon.'

Unknown to Heinz it was already too late. Alice Ziegler had been deported from Theresienstadt to Auschwitz on 15 December 1943; she died a few days later.

In December, just before Christmas, 104 Squadron, flying Wellingtons, moved to Italy and Heinz was excited to be back in Europe – 'the grand old continent'. He noticed 'the antiquity of people's faces . . . especially among the women . . . a real beauty as well as true Catholicism'. He went to Midnight Mass in the nearby cathedral (no place names would get past the censor). The service was packed with Allied soldiers and airmen, 'the high windows of the cathedral lit by the lights of the RAF lorries . . . [Still] no letter from you . . . all I got was a letter from Mary.' He was reading *Eyeless in Gaza* and asked Paul to send him *Grey Eminence*, also by Aldous Huxley, the book that Paul Ziegler had given to Mary in 1941. The cold weather of the southern Italian winter had brought back Heinz's rheumatism. Because he had Latin and French, his brother officers concluded that he was the obvious choice to forage supplies from the rural population and he came back laden with chickens, ducks and eggs, and taught his tent companions how to make wine punch.

In his letters to his brother Heinz made no mention of his personal commitments, but on hearing of a friend's 'matrimonial difficulties' he showed little sympathy. 'A husband and father's duties are quite obvious, unequivocal. It's his job to stick it out. He has to arrange things so that a continuation of the domestic life is possible. In very few cases is married life continuous bliss. Even the most delightful wife gets – after some years – on your nerves . . .' Referring to 'the lovelies' he wrote, 'No letter from Pam yet – I am most disappointed . . . Had another letter from Mary . . . (in fact a very charming letter).'

Then came a period when Heinz received just three letters from Paul in two months, and his own letters took on an uneasy tone. He had always been a protective older brother and with the death of their father this tendency increased. He was concerned about his brother's plan to become a Benedictine monk and urged him to think again. 'I very often get quite a nostalgia and longing for the old wise, tolerant and humorous . . . brilliant and kind Paul . . . who always used to be a tower of strength for me. The one who helped me when Babs went away . . . I would like him back as a Christmas present.' Heinz's skipper, Bob Avery, managed to fall into a can of petrol and burn himself, so the entire crew was grounded for several weeks and Heinz, hearing of another officer's chance encounter with a strange priest, spent a day in the mountains. He said that he found a 'Franziskan monastery' where there was a stigmatic, 'Father Pio da Pietrelcina . . . There he was, rather on the small side, wonderful eyes in a strong rustic face, laughing, patting me on my cheek, making me feel at ease. He seems to understand and look through you without the halting explanation. He didn't say much but he just radiates common sense, faith and such a happy, supreme piety – you know everything will be all right, you relax and trust . . . He will pray for us.' Heinz sent Paul two letters about his visit to Padre Pio.

At Boskenna, flower picking had started on 2 February and Mary sent a description that made him wish he were in Cornwall, in the spring sunshine and out of the bitter Italian cold. He heard about the renewed Blitz of London and was worried about Paul, who was on fire watch in Lombard Street in the City. Hearing that Paul had been visiting Quarr Abbey on the Isle of Wight he wrote, 'I hope you had a good retreat.' Time and again, he asked for more letters.

In October, 1943 the Eighth Army, advancing through Italy, had captured Foggia Aerodrome, north-west of Bari, on the Adriatic, and Eastern Europe (including Auschwitz) came within range of RAF Bomber Command. 104 Squadron was redeployed to attack German munitions factories and railway depots in Hungary. As the crew returned to flying duties, Heinz said that his new tent companions were 'extremely pleasant . . . they are such good listeners and appreciate all my jokes and tricks'. He started to reread *Pride and Prejudice* and 'got so enthralled by it that I forgot all about Ops the other day'. This was his first mention of the actual business of war.

Heinz's last letter to Paul differed from the rest. There were no enquiries about 'the lovelies' or their friends, and no reference to Hans or their parents. His handwriting was bigger, he was in a hurry to fill the standard three pages of the aerogramme; he was evidently tired. The strain of war was beginning to tell on the young professor, who had become a very old and rather sore air gunner who on most nights had to fold himself into the freezing rear turret of a bomber plane that was on

a mission to destroy targets in the old Habsburg Empire. 'Paul my dear,'
he wrote,

> Got your letter dated Passion Sunday . . . We are under canvas again
> which is bad for my rheumatism but suits me otherwise . . . I am grateful
> for any trees or flowers and all the friendly noises of the country . . .
>
> I couldn't agree more with you about Ak-ak.* As far as shells are
> concerned we are very much in the same boat. What rains down on you
> comes up against me. Let's continue to skirt round it.
>
> So long, Paul. The sun is calling and the great 'getting perfectly tanned'
> craze has broken out on the squadron. Much love and bless you. H.

Early on a Sunday morning in May 1944, the village postmistress from St
Buryan came to Boskenna with a telegram for Lady Swinfen. Mary, who
was still asleep, was called down to the hall to receive it. Feeling that the
village's chief gossip was watching to see her reaction, she took it upstairs
and opened it in her bedroom. It contained the news that Heinz was 'Missing,
believed killed'. Safely in the bedroom, Mary collapsed. 'Betty's old father
saw me lying face down across a bed and asked, "What's up?" Betty said,
"She's just heard that Heinz is dead, father." The old man said: "Oh, oh.
Poor little thing. Would she like to go for a drive?"'

Her sister Susan had received a similar telegram when she was widowed
two years earlier. Colonel McLaren had been killed in action in Burma.
Susan told Mary that 'Missing' meant nothing; it just meant they couldn't
find the body. Nonetheless, in her engagement diary for 7 May, Mary wrote
'H. missing' and underlined it.

It took a long time to track down Paul Ziegler by telephone. When he
first heard the news, he refused to believe it. Heinz spoke fluent German.
He had been bombing Budapest, not so far from home. He would make
his way back, across country, across enemy territory. All this was wishful
thinking.

A few days later the Air Ministry sent confirmation that Flying Officer
H. O. Zetland of 104 Squadron had died. Two weeks after his last letter
to Paul, Heinz's squadron had taken off from Bari on the evening of
4 May. That night his Wellington was shot down and there were no
survivors; he had become one of Bomber Command's 50,000 lost aircrew.

---

* Ack-ack: slang term for anti-aircraft fire. Shell casings and shrapnel from the
guns often fell back on to the ground the guns were defending.

Mary could not remember how she reacted. She said that she was 'shattered' and that there was no one she could talk to. She thought she probably went for a walk down to the cliffs and the sea, on the paths she had walked so often with Heinz. She had given Heinz a gold and turquoise locket which had belonged to her grandmother. Heinz put a photograph of Toby in it and clipped it to the chain of his name tag. After he was killed, she recalled, 'I went quite mad and had a whole lot of affairs.' Masaryk, on hearing the news said, 'Stupid, stupid waste. We wanted him for foreign minister.'

Even before Heinz's death, Mary's London life had become more hectic. On one occasion in 1943 things got out of hand over lunch at the Ritz. Several of the newspapers splashed the story on 23 October. The *Daily Mirror*'s headline was 'Lady Swinfen buying clothing coupons from her maid'; there was a picture of Mary and the story was a back-page lead. Betty's maid had sold her family's clothing coupons to Betty, who had put them in an envelope and asked Mary to put the envelope in her coat pocket while they had lunch. Mary did not know, or ask, what was in the envelope. Meanwhile the maid's husband, who was not in on the deal, discovered what his wife had done and informed the police. Enforcement officers from the Ministry of Food then trailed the coupons and struck in the cloakroom of the Ritz. Mary's explanation was accepted by the court but not before the story had been leaked to the press. 'Peeress in coupons racket' was just what the Ministry of Food needed to publicise its latest clampdown on the black market. In Wales, Mary's bridesmaid, Venice, followed the story with close attention in the reading room of her local public library and it was a major entry in her diary that week: 'Mary Swinfen in all the papers on clothing coupon charges.'* In London, her mother-in-law Blanche followed the story with close attention, going out to buy successive editions of the day's papers and pasting the clippings into her diary. Several of her friends thoughtfully rang to enquire whether she was the 'Lady Swinfen' who was apparently in all the papers.

For New Year's Eve that year Mary's appointments diary read, 'Meet B. Lunch Paul Ritz 12.30. P's party, Berkeley, Ciro's, 400.' In other words,

---

* Some years after the war Mary met the editors of the *Daily Mail* and the *Daily Mirror* when they were lunching at Simpson's. She said that they had apologised to her for the raw deal she had received; it was not possible to splash a 'clothing coupons story' without a pretty face.

following the party she went on to three separate nightclubs. New Year's Day 1944 read: 'Lunch, Peter, Berkeley. Meet P, 9 Ambassadors' (a fourth club). The next day was Sunday, but there was no respite: 'Nip [i.e. drink] Bruce 12.30. Lunch Richmond, George dinner.' Monday was 'P. lunch Ambassadors' and in the evening, 'Duncan, Bruce.' On Tuesday she went home to Cornwall. She had discovered a secret train, not listed on any timetable, with sleepers to Penzance. It was intended for military use, but Mary usually managed to talk herself on.

As the year passed the pace in London quickened so that it is sometimes impossible to disentangle the crossed and scribbled entries: 'Antoine's, Bon Viveur, nips, dentist, Dennis, Rules, Normandie, Café Royal, 2 New Zealanders, 1st Sea Lord Pat Cullen, Bill, Jean, Pat, Claud . . .'

With Paddy Green in North Africa and no longer able to threaten murder if she was unfaithful, Mary had two more light-hearted affairs. The first was with a Texan army officer, Lieutenant-Colonel Alex George, who was attached to the headquarters of the 175th Regiment US Infantry. He first appears in the diary on 30 March and in May he came to stay twice at Boskenna. On 1 June she saw him for the last time before D-Day, which wasn't called D-Day at the time, but the 'Second Front'. Mary's diary entry 'Second Front started' reads over the line between 5 June and 6 June, as though she had prior knowledge. Devon and Cornwall were assembly areas for the US Assault Force and Follow-Up Forces – the 4th and 29th Infantry Divisions, embarking at Brixham and Falmouth – and everyone in St Buryan knew when the invasion was imminent because the Americans told them that when they all disappeared into secured camps, it meant they were on their way. On 2 June the Americans duly disappeared and the Rivers Teign, Fal and Tamar emptied of boats. On the evening of 6 June Colonel Paynter's neighbour, Alice Favell, rang with the news that her son Teddy, a paratrooper with the 6th Airborne Division, had been killed. She did not explain how she had received the news so quickly, before the official telegrams were sent out. Later she called again to say that they had telephoned Margaret, Teddy's sister. Teddy and Margaret were twins, and she too had seen his ghost. She told her mother: 'Teddy walked into the house at 9 this morning. I have known all day.'

On 8 June Mary heard that Alex George had been so badly wounded he was not expected to live. He had wounds in the legs and back, and had lost an eye. His wife cabled from San Antonio asking Mary to go and see him. She caught the 8 a.m. train from Penzance on 15 July and was driven from Cheltenham to 'an enormous American hospital in the Cotswolds . . . for very serious cases only, chiefly for the dying and those to be shipped home to America unfit ever to fight again or to live normal lives'. She was met by the commander of the 60th General Hospital at Fossebridge and by another visitor, General Davies, and told that Colonel George had given up hope but that he might change his attitude if they could save his other eye. They gave her a strong drink and led her to the ward saying, 'Don't worry but don't let your feelings show in your face.' 'The little Texan was shaved, sightless and painted horrible colours: he could move one arm but not back or legs; from a hole near his nose oozed white fluid. This he said was his brain oozing away.' He was obstinate about the fact that whatever they said they would have to take his second eye out. Mary stayed for three nights, living with the nurses and encouraging the walking cases, who were mostly 'boys of twenty'. The nurses treated their disfigured patients 'as though they were the most eligible *beau* they had ever seen. I admired those girls tremendously. Pretty, smart, terribly efficient, made up to kill, they wrapped those poor men into a cocoon of light-hearted affection.' Mary used different tactics. She told the Texan that he should be ashamed, that he would be quite all right and that she was going to write to his wife and tell her so. But nothing seemed to help until she lost her temper and said that 'the stuff oozing out of the hole in his face could not be his brain because he hadn't got one'. On the fourth day the commander of the hospital and the eye specialist saw her off at the station and she eventually heard that Colonel George had recovered, refused to be shipped back home and succeeded in getting himself posted back to General Patton's Third Army for the advance into Germany.

Mary's final wartime fling was with the writer Simon Harcourt-Smith who, with his wife, was an old friend of Betty Paynter's. The Harcourt-Smiths entered Mary's life as a couple on 12 June. After her visit to the American Hospital Harcourt-Smith reappears on his own, in her diary now, as an attentive suitor at the end of July. In August, as the V1 attacks on London began to intensify, Mary saw him on a near daily basis during her London visits. He came to see her in Boskenna, 'to write', although in Mary's opinion he was actually escaping from the unnerving 'Doodlebugs'. He did not stay in Cornwall for long, falling victim to the old Colonel's deadly technique of the raised voice behind the door. 'How long is that fellow staying, do you know?'

'Hush, darling, he has come for a week because his nerves are bad.'

'Well, time he left.' Invariably courteous face to face, the Colonel would stalk his male guests from room to room, enquiring about train timetables in a loud voice. Not even fear of the V1s could match this barrage. Simon Harcourt-Smith fell in love with Mary. After the Colonel had muttered him out Simon wrote to her from Boodle's, to which his own club, Brooks, had been evacuated. 'My Angel, One solid hour did I wait for your call the night before last. Yesterday I was considerably compensated by your two charming letters. I tried to ring you up from Lady Richardson's. They said there would be three-quarters of an hour's delay and so I never hear your sweet voice.' He ended the letter with an urgent request, for eggs. Three days later he wrote again: 'I suppose I couldn't come to Boskenna next weekend, or you couldn't meet me somewhere? [The answer was a double 'No'.] I adore you but I could wish you poured more of your industrious correspondence upon Your Fond Admirer.' There was no signature.

One of Harcourt-Smith's advantages was that when Mary came to London he arranged for her to stay with Lord Astor at 45 Upper Grosvenor Street. She had never met Astor, who assumed she was a tart. He was repulsed, but nonetheless gave her a bed and, after bidding her goodnight, retired to the basement where he slept in the silver safe,* well protected from the Flying Bombs.

Mary finally tired of her wartime lifestyle after an incident at the Harcourt-Smiths, where she had agreed to stay in September. Mrs Harcourt-Smith, having got wind of the situation between Mary and her husband, decided that it would be more fun if all three of them slept together. But Mary thought that the Harcourt-Smiths 'looked very silly, lying together naked in their canopied bed' and went upstairs to pack her suitcase. On the way downstairs, having called a taxi, she passed her host and hostess who were making a commotion on the landing; Mrs Harcourt-Smith had sunk her teeth deep into her husband's calf. Mary took the taxi to Paddington with a feeling of relief. Her way of life had become excessive: 'too many lovers, too much to drink . . . I was on my way to becoming a very nasty person.'

Carol had finally given in to her wishes and in August, as Allied armies broke out of Normandy, his petition for divorce on the grounds of her desertion had been listed for hearing. The war, with all its 'terror and exhilaration', was nearing its end; the time had come to find a job and make plans for the children. Roger and Toby could not run wild in Cornwall for the rest of their lives, and Mary decided to find them schools. On Thursday, 26

---

* Lord Astor's friendship with Simon Harcourt-Smith led him to advance the latter £6,000 on the security of various works of art, which were valued after the war at £800.

October, she took the 9.45 train from Paddington to Oxford, where she interviewed the headmaster of Summerfields, a school recommended by Heinz's friend, Maurice Bowra. That evening she went to the Westminster Theatre with Richmond Stopford, a senior figure in MI6, to see *It Depends What You Mean* by James Bridie, starring and directed by Alastair Sim. Richmond Stopford greatly enjoyed Mary's company but, although heterosexual, did not try to go to bed with her and she found this a welcome relief. Following the performance, they went on to the Ritz for dinner.

Mary had arranged to meet Richmond Stopford because she was hoping to resume a career in MI5 and was worried lest an incident that had taken place a few weeks earlier had spoiled her chances. Towards the end of September her former lover, Raymond Lee, who was still travelling backwards and forwards to France for SOE, had asked her to lunch. When she got to the restaurant Lee was not there; instead, she was greeted by a tall man with a mid-European accent wearing a good suit, who told her he was a fellow guest. They ordered their food and the stranger asked if she knew of 'a nice English prison' that would let him in. He appeared to be sane, said he was Czech, but would give no other account of himself. Raymond arrived at the end of the meal, ordered more wine and they then moved to an afternoon drinking club of which Mary was a member. The 'Czech' continued to ask if anyone knew of 'a nice English prison' and Raymond brushed the question aside, until eventually an explanation was produced. Raymond told Mary that he had met his friend in Paris, where the Czech was in hiding, trying to avoid the *épuration*, the brutal purge of collaborators that was still taking place. Raymond had dressed up the fugitive as a British paratrooper, smuggled him into a British army unit and marched him ashore at Southampton, before concealing him for six weeks in an army camp in the Cotswolds. The 'Czech' had not appreciated this since the food had been 'frightful' and not at all up to the standards of the black market in Paris during the Occupation. He was quite determined to get into an English prison since he was sure that the French would execute him, whereas the English were 'honourable and *comme il faut*' (correct).

During the course of the afternoon, Mary stopped drinking while Raymond Lee became completely drunk. The 'Czech' drank huge quantities but remained sober and absolutely determined to get himself locked up as quickly as possible. Mary eventually told him that if he really had decided to give himself up she might be able to help and called FLAxman 6032, the telephone number of Richmond Stopford's house in Chelsea.

Somehow, Mary and the tall 'Czech' managed to get Raymond into and out of a taxi, and the three of them stood swaying gently on Richmond's doorstep and rang his bell. They were welcomed politely and offered drinks, which Raymond Lee accepted once he had settled himself comfortably on the hall floor. The 'Czech' explained his problem, Raymond interrupted with shouts of 'Nonsense, we can go to Southampton and get a boat to South America'. Eventually Richmond Stopford said he really had to go out, but if Mary would arrange another taxi to Raymond's flat, and if both men promised to wait quietly, a car would come round later.

That night the 'Czech' was arrested, held on remand and deported to Nuremberg, where he was eventually tried for war crimes and convicted of several murders. Raymond Lee was arrested, cashiered and deported, having narrowly escaped a court martial. Richmond Stopford told Mary that he himself had been looking for this 'Czech' for some time, as had Peter Hope, also of MI6. And Mary was now wondering what would happen to her security clearance. Over dinner Richmond told her that he thought it would probably be all right, although she certainly had some rather 'peculiar friends'.

It was to be several years before Richmond Stopford told Mary the full story of the tall Czech in the good suit. The story, which has never been published, sheds an interesting sidelight on British involvement in the French *épuration*. The 'Czech' was actually an Austrian Nazi named Alfred Kraus. He had lived in Paris during the Occupation and worked with the Gestapo. He was married to Princess Jacqueline de Broglie, whose mother, Marguerite Séverine Philippine, had divorced the Duc Decazes and remarried a cousin of Winston Churchill's. In England Marguerite Séverine Philippine was known as 'Daisy' Fellowes, more formally as the Hon. Mrs Reginald Fellowes, less formally as the mistress of Duff Cooper, wartime minister of information. Free from the Anglophile tendencies of their remarried mother, Daisy's French daughters, Jacqueline and Emmeline, became enthusiastic members of the Parisian collaboration. In August 1944 they were fortunate to escape with their lives. Both were caught by the Paris mob and Jacqueline, now Madame Alfred Kraus, had her head shaved in the streets of the 16th arrondissement, a relatively mild mob punishment for Frenchwomen who had chosen to marry Gestapo officers.

Meanwhile Emmeline de Broglie, a lesbian, was still in danger. She was accused of betraying a girlfriend in the Resistance who had been unfaithful to her. Her mother, Daisy, therefore asked her former lover Duff Cooper for help. Cooper, one of Churchill's inner circle, had arrived in Paris as

British ambassador on 13 September. He told her that – officially – she would have to work through the usual channels, but it was shortly after this response that Alfred Kraus, although still in hiding, succeeded in making contact with a British agent, Raymond Lee.

Alfred Kraus was unusual, perhaps unique, among members of the Paris Gestapo in managing to find refuge in England from torture and summary execution in Paris, and it may be coincidence that he was also the only Gestapo agent who was married to the stepdaughter of Winston Churchill's first cousin and the only Gestapo agent whose mother-in-law had been the mistress of the British ambassador.* Or, Raymond Lee may have been dispatched to Paris specifically to help Kraus.

But whether Raymond Lee was sent to Paris secretly to save Alfred Kraus from the mob, or whether the two men made contact by chance, Lee's action in smuggling Kraus back to England must have been partly inspired by Kraus's connections. The fact that both Stopford and Hope were looking for Kraus – a run-of-the-mill Gestapo thug – seems to confirm an unusual level of official interest in his fate. Lee's offence, in failing to surrender Kraus at Southampton, and his severe punishment of being cashiered – disgraced and dismissed – despite his outstanding war record, is another pointer to the depth of potential embarrassment. As for Mary, her role in the arrest of Alfred Kraus is further evidence of her continuing connection with military intelligence throughout the war. She would have relished the fact that her final task should have involved her in this imbroglio, whereby the English and French aristocracies joined hands to save a central European war criminal from the vengeance of the Paris mob.

As Mary entered the Ritz that night with Richmond Stopford she paused in the Palm Court to talk to two 'raffish' friends, Pauline and Sylvester Gates,† at which point a tall man came up to join them, cheerful and drunk, who invited her to dine with his party. Naturally, she refused, but throughout dinner the waiter brought Mary a succession of notes from the tall drunk: 'Why not leave that boring Mr Stopford?' 'Why not come on with us to the Milroy?' 'Why not come on and dance at Les Ambassadeurs?' Eventually Richmond Stopford retrieved his bowler and umbrella, having

---

* SOE agents then on the embassy staff included George Napier, the ambassador's private secretary.
† Pauline Gates, sister of the actor Robert Newton. Sylvester Gates, old Wykhamist, barrister; subsequently chairman British Film Institute, CBE (1944).

decided that it was time to go home to bed, and Mary switched tables – much to the irritation of Pauline Gates, who asked her whether her eyelashes were real. The evening ended with the writer of the notes, who was called Eric Siepmann, taking Mary back to her hotel, the Rembrandt, where his efforts to join her in the lift were thwarted by the 'tiny Swiss' night porter.

Mary did not want to 'get caught' again so soon after abandoning her promiscuous life; Simon Harcourt-Smith had been given his cards a week earlier. She slept alone, but in the morning she was woken by the telephone. It was the tall drunk of the previous evening: 'What are you doing?'

'Packing to leave.' Her diary shows that she was due to go down that afternoon to stay with her sister Susan in Hampshire. As she was paying the hotel bill Siepmann arrived in the lobby and persuaded her to go to a chemist's called Heppels that specialised in the 'American pick-me-up', a 'nauseous brew' designed to cure hangovers that brought tears to Mylo's eyes in *Not That Sort of Girl*. Customers of Heppels would queue in the street if necessary and Mary was well known there. Once, when she was the only woman in the queue, the man behind the counter had leaned over and asked, in a stage whisper, 'The usual, m'lady?'

Refreshed by the pick-me-up, Eric Siepmann and Mary went on to the Ritz for a mid-morning 'nip'. There they were ambushed by Betty Paynter. Eric was dressed in a mixture of Eighth Army and Royal Marines uniform, with a cracked Sam Brown, dirty shoes and an untidy beret. 'Isn't he good-looking!' was Betty's first comment. Her second was, 'He stole the spoons from Boskenna.' Since Mary was in the midst of a divorce and wanted to avoid further gossip she had to be discreet. She got rid of Betty, sent a telegram to Susan postponing her arrival and set off with Eric to find a hotel. They reached the De Vere Hotel, opposite Kensington Gardens. It should have ended where it started, but according to Mary's diary they spent three nights there and she eventually reached Susan's on the evening of the fourth day. On one of their journeys back to Heppels, Eric had said, 'It is too awful. I shall have to marry you.' Later Mary wrote a poem about their meeting that contained these lines:

> I no longer need to drift alone
> In the mist of searching
> For the door into our garden . . .

I will watch for the wind
And guard our solitude
Let no one invade it
Before your return.

'We met in the autumn and I read him *The Georgics* in bed,* and the *Four Quartets* which he had not heard as the war had rather interrupted his reading, and we lay above the sound of the traffic looking out onto the Broad Walk . . . So casually do you find your rubies,' Mary recalled.

---

* The most recent translation by C. Day-Lewis had just been published.

CHAPTER EIGHT

The Trap Shuts

'Eric Siepmann was the wickedest man I ever met.'

Antonia White

Eric Siepmann, to whom Mary now committed herself and who dominated her life for the next twenty-five years, was not a stable character. He was nine years older than Mary, mercurial and brilliant, but when drunk, a frequent occurrence, he became abusive and sometimes violent. When he met Mary he was separated from his second wife.

Siepmann was the son of Otto Siepmann, who had been born in the Rhineland. But Otto had left Germany in 1885 at the age of twenty-four and spent most of his subsequent career teaching at Clifton College with such success that, according to the *Dictionary of National Biography*, he became the country's leading authority on the teaching of modern languages and his name was 'well-known to generations of schoolchildren in Britain and across the British Empire . . . He was seventy years ahead of his time.' Otto had brought distinction to Clifton; his pupils had won a long list of Oxford and Cambridge scholarships, and they remembered him even after they had become Cabinet ministers. At work, he 'distrusted emotions and kept them severely in check', but at home he indulged a volcanic temper and frequently chastised his own children. It was an undeniable fact, as his son recalled, that 'the union of Siepmann and Baker' (Eric's mother) had proved 'singularly explosive'. Nonetheless, Eric loved his father and became very angry when he heard him described as 'a German bully'.

In due course Eric Siepmann had won scholarships to both Winchester and Corpus Christi College, but had left Oxford after one year without taking a degree. He had gone to RADA, after which he set out to become a playwright. While still at RADA he had fallen in love with a fellow student,

Benita Hume, who told him that she would marry him when he earned £1,000 a year (today's equivalent being £160,000, so he had abandoned the stage and turned to journalism. He had written a play that was produced in New York and a novel that was published in London, but his literary career had ground to a halt whereas his journalism as a foreign and diplomatic correspondent was highly regarded. He enjoyed foreign reporting but it left him feeling frustrated; it was not, finally, what he wanted to write. His marriage to Benita Hume broke up in 1929, when she left him for the romantic actor Ronald Colman and an acting career of her own. Siepmann became 'a bohemian, in revolt against conventional society', and rattled around Europe and North America, working for the *Manchester Guardian* at one moment or for Alexander Korda the next. He had a brief and unhappy affair with Antonia White, and began to build up an extensive and richly assorted acquaintance of celebrities. These included Basil Litvinoff, Lord Robert Cecil, Maurice Bowra, Montagu Norman, governor of the Bank of England (who would greet Eric with 'Well, old cock, what about a glass of beer?'), Randolph Churchill and his father Winston Churchill (with whom Siepmann collaborated on a film script), Margot Asquith, Geoffrey Household, Gerald Brenan, Nancy Cunard, Norman Douglas, Ford Madox Ford, Claud Cockburn* and so on. In other words he had a good contacts book. Yet however distinguished or powerful his acquaintances, he never managed to become part of their world. For most of his life Eric Siepmann was more or less at war with the values of his time.

Writing later about that first encounter with Mary, Siepmann recalled, 'I had met somebody who I really loved, who believed in God, and who thought that loving meant what you give and not what you take. Oddly enough, this had never occurred to me . . . It was the beginning of a new life.'

Nearly thirty years after Eric's death Mary wrote, '. . . In those few days in London, before I went back to Cornwall the trap shut; we became committed and remained together until he died. We were together twenty-five years of ups and down, of security and insecurity, of successes and failures, and I for one was never bored. There was a lot of heartache too of course; by choosing to live with Eric, I chose a very difficult path.' And

* Basil Litvinoff, arms dealer; Lord Robert Cecil, disarmament negotiator; Margot Asquith, wit and prime minister's wife; Geoffrey Household, novelist; Gerald Brenan, writer and historian of Spain; Nancy Cunard, socialite and progressive; Norman Douglas, author; Claud Cockburn, polemical Communist and novelist.

again she wrote, 'Eric once said, "The reason I love you is that you take such appalling risks." He was one of the risks.'

Mary's relationship with Eric Siepmann – rumoured to be 'German', or possibly 'Jewish' – was the cause of a further rift with her parents, at a time when the gulf between them was already wide. As the divorce approached, Mary's best friend in the family seemed to be her brother Hugh, who was about to be married. Six weeks before his wedding Hugh had written to Mary from Belgium, where he was on active service, a long and chatty letter from SHAEF headquarters in Brussels:

> I am glad, for your sake, that the business with Carol has begun. And I trust that presently you will find someone really nice with whom you will be really happy . . . If we are married in London presently I intend to commission you to collect a supply of lobsters for use at the reception. I think that we may be able to get a little champagne. I am so delighted that you like Constantia so much. She reciprocates your sentiments! All love, Hugh.

There was no hint in this affectionate letter, in which he commissions his sister to be responsible for black-market lobster from Newlyn, that Hugh was about to invite her soon-to-be-divorced husband to be his witness.

Mary always recalled Hugh's wedding as a personal ordeal; it was a big family occasion, all the aunts who had cut her out of their wills were present, furthermore Carol, who was about to divorce her, was omnipresent. In these circumstances the day was saved by the bride's mother, Etheldreda Rumbold, whose husband, Sir Horace, the 9th Baronet, had been British ambassador at Constantinople, Madrid and Berlin. Etheldreda was mistress of the occasion; she clearly regarded Farmar family politics as inappropriate at her daughter's wedding and placed Mary beside her in the reception line, as though she were one of her own daughters. So the guns of the aunts were spiked; they could hardly snub a niece who was standing beside their hostess. Large family weddings always stimulated Mary's imagination. Her description of Hugh's, in a letter to Eric, is the first recorded example.

> My brother's wedding was a splendid and agreeable performance. In the grossly overcrowded church [it was the Grosvenor Chapel] there were two themes of conversation carried on in carrying whispers. Mary's divorce, the first to disgrace the family for a hundred years, and the curious fact that Hugh and Constantia look exactly alike. There was lots

of champagne at the party afterwards, in the house of one of the late King Edward's mistresses. A racy old lady who got bored and bore me off to see the secret stair down which, as she put it, 'one can nip down secretly if surprised'. There was a fine collection of Ambassadors and their widows, gamekeepers, ex-loves of Hugh's, mobs of relations, old nannies and friends. My husband was there . . . he tells me they kick off with the case early in January. So many people went out of their way to be pleasant to me that I realised just how greatly in family disgrace I am. At the time it made me rather giggly.

But the high spirits did not last. On the following night's train back to Penzance she 'was assailed by night horrors about my family's disapproval, wept stormily, gave myself a sore throat and a headache and the feeling that I really *had* been through the mangle this time . . . Not that family disapproval has ever deterred me in any way. I just wish they'd shut up.'

Mary's exclusion from her own family became all the more public when Hugh agreed to be Carol's only witness at the divorce hearing on 11 April 1945, before Mr Justice Denning. Carol's solicitors had briefed Victor Russell, the father of one of Mary's childhood friends. At this hearing, before a young and extremely acute judge, Mr Russell had to ensure that the husband, most unusually, was given custody of his two children without blackening their mother's name. The judge asked Carol about custody quite closely. He wanted to know if Lady Swinfen had talked the matter over, and when the answer was 'No' he wanted to know if Lord Swinfen was suspicious that 'any other man' might be concerned. He accepted Lord Swinfen's assurance that he had no such suspicions at any time. Carol also said that, contrary to his wife's assertion in letters that there had been nervous tension in their relations since the start of the marriage, 'everything was going splendidly' until the christening of their second son in June 1941.

Hugh Farmar supported Carol's evidence. He said that Mary had seemed perfectly happy in the early part of her marriage and that the first time he noticed any unhappiness or coldness between them was when he flew down to Cornwall for the christening of their younger son. He too was perfectly sure that there was 'no other man in question'. Mary 'entered an appearance' but did not attend court. She had taken legal advice from George Gordon, one of the leading divorce solicitors, the previous August, a week after striking the final deal with Carol.

Hugh's decision to appear as a witness against her finally caused Mary's indignation to overflow. She wrote in letters then that the 'shock of finding out who had witnessed against me was a bigger blow than I've had for a long time'. She read the full report of the case sitting in the garden at Boskenna, 'sobbing with rage and misery'. The backwash of unhappiness left her mentally exhausted. 'Darling Hugh,' she wrote from Boskenna on 16 April 1945, five days after the hearing at the end of which the decree nisi had been pronounced.

I am terribly hurt and badly shocked to find you acted as a witness against me in Carol's and my divorce case. It is not so much the fact that you acted as a witness as the fact that neither you nor Carol ever told me you were going to. You have all along made it quite clear to me that you only saw Carol's side and never tried to see or understand mine. You are perfectly intitled [*sic*] to your opinion and I don't mind. But that you should publicly stand up as a witness for Carol and therefore against me, your own sister I can neither understand nor forgive. Mummy and Daddy told me what they thought and left it at that. Susan has never been anything but loyal and sweet and has taken no sides at all, and I am deeply grateful to her.

I have always loved you and thought so much of you that this is a great blow to me.

It is not a funny thing to be divorced and I have been very miserable and unhappy for years. I cannot understand how you allowed yourself to be put in such an inviduous [*sic*] position. Quite frankly I feel betrayed and I never could have imagined in the wildest moments of fantasy that you of all people could do anything so shabby.

If you come to Tresco I would much rather you did not come here on your way back, much as I would love to see Constantia.

While we are on unpleasant subjects I had better tell you that I also felt very badly that you had Carol as a witness at your wedding and also at the actual church wedding. It put me in a very difficult position and was I think an extremely insensitive thing for you to do. I have said nothing about it before as I realised it was probably thoughtlessness on your part during your excitement and happiness over your wedding.

I am dreadfully sorry this has happened as it has spoiled something I always have treasured – My love for you. Mary.

Hugh read this letter and then returned it, without comment.

Mary's anguish over her brother's decision to support Carol is easy to understand in the context of its time. In 1945 divorce was difficult to organise and could be socially damaging. In reaction to the sharp increase in the post-war divorce rate,* the stigma where it existed was carried on to the children of divorced parents, who were frequently regarded as objects of curiosity and pity by their peers. Divorcees were ostracised; they could not be introduced to members of the Royal Family and they could be barred from the 'virtuous precinct', the golf club, the communion rail, the Women's Institute, the Royal Enclosure at Ascot; they were fair game in the English national sport of defining a group of insiders by creating outsiders. Playground bullies ruled, for life. A divorced woman might be as happy and fulfilled and generous and loving as could be, but she was ultimately a dodgy proposition since she had already, by conventional standards, claimed to be all those things and destroyed them. That was not true in every case since where reputation was concerned it was essential to know whether the woman in question was the 'innocent' or the 'guilty' party. Following the Abdication, and the King's decision to marry a twice-divorced woman whose second husband was prepared to pose as the guilty party, public opinion had moved in the opposite direction and there had been a reaction against moral rigidity. The divorce laws had been changed in 1937 to introduce desertion and insanity as new grounds for divorce. But 'desertion', which was in effect separation, still meant that one party had to be 'guilty' of deserting the other. The divorce hearing was still a trial, with an innocent and a guilty party. Carol Swinfen's only chance of gaining custody of the children, which he regarded as the prudent course, was of presenting himself as the innocent party who had tried to keep the marriage alive while his wife, the deserter (or 'bolter' in the slang of the day), had proved indecisive and unreliable. In achieving that objective the support of his wife's brother was invaluable.

The importance of being the innocent party, even in petitions based on desertion, is illustrated by the case of the Foreign Secretary, Anthony Eden. Eden was a notorious philanderer whose conquests (all married women) included Her Royal Highness the Duchess of Kent, the Countess of Warwick, Jane Clark, wife of Kenneth and mother of Alan,† Lady Caroline Paget, Countess Beatty and several others. On two occasions Eden, according to his biographer D. R. Thorpe, 'narrowly avoided being cited in the divorce courts', once by the Earl of Warwick and once by Earl Beatty.

---

* Divorces increased from 9,900 in 1938 to 47,000 in 1947.
† Kenneth Clark, millionaire art historian and television personality. Alan Clark, his heir, diarist, Tory MP and philanderer, succumbed to unrequited passion for the prime minister (Margaret Thatcher).

On the second occasion, in 1945, an officer in Eden's old regiment, the
Coldstream Guards, agreed to take Eden's place as the co-respondent and
sit with Dorothy Beatty in her house until 2 a.m. while her husband's
private detectives watched in the street outside. Had Eden been cited it
would have signalled the end of his political career. His problem was
resolved when his wife left him; three years later he could, as the innocent
party, divorce her, after which he was able to remarry and continue in politics. Nonetheless when he did remarry, in 1952, the Archbishop of
Canterbury, Dr Fisher, criticised him in public and prohibited a church
ceremony, and it was suggested that if Eden ever became prime minister
he should play no part in the appointment of bishops. All of which helps
to explain Mary's comment that 'it is not a funny thing to be divorced'.

In the six months that would pass before the decree nisi could be made
absolute, Mary and Eric were not free to live together publicly. In fact,
they had been living apart since immediately after their first meeting. She
continued to live at Boskenna throughout 1945. Siepmann, who was still
in the Royal Marines, was working as an information officer with the British
forces stationed in France after the Liberation. They parted on 30 October,
after their three days in the De Vere Hotel, and she wrote to him that same
day, an eight-page letter, the first in a correspondence that they kept up
whenever one of then was absent from home over a period of twenty-three
years. In this letter she mentions that her divorce 'is in the January list so
I suppose it will be ground out during the next year. Viva!' She also hopes
that he is 'dropping every fourth drink'. After saying how much she misses
him she added, 'Fundamentally you have made me happier than I ever
remember . . . With you I can become the person I really am – and bearing
the grave in mind be buried as such. Dear love consider yourself kissed,
Mary.' The letter was sent to Major E. C. Siepmann RM, HM British
Embassy, Paris, c/o Foreign Office, Whitehall, London SW1, and arrived
bearing the parallel red bars of the censor's crayon.

Eric's first letter, written a week later, before he had received hers, makes
it plain that in his last few days in London he had been anything but
discreet and had told several of their mutual friends about Mary. Pauline
Gates had made sincere efforts to be nice, 'spoiled only by the wish of all
one's well-wishers to see one ruined by a "bad" woman rather than happy
with a good one'. In other words his friends, knowing Mary's reputation,
did not expect the affair to last long and were anticipating the traumatic
ending. 'The fact is,' Eric wrote, 'they can't bear to see two people happy;
it *is* an unbearable sight, which is why one should shut up about it! I will,

in future.' He mentioned the play he was to start writing and another he was still thinking about, and said he was about to set out for Toulouse on a tour of the French south-west, a region that was still in a state of semi-insurrection. He also said, 'I am playing with the idea of the great journey across the Alps from the bed opposite the Broad Walk to the marriage one . . .' Almost as soon as meeting they had spoken of marriage, for life.

Eric left for Paris three weeks after meeting Mary and in November, during their first separation, she kept herself occupied by translating a poem of Louis Aragon's that Eric had discovered on an earlier journey to Paris. Over the following six months the relationship had to be conducted by correspondence; they met only once, in January, when he was given two weeks' leave. Otherwise, they were separated both by distance and by the fact that their letters were sometimes delayed for twelve days or more. The correspondence had to be conducted through the Foreign Office in London, then carried to Paris by diplomatic bag. In France the posts were unreliable so there was an indeterminate delay while British military couriers did their rounds backwards and forwards across the country. Fighting continued on French soil for the rest of the year, the German forces counter-attacking successfully in Alsace and the Ardennes on Christmas Day; they were not driven from French soil until February 1945. Life in most of the liberated territory had returned to normal, post-war conditions before Christmas. But the reign of terror conducted by the Communist Resistance in Marseilles continued until January 1945, when General de Gaulle took steps to calm a region that he described as 'completely out of control'.

Eric's letters to Mary leave no doubt that he had fallen in love as heavily as she had, but they also provide a lively account by an experienced observer of France five months after the Liberation. In his first letter, from Paris, he reported that he was

> most comfortably installed at the Hotel Louvois – minus heat and hot water, but otherwise good – where I live chiefly because my colleagues live in the Castiglione. I am also entitled to eat there, but eat at the Crillon, for the same reason. This gives me time and quiet to think about my work and you – the only two things that matter to me – without interruption. The tour looks better than I expected. Guests of FFI [the Resistance] at the good hotel in Toulouse which they have requisitioned; and sallies to Carcassone, Albi etc., as occasion arises.

He apparently addressed the letter to 'Lady M. Swinfen' and she corrected him promptly, after which she became 'The Lady Swinfen'. 'You shall have your . . . "The" (how she loves it) . . .' he wrote next. 'In spite of your audacity in offering me advice on vocabulary and the art of letter-writing, I must admit that you have some magnificent phrases. I, too, "writhe quietly".' Mary had suggested that Eric might have omitted the phrase 'If you stick to me'. This, she said, 'conjures up visions of glue – an unattractive substance usually connected with things broken – I prefer Aragon's "*Nous serons tous deux comme l'or d'un anneau*"'. (We two will be as close as the gold in one ring.) As for the 'writhing', this was a reference to the fact that Pauline Gates, who had intro-duced them to each other in the Ritz, was having a very public affair, much to the discomfort of her husband Sylvester. Mary had written that none of the latest news of this situation 'would make Sylvester writhe quieter at night'.

On 5 December Eric wrote to ask Mary what sort of scent she would like.

> I have ordered a French woman to find you an umbrella, and please name your scent as otherwise you will get *a*. 'Bourgeois [*sic*] Soir de Paris', which Malcolm Muggeridge's beautiful secretary says you ought to have, or *b*. 'Je Reviens', which is my favourite (but which I do not connect with you). Malcolm, carrying an ultra-secret bag to London tomorrow, has refused in violent terms to carry an umbrella in it . . . Churlishly he said that if I sent one round he'd give it to the secretary whom I've described as beautiful and whom he described as 'wizard'.

Paris, Eric said, was 'sad, wet, dark at night, no buses or taxis, amazingly beautiful, cold'. The French were 'very depressed, very depressing. They mostly hate themselves at the moment, are nervous, exasperated.' Mary chose the 'Bourjois Soir de Paris'.

Shortly after arriving in Toulouse, Eric realised that he had as much work to do dealing with the representatives of the French government as he had in re-educating collaborators. British activity in this severely disturbed area, where torture chambers, public lynchings and inter-Resistance guerilla warfare were commonplace, was already highly unwelcome to the suspicious Gaullist authorities.

In May, near the end of his time, he wrote,

> . . . I cannot say that I have succeeded in my mission of understanding and cajoling the French . . . I came with a plan to avoid the obvious dishing out of brochures and propaganda German-wise. I cultivated the *Résistance*,

(*Above*) The newly married Lady Swinfen. After lunch in the City with Eric Cuddon, travelling companion and close attendant.

(*Above*) Mary in her element: at Falmouth regatta, surrounded by men. On the left is Gage Williams, who was wounded in the First World War and with whom Mary had a fling during the Second War, and on the right is Pip Holman, who pursued her energetically for ten years before and after her marriage to Carol.

(*Left*) Betty Paynter's marriage to Olaf Poulsen de Baerdemaecker, Boskenna, July 1937. The bride wore a full-length pearl satin dress. 'Olaf thought he had netted an heiress and she thought she had scooped up the heir to a Ghent shipping dynasty. Unfortunately both their fathers were broke.'

Above) August 1940: Mary playing with her eldest son, Roger. Photographed in Suffolk, where she left Roger and her pug, Pomfret, safe from the Blitz, with Aunt Rose.

(*Left*) The gates of Loyovitz, family home of the Zieglers.

(*Below*) The three Ziegler brothers, photographed at Loyovitz in 1924: Hans, Paul, Heinz's wife Babs, Heinz.

(*Above*) July 1941: The christening of Mary's second son, Toby, in Cornwall. The photo that Mary sent to friends features her brother Hugh in RAF uniform; Mary, glamorous in a dark dress and cheeky hat; Mrs Bolitho; Mrs Grant who acted as go-between for Mary and Heinz; Betty Paynter and the godfather, John Bolitho, of MI5, also in uniform and holding the baby. Mary did not send out the photo (*left*) taken with Caro

(*Above*) 1941: A rare Farmar family group – Mynors and Violet in Somerset with their daughters Mary and Susan, and their grandchildren Roger, Toby, Robin and Sally.

(*Right*) Toby and Mary.

(Above) Mary rowing Roger and Toby, off the rocks at Boskenna.

(*Below*) Some of the wartime children of Boskenna: Toby, Ann Bailey, Nicky and Roger.

(*Left*) Alice and Ernst Ziegler in the garden at Loyovitz. In 1942, they were sent to Theresienstadt concentration camp, where Ernst died aged seventy-two. Alice died in Auschwitz in December 1943.

(*Right*) To disguise his Czech nationality in the RAF, Heinz Ziegler was given a *nom de guerre*: Flying Officer Henry Osbert Zetland. He signed this photo with his RAF nickname – 'Ziggy' *July 1942*. His crew, in deference to his age, called him 'Uncle'.

Amateur actors in the film which Lady (Austin) Harris is shooting privately are here lined up (l. to r.)—MR. JOHN BETJEMAN *as a clergyman;* MR. CECIL BEATON *as a dowager;* the MARQUESS OF DONEGALL *as a Court official;* LORD BERNERS *as a king; and* MR. SIMON HARCOURT-SMITH *(bearded) as a diplomat.*

(*Above*) Two of Mary's many war-time lovers: Simon Harcourt-Smith (with sword) in costume for amateur dramatics; and (*below*) Charles Patrick Green, DSO, DFC, who once shot down four enemy aircraft in a single sortie.

(*Left*) The end of the war: Alice Grenfell with her charges – Roger, Toby and Sonya. Boskenna, 1945.

and set about a *reportage* on them. Alas, I found that the new France is not the *Résistance*, and that the *Résistance* itself – whatever its past – goes around with what is called a chip on its shoulder and positively refuses to be understood! There are schisms of the past, involving us, about which you learn painfully. (I have just been told, pat: 'The English did nothing for the *Résistance*.'

Eric was accused by the Rector of Toulouse University of 'cultivating Communists'. His main enemy was the British consul in Bordeaux, whom he described as 'wildly pro-Franco' and who thought that all left-wing French and Spanish resisters were 'red revolutionaries'. (Many of them were.) Eric realised that he had been caught in a turf war between the Foreign Office and the Ministry of Information, and that he was on the weaker side. It did not help that his French opposite number was 'a strict Catholic, ex-Pétainist and anti-alcoholic'. He left Toulouse on 1 June. His supposed sympathy for Communists was founded on his friendship with Louis Aragon and Julien Benda, both of whom he admired for their writing rather than their politics.

Mary wrote more frequently – and longer – fifteen letters in the first two months, thirty-two in all. In these she gave him a vivid picture of her new, quiet life at Boskenna and spared him none of the domestic horrors associated with bringing up two small boys. On 4 November 1944, she wrote,

I got back here last night, creeping into a sleeping house with only the parrot to greet me and he was rudeness itself. (Apart from the children who set on me like a pack of terriers at six this morning. They were heaven.) Otherwise it's been the traditional homecoming with all the horrors hoarded for one's happy return dished up with my breakfast tray and ranging from 'The cook's left' to 'The fox has eaten your chickens' and passing lightly over the fact that the children are in quarantine for measles. Ending with 'I thought I'd wait till you got back to deal with it milady'.

Roger, aged six, having been goaded beyond endurance by a twelve-year-old visitor, had thrown a heavy fir cone at the bully and hit him on the head, 'drawing blood in terrifying quantities . . . [Roger's] expression of detached satisfaction as he watched me bathing and plastering his weeping victim gave me great pleasure.' Later, '. . . There was a meeting last night to form a committee for the Welcome Home of the men from the parish who have been at the war . . . Feeling ran riot as many of the committee have kept their sons at home.' The boys were already showing different characters. 'I heard a shout of "Peace!" from Betty when I was out in the fields with Toby [aged four] and said to him "The War is over", he went very pink and said "It isn't" – His thoughts are his own. Roger is instilled with potted patriotism at school and fairly well informed. Toby prays fervently for the Japanese and Germans when he is annoyed with me.' Later she gave them 'a pair of Bantams. Toby chose the hen leaving, generously I fondly imagined, the showy cock to Roger. But with a sweet smile [Toby] explained to me that the hen would lay eggs and hatch out little chicks which was beyond the powers of the rooster.'

Life in Boskenna as the war wound down still amused her. The wounded soldiers and airmen no longer visited, but others did. 'I am bored at the prospect of Geordie and Clare Sutherland invading next week. They *insist* on coming, she to stay here and he nearby in Penzance. I don't mind him really he is stupid but quite nice but she drives me scatty, Mrs Emanual's sister. Having them about is as unrestful as a badly-furnished room.' In her next letter she covered the visit:

> Romie Brinckman brought her mother-in-law for the afternoon. A splendid specimen of the dying aristocracy. Very like Queen Mary even to The Toque and The Daimler. A great gardener, she toured the garden rolling out the Latin names of all the shrubs so glibly that I began to suspect she knew she was safe, that Romie and I knew none of them. I only caught her out on one. She is recovering from a heart attack brought on by being heavily fined for getting too much or too little meal for her hens. This happens to all of us however hard we try to be honest. I adore old ladies. This collects swans (china and glass ones) she tells me she had eight hundred but that the Blitz had taken its toll. Romie kept hissing in my ear 'Don't make her walk too fast or she'll die before she's changed her will'. She is vastly rich and Romie the new daughter-in-law. I enjoyed her . . . Geordie Sutherland gave me a good laugh last night. He never has recovered from being a Duke.* He rang up in a petulant tone in answer to a telegram I'd sent him to say it is impossible to get him suites of rooms in local hotels at short notice. 'But did you use MY name?' I bellowed 'Of course I did and it had no more effect than mine'. He rang off. I wish him stuffed for the nation.

That spring the flower picking took place as usual at Boskenna. 'Every year I am surprised afresh by the spring here,' she wrote on 28 February.

---

* 5th Duke of Sutherland; inheritor of 1.3 million Scottish acres.

Impossible to get used to the flowers. Narcissus and daffodils being packed off by the ton to market. And everywhere flowers, mimosa, violets, primroses, anemones and many more . . . Every available man and girl is picking, bunching, carting or packing and the maws in Birmingham, London or Bristol clamour for more . . . today the sun was hot and the sea and the sky violently blue and the children tumbled into a cart full of daffodils looked absurd and vital and I wanted you there very badly to see it all.

Her next letter described two days of

blue and gold. Frost in the morning followed by hot sun. I worked in the flower field most of yesterday as we were short of labour . . . For an hour Toby and I struck and sat under a flaming gorse bush which looked exactly like scrambled egg on toast in the brown bracken, but smelt hot and delicious. I read him *The Georgics* which he affected to like. Then we worked again. The horse is called Albert and gets very bored . . . On days like this everyone sings as they work and there is a strong similarity to a pagan festival and I feel very near the earth . . .

Colonel Paynter's activities were a frequent diversion. He was seventy-nine years old but had lost none of his *élan*. When wartime restrictions threatened to close down the transportation of Cornish flowers by rail to London and ruin the local economy, the Colonel simply switched to smuggling. Boskenna's flower farms were soon producing more than he could sell locally, so he contacted the commander of the local US base and came to an arrangement. The transport of flowers by road was not authorised, but the police were not allowed to stop US military vehicles. At night very large American lorries would draw up at the back of the house and the gardeners and all the farmworkers would load them with flowers, after which they disappeared up the back drive with doused headlights. Alec Beecham, the local MP, knew what was going on and found his visits – he was courting Betty – increasingly nerve-racking. One busy night Alice came into the drawing room and said the constable had come to see the Colonel and she had shown him into the library. This caused great alarm to Betty, Mary and Mr Beecham. Colonel Paynter finished his coffee, then wandered off to the library. He returned chuckling. 'Came down the front drive,' he said. 'Some people take fright much too easily.' The commander of the US base and several policemen were in due course arrested and charged, but Colonel Paynter, who was still a JP, was never bothered.

After four years of living at Boskenna, Mary's affection for the lawless Colonel was still growing. In January 1945 she wrote, 'My Darling, It's so cold here . . . No telephones working and no signs that they will ever work again . . . Everything drips in a beastly thaw from the eaves to the Colonel's nose.' In April the Colonel, feeling the sap rising, set out for London on his favourite jaunt, in search of dancing girls, usually at the Windmill. He is going to 'take Jean Batten out dancing', wrote Mary. 'I do love his utter lack of self-consciousness at eighty-one.' (He was actually seventy-nine.) When the war ended he told Mary that 'the only difference the Victory is going to make is that we shall gradually stop feeling guilty when we enjoy ourselves'. In Penzance a Victory Parade was organised and as commander of the Home Guard, Colonel Paynter turned out. He marched three miles in the after-noon, 'coming back to tea undefeated. He answered my anxious enquiry with the retort that he wears out "three partners in the Flurry Dance" so this was nothing. I love him.' When Mary went to meet Colonel Paynter at the station on his return from London, Hugh and Constantia got off the same train. They were going on directly to the Scilly Isles. 'It was a mixed pleasure for Hugh,' Mary wrote. 'He eyed me rather like a horse passing a tractor . . . [but] . . . having bowled the old boy off his feet in a totally unexpected attack I feel revoltingly magnanimous.'

Another favourite character in Mary's letters was her trusted old confi-dante Mrs Grant, who in 1941 had discreetly alerted Heinz to the birth of Toby. Widowed in the Boer War and living out her life in great style on £300 a year, Mrs Grant, by then in her seventies, once told Mary that her 'jolliest' times had been when she was in her fifties – 'By far the best lovers, my dear.' In May, Mary took her to a concert given by the Penzance Orchestral Society. 'Armed with a mass of musical instruments [the orchestra] began the programme by battling through *The Bartered Bride* . . . glaring at one another they fiddled and trumpeted faster and faster.' They were playing with a professional pianist, Michal Hambourg, and Mary's 'heart warmed to her when I saw her go pink and begin to shake with giggles as the orchestra bolted'. Later Mary made friends with Hambourg in 'the Mayor's Parlour while the orchestra massacred Beethoven's Second Symphony. Never have I heard it sound so like *The Ride of the Valkyries* . . . Feathers flew and Mrs Grant's comment, made in a clear voice during a quiet passage, that "the conductor seems to be making a soufflé", could be heard all over the hall. When Mary in great excitement telephoned Mrs Grant to tell her that she had just received 'physical support from America yesterday in the guise of two most elegant bust bodices in answer to a *cri de cœur* to a friend in New

York . . . she said unkindly I thought, "What are you going to put in them, Darling?" ' Eric told her to tell Mrs Grant that there was 'plenty'. Mary gave him two other items of information. Hitler had just been accorded a full-page obituary in *The Times* and in December, Boskenna had been roused by a 'macabre' night-time search for a missing coastguard.

Considerable hue and cry over the telephone and storm lanterns and torches bobbing along the cliffs, starlight and bitter cold, beautiful and frightening. The children knew all about it before anyone else. He was found dead in a blue mackintosh by his brother, having fallen over Lamorna Cliff . . . The search parties ended up here, keening in the kitchen and drinking beer. The parrot joined in with some pithy remarks and made me giggle. He has about as much tact as my Aunt Violet.

Mary found something unconvincing in the searcher's account because she added, 'Personally I think one of the elementals gave him a push.' She had thought it odd that no one began to organise search parties until dusk, although the coastguard had been due back from his beat at midday. In her brief description of this incident there are several factors that marked her imagination and re-emerged in her writing forty years later: the fall of a coastguard over a Cornish cliff, the tactless intrusion of a parrot, the sinister possibility of a push, the inappropriate involvement of children in something 'beautiful and frightening'.

In the eight months that separated their first meeting and Eric's final return from France, he and Mary spent less than four weeks together; their continuing relationship was entirely dependent on their correspondence and might have died away without it. 'Aldous Huxley says', Mary noted, 'that loving by letter is a difficult and dangerous thing since in absence each tends to idealise the other and reunion leads to disappointment. I don't agree . . . You are I think unaware of what you have already given me, a security in time which no one else has ever given. For that I can say I can love you for ever.' In fact, what characterised their expressions of love was not anguish or frustration but optimism – and surprise. Realising at the beginning that they were in for a long separation, they agreed that they would simply have to rely on mutual faith. Mary then wrote, 'One aspect, a simple one, seems to be that having found one person in whom I have faith I am in a fair way to growing smugly impervious to the winds of malice. It's a startling and enjoyable feeling, rather like meeting God at a party.' That came in a fourteen-page letter and she wrote again on the following day (3 December), 'I must have changed as

Alec [Beechman MP] looked at me the other day and said: "I don't know
what's happened to you, Darling, but I'm very glad".'

No doubt the clues were everywhere. Mary had been repainting the
nursery rocking horse: 'I have given it eyelashes like ostrich feathers, spots
like American bruises* on its haunches, and as for its mane and tail – Well!'
Eric tried to match her high spirits, but sometimes became depressed. He
pinned all his hopes on his future as a writer. He was already in debt and
supporting an absent wife who detested him but his impending success as
a playwright would solve everything. 'The play', he wrote on 14 May, 'is
completely held up . . . but 60 pages of notes for "Is there a New France?"
round themselves off nicely at the Capitulation ceremonies. I had luncheon
yesterday with Julien Benda,† the writer, and he greatly approved my title
and subject.' Later he wrote, 'I shall never again take on a life of bluff; by
which I mean propaganda or the cheaper if more lucrative journalism. I
mean to free-lance for a living, and get my plays put on.'

Mary, for her part, foresaw no difficulties about Eric's divorce, her own
was almost complete and her commitment was now total. Before Christmas
she had told Eric that her bitch True had 'slipped up with some low-suitor'
and that she felt illogically disappointed to find that she herself had not.
'I have never loved before without knowing I could somehow manage
without it. Nobody can really hurt me except you now . . . I feel a great
enthusiasm for the future and no modesty about telling you so.' And again
– 'We are travelling down a path which neither of us has ever travelled
before . . . I want so much more for you than I seem to give in my letters . . .
I want to be extremely extravagant with my love as between this and the
grave there will never be enough time to spend it.' In a letter written two
weeks before his return she signed off – 'I love you. It will take me years
to show you how much, M.' And the last letter Eric wrote from Toulouse,
just before setting out for Paris on 30 May, finished, 'I feel like giving the
future a square look in the eye with you; an intimidating look. The wolf
has been at my door before, but this time he is going to get a surprising
reception . . . Darling, I adore you! Facing disaster with you is exhilarating.
Let's make an end of disaster. E.'

---

* American bruises: Wartime slang for love bites.
† Julien Benda: left-wing critic, moralist and anti-Marxist. He coined the phrase
'*la trahison des clercs*' to describe intellectuals who betrayed universal truths by
descending into the political arena.

PART THREE

1945–1970

CHAPTER NINE

The Face at the Window

'Eric, I am going to be bloody . . .'

Phyllis Siepmann to her husband in 1946.

The conflict was over and after the first elation Mary noticed a widespread feeling of 'sadness and emptiness', the after-effect of war. 'There are so many shocks and disappointing surprises in the first years that one becomes battered into insensitivity and unable to rejoice,' she wrote. Like many thousands of others, Mary and Eric were now faced with simple practical problems that added to the overwhelming sense of anticlimax. Where to live in bombed-out London, how to pay the rent, where to find a job? They could not get married until Eric was divorced and they had no savings.

Mary left the children with Alice Grenfell at Boskenna for a few weeks. She and Eric moved into lodgings at 31 Smith Terrace, Chelsea, where they spent most of the time 'merrily making love'. In September, when Mary was back in Cornwall, Eric found a more expensive room at No. 39 in the same street. Here the landlady, Mrs de Vos, used to bring up meals on trays to keep up their strength. They were living on £45 a week, and the rent was 9 guineas (£9.45). There was no bathroom and the lavatory was at the far end of the garden. There was a hip bath which Mrs de Vos, who was a romantic, would make her husband fill for them by carrying the hot water up in buckets. In the evenings they would frequently dine at the Ritz, where Mr de Vos was the wine waiter. There was no better place for consolidating their relationship and it was as cheap as anywhere else because no restaurant was allowed by law to charge more than 5/- (25p) for a set meal.

The man Mary had fallen for was a complex character who had considerable ability as a journalist and a linguist. He had translated Molière and, according to a glowing reference supplied for him in September 1945

by Sir Walter Monckton,* he spoke five languages, including Hungarian.
But despite his capacity to excel at various practical and well-paid activities, his real ambition was to make his living first as a playwright and
then as a novelist. His pre-war novel had taken him six weeks to complete
and he was always convinced that he could repeat this feat. Mary said,
'He was one of those people who boil with ideas, he always had far too
many ideas for one novel. He would never slow down and cogitate and
rewrite. He would have a brilliant idea and get bored after one chapter,
and he was a terrible chucker away.' He also had a self-destructive streak.
Antonia White, who knew him as a young man, once wrote that she had
wanted 'to rape him'. Their brief and unhappy affair had given her some
insight into Eric's problems:

> ... He is terribly split and divided against himself ... naïf and
> childish ... but with a much keener drive of mind and imagination too.
> He goes pretty deep into anything that really interests him with a real
> German thoroughness ... His mind strikes here and there like a sharp
> searchlight, but whole tracts are unilluminated ... Innocent, muddled,
> terrified he has built up this swaggering, cynical, Byronic self as a defence.
> But his cruelty, his impulse to destroy his own happiness and that of the
> people nearest him is very deep indeed ...

She eventually decided that Siepmann was 'the wickedest man I ever met'.
    In Mary's experience, Eric was sometimes violent, always volatile and
extremely jealous. He made her give him a complete list of her previous
lovers and she was so worried by his explosive temperament that she
destroyed all her diaries soon after meeting him, 'I didn't want him to read
them and so I put them in the boiler at Boskenna,' she said.† Two years
after meeting Mary, Eric recorded his dark suspicion that she had 'fallen
in love with the Young Tennyson in the National Portrait Gallery'.

Soon after Eric's return to England, Mary took him down to Cornwall to
meet the children and Colonel Paynter. The Colonel must have been very

---

* Sir Walter Monckton KC, later 1st Viscount Monckton, wartime Director-
General of the Ministry of Information, later Solicitor-General and Minister of
Defence, political and legal fixer, friend and adviser to the Duke of Windsor.
† The diary for 1944, year of Heinz Ziegler's death and her meeting with Eric,
somehow escaped.

fond of Mary because he took to Eric at once and they soon fell into the habit of playing a daily game of chess. Eric spent his few weeks of leave at Boskenna – he was still in the Royal Marines awaiting demobilisation – then returned to the care of Mrs de Vos, determined to finish his play and find more suitable accommodation. Mary wanted everyone, including Roger and Toby, under the same roof. Their correspondence at this time shows how the drama of their world, the war, has been replaced by a completely different miniaturised drama of private life. The bombs and destruction were a thing of the past but the dangers ahead, though less dramatic, had the same potential for destroying personal happiness.

The happiest years of Mary's life were the twenty-four years she spent with Eric, a period launched on the optimism they shared in 1945. But this optimism had first to overcome the problem of her family. When Mary's parents came to London they stayed quite close to Smith Terrace. And her brother Hugh also lived in Chelsea. In July, just before a family wedding, she warned Eric that, 'My mother, father, brother, sister, niece and pregnant sister-in-law will all be rampaging round Chelsea from tomorrow. Buy me a mask.' In order to avoid embarrassment Mary decided to explain the situation to her parents. 'They were both quite horrible. They sent my sister round to make a scene. They tried to enlist my brother, but he and his wise new wife steered clear . . . They persecuted Carol (again) who complained (to me).' Eric eventually went round to see Mynors but they never met again. Eric said that Mary's father had behaved 'like a Victorian'.

Mary discovered that her family's chief ground of complaint against Eric was not his unstable record, nor the fact that he was married. He was, apparently, 'German'. It was true that Eric spoke German and that his father, Otto, had once been German. But old Otto Siepmann had married an Englishwoman and his two older sons, both born in England, had fought in Flanders in the same trenches and under the same flag as Mary's father. Eric himself was still serving in the Royal Marines. To describe him as 'German', let alone vilify him for it, was prejudice taken to the point of self-parody.[*]

In August, while Mary was struggling to set up home with Eric, support him while he found a job, look after the children, divide her time between

[*] Had Otto ever heard of it he would have been reminded of the anti-German feeling he encountered among the staff at Clifton College during the First World War. Otto – now in his mid-eighties and living in retirement in Berkshire – was shortly to die of heart failure, having doubled his heavily taxed tobacco consumption in 1939 as his contribution to the war effort.

Chelsea and Cornwall, and fend off her enraged parents, she became pregnant. She had been half hoping that this would happen and had already chosen the names Hyacinthe and Dominic. She had thought she was pregnant in July, but it had been a false alarm. She then decided that she would rather not use contraception: '. . . If it is humanly possible I want Hyacinthe-Dominic to be born when they want to be.' In other words she deliberately became pregnant. Then, trying to reach a decision about her pregnancy, Mary wrote a series of letters from Boskenna to Eric, who was in London. On 25 August she was still happy about the future – 'I feel very well and completely unworried' – but on the following day she was feeling so ill that she considered giving up smoking and one day later she was having serious doubts. 'I am thinking very hard about H-D,' she wrote.

> The more I think the more inconvenient they seem to be. It isn't as you know that I don't want them, it is the problems we have already looked at. That it's very unfair on you even if you get started straight away in a good job. That it may turn out to be unfair to them. That thinking it over here I believe it might make things more difficult for Roger and Toby to be with us and I am sure that I should not be able to laugh off a bogus story about it. At the moment I am *afraid* of the difficulties . . . I want our children to have the very best start we can give them and this doesn't seem to be it! . . . I have talked to Betty who is prepared to help and in such a case is a very loyal friend. She is naturally in favour of a riddance as indeed I was for her in the same case. Nor do I blame her. Mrs Grant I also told. She was heavenly and most concerned. Please my love don't think I've been influenced or have panicked. I haven't. I've just been thinking hard and unemotionally. We are only starting our Alpine climb and I want to be a help to you not a drag! . . . Think about it too and let us decide when I get back to you on Friday night . . .

Eric meanwhile had just written to her, blithely, from Smith Terrace: 'Am I having this baby or are you? My imagination is affected, and I see babies everywhere. As I walk in Battersea Park they sprout like mushrooms around my feet . . .' Having posted that letter, he received the news that she was having second thoughts and without waiting for their meeting at once supported her new position. 'I shall *hate* getting rid of it,' he added, 'and I dread the personal experience for you.' This letter was posted two hours after the first, so they would probably have reached Mary by the same post, and she was clearly more convinced by the second than by the first.

Mary told him not to 'worry about ways and means as they are all set, safe and painless'. In fact, abortion was expensive and quite difficult to organise in 1945. The only legal justification for it was a serious threat to the health of the mother and 'stress' was not regarded as a threat to mental health. In these circumstances it was usually necessary to go to a 'back-street' abortionist, who was not always competent or even qualified. Nonetheless, Mary decided that another baby would be too much to handle. Her parents' fury about Eric had been a great worry to her. In one letter to him she said, 'Forgive the emotional storm I set going over my parents. You were so wonderful over it and I never said Thank you properly.' She was exhausted by the struggle she was having with her entire family and could not face adding another scandal to their long list of complaints: too many affairs, divorce from Carol, black-market dealing and living with a married 'German'. So she lost her nerve and 'took the advice of worldly friends'. Despite her assurances to Eric the operation was carried out in London under local anaesthetic at the home of a doctor who lived in a block of flats opposite a police station, following which she went home by taxi. The doctor was 'central European', a description in her memoir of 1958 which she subsequently crossed out, but which makes it sound as though the operation was performed by a refugee doctor whose qualifications were not recognised in England.

Mary later regretted her abortion and described it as 'cowardly'. She always thought of this missing child as 'Hyacinthe'. Many years later, at the age of eighty-eight, in her final attempt to complete her memoirs she included this passage: 'I have not written a word of this for months [a gap of almost two years] grinding to a halt for no reason in Smith Terrace and yet I know the reason I do not want to write about it. I got pregnant and had an abortion and I do not want to write about that.' Her second attempt to set down an account of her life ended three pages later.

In September 1945 Eric was demobilised, and in October Mary's divorce became absolute and she could start to live with Eric openly. They found a house, still in Chelsea, at 29 Donne Place. Mary discovered that Eric had never in his life boiled an egg. One day, feeling unwell, she went to bed. Presently a voice floated up the stairs, 'How do you turn the gas on?' and she was back on her feet. With the help of Sir Walter Monckton's reference Eric started a good job as a press officer with British European Airways (BEA). And then, when everything seemed to be going right, it all went wrong again.

Phyllis Morris had married Eric Siepmann in January 1941. She was an athletic and attractive woman, a champion skier and an Oxford graduate at a time when few women went to university. She had been living with Siepmann for seven months before their marriage; he was already an officer in the Royal Marines waiting to be sent overseas. Before his unit finally embarked there was a series of delays, described by Evelyn Waugh (a fellow officer in 8 Marine Commando) in his *Diaries*. During this period Siepmann subsequently said that he was put under considerable pressure by Phyllis to marry her. She contacted his fellow officers, asking them to plead her case, and she told Eric that since he was bound to be killed in the Commandos it would be a waste of a widow's 30s. pension if he did not marry. He found this blunt argument persuasive. She also wanted to get out of the WAAF, in which she held the lowest possible rank. In the event, Siepmann's unit never saw action in Crete but was left behind in Egypt, where Phyllis eventually rejoined him in August 1942. Here, they attempted to establish their marriage, without success. Siepmann drank far too much and was violent towards her, and they separated for good in December. By that time he was an intelligence officer in charge of press and public relations for the Eighth Army.

In August 1944 Siepmann returned to Europe and was sent almost at once to France to work in 'psychological warfare' (propaganda) in a country that was regarded as largely collaborationist. It was while he was on leave from this posting that he first met Mary. Meanwhile Phyllis had remained in the Middle East. At some time in 1944 she had written to Eric's brother, Harry, who was a director of the Bank of England, asking him to contact Eric in order to tell him that she wanted a divorce and needed the evidence. Eric naïvely supposed that his divorce was therefore 'in the bag' and that all he needed to do was provide Phyllis with evidence of adultery. After talking the matter over with Mary, Eric sent Phyllis two hotel bills showing that he had stayed with an unnamed lady in London, in the Park Lane and Normandie Hotels, in January and February 1945. He also told her that he would pay all the costs of the divorce case. Mary had written to Eric on 18 July, 'Phyllis should be getting your letter any day now. I'm praying steadily.' But Phyllis made no response to this letter and continued living in Beirut, where she was working in the British legation and enjoying herself and where she won another skiing competition. Throughout this period Siepmann was paying Phyllis a monthly allowance, but the correspondence suggests that Eric's solicitor of this period, Mr Rutherford, of Ralph Bond and Rutherford, was often hard to contact and of little help. Eventually, in April 1946, Eric received a letter from Phyllis who said that she was returning to England, that she needed a loan and that she had lost the two hotel bills he had sent her as evidence for their divorce.

Alarmed by this new attitude, Mary made the mistake of changing her name by deed poll to 'Siepmann'. In June 1946 Phyllis wrote to Eric again, this time from Paris, saying that she loved him and needed him.

Eric and Phyllis Siepmann met in July 1946. They had not seen each other for three years and Mary had told Eric to be careful. But when Phyllis confirmed that she was willing to have a divorce he incautiously told her about his relationship with Mary and of how they planned to get married. Trusting completely in the goodwill of Phyllis, Eric spontaneously provided her with the details of his life with Mary, including many private details of Mary's life before they met. Mary was at this time in Boskenna. Eric and Phyllis continued to meet in London and make their plans over a period of several days, at the end of which Phyllis said, 'Eric, I am going to be bloody; I am not going to divorce you under any circumstances.'

It is possible that when she had written to Harry Siepmann in 1944 Phyllis had met someone she wanted to marry in Beirut, but that this relationship had ended, leaving her without money and with no prospect of happiness. She had returned to England to find that Eric had acquired a job and an attractive mistress who was calling herself Mrs Siepmann, 'stealing' her husband, her identity and a large part of the available money. Up to that point Phyllis had achieved very little in life, but the energy, ingenuity and ruthlessness that she deployed over the next six years showed that she had missed her vocation. Having, as she saw it, been scorned, she became the embodiment of one of the ancient Furies. Today her behaviour would be called 'stalking' and it would be fair to say that Phyllis was so good at it that she broke Eric Siepmann as a journalist. She opened her onslaught with a letter to Mary, written on 11 July 1946, just after her frank declaration refusing Eric a divorce.

'I well believe,' she wrote, that 'he feels very fond of you. He does of all of us – in turn. Unfortunately for you I met him before you and took a risk which nobody had taken for 20 years – and married him for ever, meaning to stick to him for ever because I don't think I'll ever love anyone more than I do him.' On the same day she sent letters to Eric, to Carol Swinfen and to Eric's sister Edith, who was married to an Anglican clergyman. To Carol, a complete stranger, she said, 'I have been wondering how Mary could live financially without being somebody's mistress . . . I would like you to stop paying her while she continues to live with Eric . . . Please let me know your views.' And to Eric she wrote: 'I didn't marry you to divorce you – mistresses

are one of the painful adjuncts of marriage – like self-sacrifice – I'm prepared
for one of the "Herculean efforts" on which you congratulated me in Cairo.'
   On 29 July Eric wrote to Mary, 'We shall weather our difficulties. Rocks,
after irritation and involuntary tears, come out of eyes . . . I couldn't bear
her interferences with my "soul" . . .' He also replied to Phyllis's first letter
pointing out that she had been the first to suggest a divorce, that he still
had the letter she had written to his brother in March 1944 and offering
her a larger allowance as long as it was paid through a solicitor. But Phyllis
was up and away. She wrote to Mary's lodger at Donne Place, a young
woman called Christina Sandberg, saying that there would be no divorce
and that Eric had ill-treated her physically and mentally in Cairo. And then,
opening up a new front, she turned to Eric's employers at British European
Airways:

> Please forgive my writing to you on a very painful and personal matter. I
> do so because I think there is a faint chance that you may be able to help
> me over my husband who is working in your organisation. I have just
> arrived back from the Middle East, after not seeing my husband for three
> years, to find him living with another woman . . . Before our marriage there
> was a series of such semi-permanent liaisons, which were mostly ended
> by force of circumstances. I would like this one to end quickly in the same
> easy way.

In October Phyllis, carrying a suitcase, gained entry to the house in
Donne Place and refused to leave. Eric was at the office and received a
telephone call from Mary, who had come face to face with Phyllis for the
first time. He returned home and repeatedly asked Phyllis to go. When she
refused he threw her out, using the minimum of force; nonetheless Phyllis
put up a violent fight. Mary must have been involved in the struggle because
afterwards Phyllis threatened to sue her for assault.
   Throughout this time Phyllis continued to correspond with the management of British European Airways, which Eric found humiliating and highly
embarrassing. She also started a correspondence with a colleague of Eric's
in the office, Miss Gow. Whereas most of the men who heard from Phyllis
tended to discourage her politely, a waste of effort that merely encouraged
her to redouble her efforts, Nancy Gow, who liked Eric, used a different
technique. She engaged Phyllis in correspondence, suggesting that Phyllis
was simply mistaken, that Eric was an intelligent and effective member of
the human race, that Phyllis's most outrageous suggestions left her un-

convinced: 'I think that you and your psychiatrist must be suffering from a misapprehension regarding your husband . . . I have seldom met anyone for whose ability and character I have greater respect and admiration.' Miss Gow's style – laconic, detached, quizzical – was either completely humourless or evidence of a deadpan wit. In either event she was more than a match for Phyllis. Miss Gow added that she was quite happy to meet Phyllis if a meeting was suggested, so that she could repeat her assurance that no, Eric was not a drunkard, contrary to his wife's view, and that the idea that 'no little Arab boy in Cairo was safe while Eric had been there' was implausible, not to say totally mistaken. Phyllis seems to have found this response quite wearing so she switched back to a much softer target, an Old Etonian peer being a pushover for a woman of her mettle. On 3 September 1947 she wrote a letter to Lord Swinfen: 'I am now told that I can get . . . Legal Aid and bring a separation suit in the High Court on grounds of drunkenness, cruelty and unnatural vice . . . Eric has homosexual leanings and in Cairo on several occasions . . . made advances to little boys in front of friends . . . It is useless to hope that out of a sense of fairness you would help me . . . but you may for your little boys' sake care to intervene.'

In November 1946 her tone with the management of BEA changed and became that of a blackmailer. She wrote of her urgent need for money and of how she was beginning to think that the only way to get it was to make a scandal; she was hesitating solely because of the possibility of 'harmful publicity'.

Eric's position became embarrassing and unbearable. In May 1947 Phyllis got into his office while he was away and intimidated a young secretary. His colleagues had already noticed a very great change in his physical and nervous condition. He had lost his concentration, he became easily upset, he was unable to do his work properly and he had the feeling that he might lose his job. In June 1947 Eric resigned from BEA.

Eric's father, Otto, had died in January of that year, leaving five surviving children and an estate of £9,257. Eric and Mary therefore had enough money for a holiday, well away from Phyllis, so they flew to Marseilles at the end of July and visited Aix and Toulon and St Remy, and planned their new future as writers. In Marseilles, Mary noted in her diary that 'the brandy tasted of soap'. Eric hated working in an office at the best of times and they hoped to be able to keep going until they could sell their work. Mary had already lunched with a leading literary agent, Spencer Curtis

Brown, and had proposed a novel in which he was interested. Eric, as always, had several projects under way. On their return, still deep in unmarried disgrace with Mary's family, they went to stay with Eric's sister Edith, who had married the Vicar of Bagshot, Wing-Commander the Rev. Ralph Bankes-Jones. Her husband was away so Edith lodged them in his bed. 'If you can't get married couldn't you at least have Eric's child? It would be so good for him,' said Edith. Mary reminded her that she was a parson's wife. 'Oh, what does that matter,' said Edith. Her husband then returned home unexpectedly and strode into the hall declaring, 'This house *stinks* of adultery.' Mary and Eric decided to leave London and head for the West Country. Eric's inheritance would provide enough money to buy a cottage; it would be the start of a new life.

In *Part of the Scenery* Mary referred to this period of their time together: 'Eric worked on his novel, I tinkered with mine.' Earlier, on first reading her book, he had written,

> Some bits are so good . . . that they show that you have it in you to do something really good . . . the chief point and the ultimate effect is that you have written a novel that is well above the average, beautiful and amusing in parts (funny and beautiful is, I feel sure, your line . . .) and full of promise as a first novel. I am frankly amazed!!! . . . You have a 90 per cent chance of getting it published and a 50:50 chance with a good publisher. I should send it first to Collins, and then to Gollancz. (It might be best, after all, to use Curtis Brown?! You do owe him the suggestion!)

And in another of his letters Eric wrote, 'Do you know I am glad this woman persecutes me – it keeps me alive, and balanced (this memento of how not to live) and *drives* me to write! I am only sorry that it should affect you.' But this comment was no more than bravado.

Before setting out from London Mary collected the boys and the dogs, then they all went down to Pinchaford in Devon for the rest of the summer holiday. They stayed in a boarding house and Eric set to work in an outside room. After a few days he looked up and saw Phyllis's face at the window.

CHAPTER TEN

The Shadow in the Street

'Julia had an empty tin in her hand, its jagged lid threatening his face.'
An Imaginative Experience

She was in festive mood, wearing a yellow aertex shirt. She came inside and said, 'Writing a masterpiece, I suppose.' Then she asked for £4 a week (up from £3) and a glass of water, and when the water was given to her she threw it in Eric's face. The next day she came back to the boarding house and found the two little boys playing on the lawn and tried to talk to them. When the landlady asked her why she did not divorce Eric if he was such a bad man, Phyllis replied 'that she would never let him go and that she would hound him wherever he went'. After that she agreed to leave and meet Eric at his solicitor's in London. Then she waited until Eric had set out for London before returning to the boarding house at lunchtime. As Mary recalled it, 'She made a magnificent entrance during the hotel lunch, bursting into a dining-room full of God-fearing holiday makers and their children, shrieking: "There's that Scarlet Woman, Lady Swinfen" and struck me violently. I was terrified. Roger said, "Mummy, that woman hit you. Why didn't you hit her back?" My knees knocking together I said, "I think she's dotty, darling," and the gardener ejected her far more violently than was necessary and the local police were called.'

Eric was staying in London with Carol, and together they advised Mary to take the boys to the Clarence Hotel in Exeter, where Eric met them the next day and they went to Chagford in the middle of Dartmoor. Mary's diary for 1947 covers these events as '*August 26*, "Dentist 10.30 Assault." *August 27* "Flight to Chagford"'. At Chagford they stayed in the Beverley, a small private hotel. The summer holidays resumed their orthodox course and the diary entries read 'river', 'gymkhana', 'ride bog', 'carnival'. Mary made friends with the vicar and sometimes went to church. The boys went back to school and on 1 October her diary notes, 'Started work on *Henrietta*.'

Phyllis meanwhile had not been inactive. In September a telegram had been delivered to Carol's house in Ovington Square, addressed to Eric. It read, 'Are you spiv drone heel or butterfly that instead supporting wife you require her to work stop Please telephone solicitors stop You will sign agreement accordance written promise stop Alternative another personal discussion.' When this failed to have any effect, Phyllis dashed off a few lines to Eric's sister suggesting that Eric was habitually drunk and liked to make sexual advances to little boys. She then resumed her investigations and tracked Eric and Mary down to the Beverley Hotel in Chagford, but this time she made a mistake.

The Beverley Private Hotel was run by Major Trevor Hughes and among his permanent guests was an old lady called Miss Drake. On 20 October Miss Drake's breakfast was ruined when she received a letter, out of the blue, suggesting that that nice Mr Siepmann with the pretty wife, whose table was just across from hers in the dining room, was in fact a violent, adulterous, alcoholic, wife-beating child molester – but adding reassuringly, 'It is wrong to blame or condemn him . . . my husband is irresistibly compelled to ill-treat all his women owing to a deep and unconscious mother-fixation which can only be cured by psychological treatment.'

Dusting Miss Drake down after this upset did not put Major Hughes in a good mood. Several days later Phyllis turned up in Chagford, intent on a renewed frontal assault. Eric refused to see her, so Major Hughes walked her up and down the lawn outside the lounge windows while she abused Siepmann in a loud voice as 'a Bluebeard and a sadist'. When she refused to leave, the Major locked his guests inside the hotel and set out to find the village constable. On his return he found Phyllis tapping on the windows of the lounge and denouncing him for running a hotel that was being used for 'immoral purposes'. While he was ejecting her from the premises she set about him, and both she and her dog bit him in the leg.

Subsequently she summonsed him for assault. Major Hughes cross-summonsed her for assault and battery. He won his case, she lost hers and the result was that she was bound over to keep the peace. This meant that if she caused another rumpus in Chagford she would be locked up; and the practical effect of the case was to make the village on Dartmoor a safe haven for Eric and Mary for as long as they remained in the parish. Since Phyllis had gone to the trouble of contacting the vicar, all the publicans and every shopkeeper and bank manager in the place to denounce her husband along the usual lines, this was for her a bit of a setback. For Eric and Mary it was a liberation.

Mary's diary tracked the progress of *Henrietta*: 9,700 words 'written and revised in the first week, and by the 27th of December it was finished'. By 4 January 1948 it had been cut back to 70,000 and retitled *The Glass Bugle*. Eric remained a stern critic. He was in Chagford working on a short story and a novel, and on 19 March he wrote to Mary who was staying at Ovington Square, 'Be in good heart about your book; I'd rather you sold a perfect one, and I should like you to change this one. So many chapters are really good – and several almost drivelling! These are the pains of learning, *without which we'll never achieve success*. There isn't an easy way . . .' Mary had already chosen the pseudonym that would make her famous forty years later. At first she had thought of using her grandmother's maiden name, Wellesley, but her brother Hugh – who was trying to help her find a publisher and who had introduced her to an editor at Hutchinson's – advised her that there was a real-life cousin called Mary Wellesley who lived within a stone's throw of Buckingham Palace, and that she must not embarrass the family. Thwarted yet again in the cause of respectability, Mary decided instead to make a teasing reference to the Wellesleys' original name. In April Eric informed her that he had sent 'Cassell's a most intelligent letter from "Mary Wesley"'. Eric had by this time abandoned his own novel and was writing two plays and a book entitled *Liberations*, about France. Mary lost confidence in *The Glass Bugle* and in Curtis Brown who had advised her to "re-write it *down*", for a more popular readership, so she threw it away.

Although Eric and Phyllis had never been close, he had confided in her on many occasions with the drunkard's brutal and reckless candour, so he had made himself vulnerable and she knew how to hurt him. During the course of her long persecution she sent hundreds of letters to Eric's and Mary's friends and family; Nancy Gow had seen the effect of this campaign on Eric when he was still at BEA, of how he gradually became incapable of doing his job so that he ended 'like a pricked balloon'. Eric recalled how Phyllis haunted Donne Place where he lived and Hill Street where he worked and of how he saw her 'only too repeatedly', and how she would pass him in the street, muttering. And Eric's brother, Harry Siepmann, who received a barrage of nuisance calls in his office at the Bank of England, said that in his view, during the worst period, Eric was reduced to such a state that 'he might even I feared think of desperate things'. Nor in the safe haven of Chagford, shielded by the village constable and Major Hughes, could Eric find complete peace of mind. Phyllis switched her written assaults to open postcards and was enjoying herself. She began to taunt Eric about his failure as a writer.

On 31 March 1948 she wrote a postcard to Eric Siepmann Esq., c/o Lloyd's Bank, Chagford, via Newton Abbot: 'Dear Adolescent Husband, Drunkards, I found you still (after 25 years?) writing your play about a drunk. To speed you up I suggest:- Title:- "One over the Eight" or "Shame is the Spur". Characters:- Mr Siepmann played by Major Jekyll-Hyde. Mrs Siepmann played by 9 of your ladies in turn with the Grand Finale of Mary Lady Swinfen as No. 9. One over the Eight!' Five years before she died Mary wrote, 'We were never safe from her . . . Thinking about that period now I don't know how we bore it: telephone calls in the night, a figure following me in the street, terrible letters written to everyone we knew accusing Eric of being an alcoholic, a murderer, a womaniser, a homosexual, a wife beater, a child molester . . . and of buggering my children . . . a lot of people found it funny at the time but I do not . . .'

In November 1947 Eric sued Phyllis for divorce on the grounds of her wartime desertion, and this had the effect of temporarily interrupting her visits and physical attacks. Then, in the spring of 1948 Mary at last found a house in Cornwall, at Lansallos, near Fowey. It was called Peakswater and it 'seemed perfect'. With the money left to them by Otto they bought it. The property was bordered by a trout stream and included an orchard and several 'good-sized fields'. Eric believed that with ten acres one could plant £50 worth of potatoes and harvest them for £250 although the labour involved did not come into his calculations or his timetable. In her published memoir of the West Country, *Part of the Scenery*, Mary remembered Peakswater as the scene of an idyllic interlude when their plans to make their way as writers nearly came off. But the correspondence shows a less tranquil reality. Eric found their new neighbours so irritating that he would return to Chagford from time to time to write. As the pressure on him to sell a book increased and Phyllis's postcards continued, his mood darkened and Mary became discouraged. On 9 August 1948 he wrote in reference to the Peakswater neighbours, 'I did not escape an office to be pinpricked by bumpkins.' He added, 'I wrote you a long letter last night about your tears and my bloodiness and your terrible threat to fall out of love (with house or me?).' But when it came to his work he remained boundlessly optimistic. By the end of the month he was still in Chagford, but had moved away from Major Hughes's boarding house to the Easton Court

Hotel, where he was given a peaceful room with 'a solid table and chair'. This encouraged him; it was owned by Caroline Cobb, who offered special terms to struggling writers. Eric's friend Patrick Kinross, who had recommended it to Evelyn Waugh in 1931, had been staying there himself the previous December when both Mary and Eric were living in Chagford and they had seen quite a lot of him. By the end of November Eric had finished one of his projects; he had an appointment at the Bodley Head on 29 November, but it came to nothing and in Mary's words, 'Gradually, since no publisher evinced any interest we ran out of money.'

Eric's health was another cause for concern. Dr Whitcombe of Queen's Gate in Kensington examined him at this time and found that he was still subject to 'acute mental worry' and insomnia caused by 'the persecution he was suffering at the hands of his wife and his concern as to the effect it was having on his ability to earn a living'. That Christmas Mary and Eric were at Peakswater with the boys, both now at Summerfields Prep School in Oxford, where Toby had become a ferocious chess player, already capable of beating Mary. 'His smug smile of nonchalant triumph as he snitched my Queens is odious,' she reported. After Christmas Mary put Roger and Toby on the train to Penzance, and they went to stay with the Colonel at Boskenna for the annual pantomime. The pantomime was the Colonel's high point of the year; he had a thing about 'principal boys', several of whom he had persuaded to dance naked on the lawn at Boskenna. Mary mentioned one of his girlfriends coming to dance with him on the lawn in 1945: 'She is a recurring phenomena [*sic*] and of truly devastating gentility.' Another came with her mother as chaperone, and the ladies danced together. For the visit of Christmas 1948 Toby remembers that the Colonel ate too much rabbit for lunch, his favourite dish. They went to the pantomime in Penzance as usual, but the Colonel felt unwell and had to leave during the Wednesday matinée performance.

The lights finally went out for Camborne Haweis Paynter on 11 January 1949 and with him went the magic of Boskenna. Two world wars had done for him and his class, and Mary remembered him saying in 1946 that he was 'having great difficulty in showing a tax loss on the estate accounts'. Despite all his ingenuity he had been forced to sell land and so he passed on less property than he had inherited. Jenifer Murray was told a story in the 1970s, twenty-five years after Colonel Paynter's death, that he had died in a hotel in Penzance in the company of one of his fancy girls after another visit to the pantomime, and that Betty and Mary had been called from Boskenna to deal with the situation. Since he was already dead and weighed a trifle, they had put him into his trousers, shoes, overcoat and hat, and walked him through the hall to his car, where his body was propped up and driven home. This would have been an appropriate exit, but Mary's diary shows that she was in Peakswater with the children when the Colonel died and Betty, according to Jim Hosking, was in London. So the last march past the reception desk seems to be as much part of his legend as the story that he had dispatched his wife by frightening her hunter over a cliff. Legends sprouted round Camborne Paynter. Even in 2004 eyes lit up in distant parts of West Cornwall among the wartime generation when they talked of Boskenna in his day. For Mary, his death reminded her that the carefree days were over and of how much life had changed since 'the death rattle of life' in Boskenna's wartime corridors. The Colonel's last words were 'I knew there was a catch in it'.

In November 1947, when Eric had followed his lawyer's advice and sued Phyllis for divorce on the grounds of her desertion, he had made a mistake that cost him thousands of pounds. He had to drop the action early in May 1949. Even as the year started Eric realised that writing would not suffice and that he would have to get another office job – as far away from Phyllis as possible. He and Mary dined in London with Malcolm and Kitty Muggeridge in February, and Muggeridge recommended him to the *Sunday Times*. To their delight Eric was quickly offered the post of Berlin correspondent, a key position at the time of the birth of West Germany and the Berlin airlift, when the city was the likeliest flashpoint for the start of the next world war. Mary wrote to him on 29 March 1949, 'My darling love, I have been thinking of you a great deal to-day and of the start of your new adventure tomorrow . . .' After only one year she was preparing to sell Peakswater and ended, 'I feel such gratitude to God that I have you to love.' The next week she wrote again, addressing the letter to the British Press Camp in Berlin, saying that an estate agent in Fowey was recommending a price of £4,000. 'I am only going to deal with people who know the wants of the upper classes,' she added, 'who are the only people likely to want this house. The others are waste of stamps.' Mary was counting on Betty's help in placing an ad in the London press, but this must have fallen through because on 17 May she switched to another ally. 'Darling Carol,' she wrote. 'Thank-you for trying to get hold of Betty for me . . . as you know she never answers letters. I was fined fifteen shillings for the dog licences – which wasn't too bad. I enclose a copy of the advertisement I want put in *The Times*.' The ad was for a 'recently modernised 18th-century house between Fowey and

Polperro, 2 miles from the sea with 5 rooms, a dairy, all modern conveniences such as a WC and hot and cold water in the bathroom and a Raeburn cooker'. It went with ten acres and a four-roomed cottage, and the asking price was £4,500. When the house was sold most of the proceeds went to paying off the solicitors after Eric's failed divorce case. Mary eventually set off to join Eric in Berlin on 3 June, unaware that Phyllis had already launched her most devastating campaign.

The news of Eric's renewed good fortune was all the encouragement Phyllis needed and, with divorce proceedings against her dropped, she felt free to recommence face-to-face operations. At first she tried her usual line of attack. She wrote to the editor of the *Sunday Times* on 13 May 1949, when Eric had held his job for just over a month, saying that his appointment abroad was preventing her from suing him for maintenance and referring to his drunkenness and physical and mental cruelty. Then, anticipating Mary's arrival in Berlin, she managed to get the Passport Office to confirm to her that Mary had been issued with a passport in the name of Siepmann.

In Germany, Mary was enjoying herself. Berlin held 'a terrible fascination'. Her first impression was 'of people putting all their possessions into perambulators and pushing them from East to West. These refugees were not at all welcome to other Germans. We [have] a Bavarian cook and Berlin chauffeur, and we all . . . try to correct each other's accents'. Mary was upset about the way in which many people in the city were living. 'I was talking in English to a friend, saying wasn't it terrible, they were all in holes in the ground while we had these comfortable apartments, and the cleaning lady looked up and said in perfect Oxford English, "Don't upset yourself about it, Mrs Siepmann. We would have done just the same to you if we had won the war".'

She got a commission from *20th Century* magazine and tried to describe the ruined city, writing of 'the ugliness, young men with stumps and women with grey-faced children'. She was struck by the way in which the Berliners 'would write the names of relatives they were searching for on lamp posts and walls, hoping to find them again', and of how living in Berlin was like 'passing through the Looking-Glass' into a world of bombed-out defeat. But none of her articles was published. Her editors, she discovered, 'just wanted to hear which member of the Scots Guards had broken his ankle playing football'. Before long Mary was brought back to English reality by 'Eric's pestilential wife'.

In London Phyllis's letters had been passed to the foreign manager of the *Sunday Times*, Ian Fleming, formerly of Naval Intelligence and not yet the author of 'James Bond'. Mr Fleming started off with resolve. He told Phyllis that he already knew that Eric had 'unhappiness in his married life' and that this was of no concern to Kemsley Newspapers, his employers. Further correspondence, said Mr Fleming, would therefore be fruitless. But Phyllis was just getting into her stride. Unlike Ian Fleming, she did not have a foreign department to run. In fact, she had nothing at all to do except destroy Eric and Mary. Her next letter was a master stroke. In June she wrote to Fleming to ask, 'Do you yet know whether my husband is returning to London immediately as a result of the Foreign Office taking action over his false statements to them which enabled him to get another woman into Germany as his wife and into married quarters?'

In the England of 1949, and even more so in the military areas of occupied Germany, regulations were king. Phyllis had struck a shrewd blow. Eric had to answer awkward questions and Mary pinned a four-leaf clover into her diary on 27 June. But Phyllis continued to pester both Ian Fleming and the editor of the *Sunday Times* until in August she forced her way into the office. Ian Fleming lost his temper and told her that he did not believe in a word of her allegations and that she must think she was 'God almighty' to carry on in this way. Phyllis thereupon wrote to Lord Kemsley, the proprietor, complaining about Fleming's attitude and appealing to his Lordship's 'sense of fairness'. She also threatened to have a question asked in Parliament about the newspaper's role in getting Mary into married quarters in Germany. By this time Ian Fleming had had enough and he threw in the towel. Rather than warning Phyllis off for trespass and breach of the peace, he recalled Eric from Germany and suspended him for three months, saying that he could return to Berlin if he settled his disagreement with his wife. Eric thereupon resigned from the *Sunday Times*. It had taken Phyllis only five months to destroy his second post-war job. In explaining his feeble decision, Fleming said that Phyllis's letters and her habit of turning up in the building with the police had made it impossible for the foreign department to carry on normal business.

Back in England at the end of the school holidays, Mary and Eric returned to Chagford, cursing '007' for his lack of resolve. They hoped it was a one-off, a freak victory by 'PKS', as Mary usually referred to her. On 4 October Eric went back to London for a meeting with David Astor, the editor of the *Observer*, and was offered another very good job, this time in Paris. It would start in May, but Astor wanted Eric to go over on an extended reconnaissance before Christmas. With Mary, Eric flew to Paris on 19 October and that evening, back in business, they met Robert d'Alsace at the Deux Magots. The engagements began to fill up in Mary's diary: 'dine Gourmets', 'lunch Petit Riche', 'cinema Fernandel', 'Elysée 0151', 'lunch Colette Boyer'. Yet within two days Nancy Mitford telephoned Eric to say that Phyllis was on to them; she had arrived in Paris and was raising hell. Not wishing to give Phyllis further ammunition, Mary left Paris on 3 November and did not return, but despite her discretion David Astor gave in even more quickly than Ian Fleming. In November Phyllis wrote several letters to 'the Editor', in classic vein. In one she said, 'I ask you to use your authority over my husband to make him conform to the minimum code of decent behaviour exacted by society from every man in a responsible post – a code which demands that he supports his wife adequately and that he does not pass off other women as his wife.' Then she wrote a personal appeal to David Astor:

> I have just learnt to my great surprise that it is you who now edit the Observer . . . I never suspected that someone who knew Eric of old had offered him a job . . . I remember him writing to me about you when you were both in the Marines, an organisation from which he quickly escaped to journalism the moment he reached the Middle East . . . He now seems to have reverted to his gigolo life . . . and sends me not a penny . . . Our Consuls cannot move in the matter . . . I am one of those who (with Princess Elizabeth) bewails present day moral timidity in England . . . and I do not believe in the right of *any* man to go to the devil in his own way – particularly one's husband. Do you I wonder?

Before Eric was able to take up his post with the *Observer* in Paris, David Astor paid him £500 and withdrew the offer of employment. Astor had won the Croix de Guerre in 1944 but he proved just as hopeless as '007' when it came to dealing with Phyllis. He explained his capitulation by blaming Eric, saying that he had not been frank about his reasons for leaving the *Sunday Times* and adding, 'and I saw no reason why I or my newspaper should run the risk of unpleasantness with the British Embassy in Paris because of his wife's behaviour.'

In Chagford once again, Mary decided to start making cheese, as she had done in Boskenna during the war. This time she would do it on a commercial basis and on the back of an envelope she set out a plan of campaign: 'A good name. Plain cartons, labels. Weighing machine, basins, muslin, string, salt, pepper, paprika, onions, chives (fennel), (vinegar).' This looks like a recipe for making what was known as cream cheese, popular after the war when there was no cheese in the shops. The basic ingredient was sour, unpasteurised milk that was suspended above a sink and allowed to drain through the muslin until it stopped dripping. A rough-and-ready version was popular among boys at prep schools, using grey woollen socks in place of muslin. Eric, battling on with a book, wrote to thank her 'This is a gallant effort of yours and it makes me feel that I haven't done enough to make our future secure.' On 12 May 1950 he wrote again, congratulating her on earning £10 from a 2lb cheese order, presumably from a local dairy. Henceforth it would be a joint effort in cheese and literature, and he urged Mary to earn £5 a week. Eric was optimistic. He had just finished a play called *Don Juan* and thought he might offer it to Laurence Olivier after Christopher Fry's *Venus Observed*, written for Olivier, received a poor notice in *The Times*. For an unknown playwright to approach the greatest star on the London stage might have been thought optimism bordering on delusion by a less loyal wife, but Eric was not deluded, entirely. On 16 May he wrote from London to tell Mary that 'Freedman, the best agent in America, has taken up my play'. Freedman had described it as 'a very capable job of writing. It is just a question of whether it will sell at this time. Maybe I can find an actor for it.'

But the writing was to be interrupted once again. Eric's health, which had improved in Berlin and Paris, collapsed – a reaction to Phyllis's victorious assault on the *Sunday Times* and the *Observer*. Dr Whitcombe saw him several times in 1949, and by the end of the year 'his condition worsened and he appeared to be developing into a nervous wreck'. He suffered from depression, bad headaches, digestive trouble, his reflexes were exaggerated and he had a tremor of the hands. He was getting into 'a state of acute nervous breakdown'. In January Eric had lunched in the City with his brother and Bernard Rickatson-Hatt. Mary had them in her address list at the back of her diary as 'Harry and Hatt MON 6666', the number of the Bank of England. The Rickatson-Hatts were friends and prepared to mount a rescue operation. The Bank's network quickly produced the possibility of a position at Portals Ltd, the paper-making firm that supplied the paper for the Bank's notes. Eric was offered the position of overseas sales manager, a post that demanded languages, political nous', a feel for public relations and some business experience. It could have been designed for him. The contact at Portals, a family firm, was Francis Portal, who had been an exact contemporary of Eric's at Winchester. Eric wrote, 'I like *him*.

Very quiet, precise, small and not at all lacking in sensibility. (I decided Wykhamist manners are best – and a relief).'

On 15 May 1950 Eric wrote to Mary to say, 'I have thought it over and accepted. I feel sure we could not do better.' In breaking the news Eric recognised that his new job would entail long separations, but mentioned the possibility of some foreign travel together and added, 'I prefer it to "public relations" and to Paris, which is poison to me since all the Toulouse hangovers have installed themselves there . . . All I live for is our future together, and our home is worth working for and must be earned. And it will be nice to have some money! We both need clothes . . . So I send you all my warm love, and long to hold you by the hip-bones. *A toujours.* PS I am so lucky to have you, I can't count my luck.' Mary abandoned her muslin and cheese basins, and waited for Phyllis's next move. But, after nearly four years of persecution, there was a gleam of hope.

When they sold Peakswater Mary and Eric had had to pay Edwin Rutherford, their solicitor, a sum of £2,900 for the failed divorce on grounds of desertion, so they had no savings. Then, out of the blue, Violet sent Mary her share in a legacy from the long-dead Uncle Charles, £5,000, and Aunt Rose's second husband, Uncle Humphrey, sent her a cheque for £500 – why, she never discovered, as he died almost as soon as the cheque arrived. Eric noted that Mary had wept when Aunt Rose died, two years earlier. Humphrey and Rose had been among the few members of her family who had never criticised her. Now, with this windfall, they had given her an unexpected chance. She would drop Edwin Rutherford, an eccentric, not very self-assertive man, and employ George Gordon, the solicitor who had advised both her and Carol six years earlier. She went to see Gordon in his Brook Street office and told him the whole story, and he said, 'How absurd. Eric divorces Phyllis for cruelty.' This made a change from Rutherford whose liveliest contribution, during countless previous discussions about divorce, had been when Mary's terrier suddenly jumped on to his desk to have a look at him and he exclaimed, 'Damned good dog that. Got a bit of hound in her.' When Mary told Rutherford that she was switching to Gordon, Dadds & Co., he advised against, on the grounds that they were 'the cleverest and most expensive lawyers in London'. It was a considerable gamble, but it paid off.

Siepmann v Siepmann came to trial on 23 July 1951, lasted three days and received widespread publicity. Eric produced over 300 hostile letters that Phyllis had written to his friends and employers and called sixteen witnesses, including Peter Quennell and Robert Boothby MP, in a contested

High Court action before Mr Justice Havers, who did not usually sit in the Divorce division but who had been educated at Winchester. Eric's counsel was Melford Stevenson KC, later a celebrated and brutal judge, whose brief was marked at 150 guineas. Phyllis, who had by this time exhausted the patience of half a dozen firms of solicitors, was represented by Mr Trevor Reeve, also an old Wykhamist. Most of the proceedings were taken up with the examination and cross-examination of Eric and Phyllis. Eric adopted a policy of total frankness and emerged from it very well. And Melford Stevenson, who afterwards said that he looked on the case as 'a crusade rather than a professional duty', proved just the man to deal with Phyllis.

The evidence in the case showed the extraordinary thoroughness of Phyllis's campaign. Not only had she extracted information from the Passport Office and arranged to have a question asked in Parliament, she had at one point persuaded the Ministry of Labour to carry out a special investigation into Eric's business affairs. She had driven her husband out of three jobs, mounted two violent assaults, persuaded Mary's parents to put her up for the night and charmed them into betraying and criticising Mary, wormed her way into the confidence of Eric's sister, persuaded one of his old friends to talk about his childhood and persecuted a director of the Bank of England. One of the few who had outwitted her had been Colonel Paynter. When she turned up at Boskenna, on her rounds, she was shown into the library where she ended her usual diatribe by asking whether Lady Swinfen had had many lovers during the war, and the Colonel had replied, 'Good-lord, yes. Dozens of them I dare say. Your bus leaves in a quarter of an hour. You'd better hurry if you're going up the avenue.' The Colonel's reply completely flummoxed Phyllis, who did not believe him. After Colonel Paynter had shown Phyllis out he said to Alice Grenfell, 'Her ladyship seems to have got hold of a veritable Bluebeard this time.' But Alice already knew; she had been listening to the conversation through the library keyhole.

Phyllis was not only a talented extractor of information, she was ruthless in how she used it. She told Ian Fleming that both Mary and Eric had described Carol as 'a crashing bore' and that Mary's parents considered him to be 'a weak husband', knowing that all this would get back to Mary and possibly to Carol. And she passed on what Mary's parents had said about Mary – that she had 'never worked nor even been trained, except in Domestic Science', and that she was so 'headstrong, they had never been able to do anything with her, and they would never have anything to do with Eric'.

But the tactics that had worked so well with neighbours caught off guard, or in a busy newspaper office, or against distracted government clerks, did not work at all in the High Court. Even when Phyllis was being questioned by her own counsel she made a bad impression. Melford Stevenson interrupted to ask if she might stop staring at Eric and address her answers to the judge. Phyllis had a sense of humour; when telephoning Bridie, Mary's Irish maid, she would announce herself as '*The* Mrs Siepmann', a reference to the correct written form of addressing a peeress. But as her allegations became wilder and more enthusiastic the judge had to ask her to try to restrain herself and when she paid no attention he expostulated, 'Really, madam.'

Phyllis made the most of her opportunity in the witness box to attack Mary and in answer to the question 'Do you feel very bitter against Mary Siepmann?' she replied, 'I feel that she is a most terrible woman who is more or less a blot on society . . . I feel she is a very wicked woman because of her past, because she left a man who nobody can find any fault with and left two children aged two and five.' (In fact, Mary had never abandoned her children.) Seeing the impression she was making on the judge, Melford Stevenson encouraged her. 'Is there anything more unpleasant you would like to say about her?' he enquired politely. And when he asked her if she felt any sense of shame about her letters she replied, 'I am trying to expose an extremely wicked woman, an absolutely ruthless, wicked woman . . .' Eventually Melford Stevenson destroyed her credibility with one question. She had claimed that the object of her campaign had been to encourage Eric to see a psychoanalyst so that he might be cured of his homosexuality, which was, in her diagnosis, caused by his mother fixation and was leading to his drunkenness, and so counsel asked her whether it had occurred to her that her conduct might damage her husband's health. She replied, 'If a person is exposed in his wickedness, I suppose it might always damage his health . . .' and the judge at once commented, 'You realised that did you?' Finally, having reduced Phyllis to tears with a skilful change of pace, Melford Stevenson cut short his cross-examination; to continue it, he said, would not be 'a useful employment of the Court's time'.

In his judgement Mr Justice Havers said,

> I have had an opportunity of seeing [Phyllis Siepmann] in the witness box and I have heard her, when she has been asked questions, take almost every opportunity she could of slipping in some damaging and highly pre- judicial statement, either about her husband or about Mary Siepmann,

and in my view she is not a reliable witness . . . I am quite satisfied . . . that she was filled with hatred and bitterness against Mary Siepmann . . . that she was filled with malice and hatred against her husband . . .

He said that Phyllis had 'commenced a course of conduct consisting of wilful and unjustifiable acts which . . . inevitably would cause pain and injury to her husband's health . . . would be likely to result in his losing any employment which he might have and . . . make life . . . unbearable'. The letter to Lord Swinfen about Eric posing a threat to the boys was described as 'disgraceful, diabolical and wicked'. Of the postcard about Eric's failure as a writer the judge said, 'It is difficult to believe there could be any communication of any kind which shows more malice and hatred for both these people . . .'

He concluded that the relationship between Mary and Eric had not caused the breakdown of Phyllis's marriage, which had broken down before, and that Phyllis's conduct had very much affected Eric's physical and mental health, and had amounted to cruelty. At the end of the hearing he pronounced the decree nisi. Phyllis appealed six weeks later, on the last available date, but the only effect of this move was to prolong proceedings by three months. The decree absolute was finally issued on 8 April 1952, and when Mary and Eric were married two weeks later Nancy Gow was a witness.

Three days after the judgement Eric had written to Ovington Square, 'My dear Carol, . . . I can't let our victory go by without letting you know that I am aware – and so is everybody – that your behaviour to us throughout has not been just wise and decent, but magnanimous in the literal sense of "big" . . . Mary stood up to the strain very well . . . with only small cracks, and I am positive (*pace* Hugh and the Farmars) that her presence in court did not only my case but her good. The judge went out of his way to exculpate her. Thanks again . . . Yours ever, Eric.' The case had taken all the money they had and left them in debt, but it had been worth every penny.

Phyllis's campaign did not end with the divorce. She started on another series of letters, this time to the directors of Portals, but that firm merely handed the packages to its solicitors who filed them for the record. In January 1953 a bulky envelope with the familiar looping writing addressed to 'The Lord Swinfen' arrived at Carol's London house. In it was a note and a copy of 'evidence' that Phyllis claimed had not been admitted at the divorce hearing. The note said, 'Eric won his petition by wholesale perjury – I hope he will be brought to justice by the DPP.'

After their marriage Mary and Eric decided to have a child but Mary remained sufficiently worried to say that she could not go through with it if Phyllis were to start again. Her solicitors told her that if this happened it would be a simple matter to get the first Mrs Siepmann locked up. In fact, the birth of Mary's third son, William, in December 1953 did start Phyllis up again and Portals reported that 'the usual circular' was being sent to all the directors. Again, Mary's solicitors reassured her in a letter dated 21 January 1954, advising her that Portals attached 'no importance to the affair'. They also advised against libel proceedings, since Phyllis was apparently out of the jurisdiction, writing from France, but they added, 'The main thing is to be able to deal swiftly with any physical molestation occurring at or in the neighbourhood of your home.' Phyllis in the flesh did not reappear. But magistrates' courts are ineffective against phantoms and, as Mary wrote later, 'her shadow haunted me for years . . .'

CHAPTER ELEVEN

Going Straight

'I belong to the dubious, the ones who do not fit . . .'

Mary Wesley

For three years following her marriage to Eric Siepmann in April 1952, Mary's life was settled, contented and free of unpaid bills. Phyllis had shot her bolt. Eric had a well-paid* job that he could manage successfully without undue strain. They lived comfortably at Knoll House, Broughton in Hampshire and their son, Bill, was born in December 1953, in Winchester General Hospital – by caesarean section. Mary by then was forty-one.

The Stalker, who had played such an important role in the early years of Mary's relationship with Eric, was no longer their preoccupation. Instead, their correspondence reflects Mary's concern for her children. She was struck by the growing differences between the brothers, Roger and Toby. Toby, who had worked out the advantages of possessing a hen in place of a rooster at the age of four, is described at one point as 'a fiend'. 'The poor child [Roger] seems quite defenceless against Toby's imaginary tales of horror,' his mother wrote in July 1945. Despite these differences Mary and Carol cooperated easily on the question of the children's upbringing. 'I know I can manage Carol,' she had told Eric in 1945, about the question of keeping the boys with her when she and Eric first lived together publicly. What she did not know, and was never certain about, was what Carol knew about Toby.

In April 1947, Mary lunched with Carol and reported the conversation to Eric. They had 'decided to send Toby to some other school than Eton, as he might overshadow Roger. We did not really make any final decision naturally

---

* The salary was £4000 a year; the equivalent today would be £206,000.

but it opens new vistas. Winchester? . . . I am beginning to feel terribly sick about Roger's first nights at school.' Roger had been sent away as a boarder to Summerfields in Oxford in May 1947, aged eight. 'Roger is with me for the day. Poor little boy I wish he were gone already – we seem to hang suspended . . . Roger is quite unlike Toby. He – like Carol – is fanning about doing nothing while I write to you. I must stop and occupy him.' In March 1949 she wrote to Eric, who was in Berlin, describing the boys' arrival at Peakswater from school.

> The little boys arrival was very nice . . . They stepped straight out of the train into my arms and there was much shouting and hugging. Pebble was *rapturous* leaping up to kiss the little brothers faces and particularly pleased to see Roger. They were in the nicest form I've ever known them arrive in. Jumping up and hugging and bouncing like puppies all evening. Roger most affectionate and Toby running in twice from the orchard to hug and say 'I'm so glad to be here' with great voluptuous sighs . . . They are eating like wolves and to-day is over without a tear or a cross word.

She added, 'What did you think of Toby's hair? Isn't he a fright. He tells me that he chopped off some (other) little boys hair too, "Parson's, in all the wrong places". Poor Mrs Parsons! Whoever she may be.'

In 1951 Mary forwarded a letter she had received from Roger to Eric, saying she was very pleased with it.

> I am beginning to love that child more and more. I think it is because I have only lately begun to defend and fight for him and one loves what one cherishes . . . Toby I have always fought for, even from months before he was conceived when he was just an Idea. I blame myself for not real- ising long before how urgent is Roger's need. I knew it in my brain but my heart was not alive enough. I think I can now be a fierce mother for him. I pray it is not too late. I believe men need fierce mothers as greatly as they need tenderness.

Later that year, still living in Chagford when Eric had just started in Hampshire at Portals, she wrote again about the boys: 'Being a mother is very interesting. I am anxious to be a good one. In a way it is easier to be a good mother to Roger, certainly he is being very nice and yet in the middle of his niceness, pop! *He is Carol* and I get a terrible claustrophobic feeling that I used to have when we were married. I see nothing of myself in him as I do in Toby where I see both myself and Heinz obstinate *en tête*, glaring back at me thwarted.'

In January 1951 Roger was taken away from Summerfields and sent to a prep school in Cardiganshire to be coached for Westminster School's common entrance. Mary felt very badly about this and Roger's god-father, Roger Mynors, by now Professor of Latin at Cambridge University, wrote to her from Treago, his family home in Herefordshire, approving her decision to switch Roger away from Eton. 'Eton would have been very nice,' he said, 'but it *was* a risk, being so near "the edge", and also if Eton doesn't do its best for a boy . . . it can do such an irrecoverable worst!' Roger said that he liked his new school but continued to write long letters to his mother in which there is sometimes a note of anxiety. 'Did Pebble miss me when I had gone? . . . Daddy has sent me some of the new stamps. I am going to use the first on you.' He is determined to write correctly and to make it a real correspondence in which he takes up points in his mother's letters and enquires politely about family and friends. 'What did Mrs Clarke give to Toby? Please will you thank her for the clown. It is most amusing. What does Tobys* do, mine goes up and down. I expect that you have already tried mine out. I think this because one end had had one of the things that keep it shut torn off . . . There has been snow on the opposite mountains for most of the term . . . Please will you send me some fruit as I have not got any. Much love from Roger.'

Compared with the letters Roger wrote to his mother from boarding school, those from Toby show no anxiety about what was happening at home. Enquiring about the dog, Toby was more interested in whether it had caught a rabbit than in whether or not it missed him. But whereas the younger boy's letters are slapdash, perfunctory, mischievous and dis-organised, typical of a busy boarding-school boy, Roger's show that he is facing a life full of problems; that he is someone who wants to live life in a straight line, who is disturbed by unexpected change. 'I am so glad that you have got your new house,' he wrote in February 1952. 'I never knew that you had bought one. Is it in or out-side Andover? Is it nearer Erick's job than Basingstoke or Kingsclear? What does it look like? Has it got both a front and a back door? How old is it? How many floors has it got? How many rooms has it got on each floor? When will

---

* Text with the original spelling.

you be moving in? How far is it from Andover? Is it in a village, if so what is the village called? Please will you tell me when you move from Andover?'

This letter referred to Mary's and Eric's new house at Broughton in Hampshire; in the previous four terms Roger's letters to his mother had been addressed to a succession of four different hotels.

When his son was born, Eric had decided to celebrate his new, unaccustomed respectability and while Mary was still in hospital went to see the Rector of Broughton, intent on making a 'clean breast of things'. The Rector, Norman Powell, was a strong chess player, fifth on the Hampshire county board; the village cobbler, a Russian émigré, being No. I. Mr Powell received Eric courteously and, after hearing his confession, reassured Eric that 'the Village' knew nothing of their background. The only criticism had been about Mary wearing trousers. He was confident that Mrs Powell would not repeat any indiscretions concerning the previous marriages, or the 'living in sin', all of which was news to him. He told Eric that he regarded him as a prodigal, that there was no impediment to Bill being christened and that all would be well.

Meanwhile, Roger was having his tonsils removed in St Thomas's Hospital, London. He wrote to Mary just after the operation:

Dear Mummy, Thank you very much for the graps* that you sent me. They are deliciouse . . . They arrived while I was in the operation theatre . . . The first indication I had of them being here was when I started coming round at about 12 o'clock . . . At the moment I am spitting out blood and flem. A lot of the blood is conjealed. I can see the river Thames if I sit up . . . The ward is a large one with about 30 patients in it . . . I am in the second bed from the end.

He makes no mention of his youngest brother, whose birth three weeks earlier had prevented his mother from being with him when he was ill.

Mary brought the baby home three weeks later, and Alice Grenfell came from St Buryan to help her to look after him. With Alice back in the nursery it was a natural development to invite Sonya, Betty Paynter's daughter, who had been more or less abandoned by her mother in a school in London, to come to stay at Broughton on most weekends. Mary began

* Text with the original spelling.

to treat Sonya as a daughter in a family that now seemed to have a reason-
ably predictable and secure future. In later life Sonya said that Mary had
rescued her, taken her into the family and given her a happy childhood.
Toby remembers their move to Broughton as the beginning of family life
(he was then aged eleven) and the time when his own relationship with
his mother 'really started'.

In her new-won haven and her new respectability, Mary had time to look
around. She encouraged a friendship between Toby and a village boy known
as 'Jacko'. In a village where everyone voted Tory or went to the Baptist
Chapel, Jacko's parents, the Butchers, voted Labour and went to the pub.
Mary remembered them as giving 'a general impression of roughness and
inspiring fear'. Their son was a bit older than Toby and taught him how to
poach by tickling trout. Richmond Stopford came to stay and asked if he
could join a poaching raid on the woods of a neighbouring landowner. When
they were disturbed by the gamekeeper Toby, Sonya and Jacko managed to
run away, leaving the former MI6 Head of Station entangled on the barbed
wire.

During the years at Broughton – the years of 'going straight' – Mary
was not just laying the foundations for a strong family life; she was also
attempting something much more difficult. With Eric's divorce and their
marriage, 'Mrs Siepmann' had become a legal and social reality. The clan-
destine life to which she had been addicted during the war was now a thing
of the past, she no longer had to divide her personality into a number of
watertight compartments, and with this new conventional identity she was
free of any patronising family interference and could try to repair the
relationship that was of first importance to her – her relationship with her
father. In this attempt she used her children as a bridge. Mary once said,
'I *think* my father loved me'; her hesitation being caused by the fact that
her mother had told her that Susan was her father's favourite. In fact, there
is plenty of evidence that Mynors did indeed love his 'wild' and alarming
daughter but that he did not find it easy to express his love. Instead, he
showed his concern for Mary's children and tried to use his influence to
help Roger and Toby take up the sort of life he himself would have liked
them to lead.

In 1954 he arranged for Toby to be proposed for membership of the
MCC. (The form, forwarded to Mary, was never filled in.) Then in 1955
there is a series of letters over a period of nearly twelve months in which
Mynors and Mary try to settle the question of Roger's future regiment. 'I
believe,' wrote Mynors in one of these letters, that 'it is the mission of one

generation to give to the next the advantages they can offer. That is the purpose of their lives. The handicap of milling in the ruck is terrific and I need not dwell on the conditions of University life today . . . Every Blessing, Your Daddy.' The letters, in which Mynors always addressed his youngest child as 'My Precious', show Colonel Farmar in his element. He was working his contacts and pursuing traditional Farmar family values, and Mary went along with it.

Mynors quickly established links between the Farmars, the Wellesleys and the Coldstream Guards, as well as links with three other regiments, one of Fusiliers, one Light Infantry and one Rifle Regiment. The novelist and regular army officer Simon Raven set out the social distinctions relevant to this choice in an essay published in 1959. To join

> a regiment of Foot Guards it is preferable to have been at Eton, Winchester or Harrow, though one would be tolerated if one had been at another of the 'big six' public schools or one of the more reputable Roman Catholic concerns. It is also either essential or very desirable to have at least £150 a year of one's own. To go slightly downward in the scale, to be commissioned in one of the Rifle Regiments requires an almost similar educational status, though there is less direct emphasis on Eton, Harrow or Winchester: again, the Rifle Regiments are said to worry less about private money, though some of the officers are extremely rich. After this we descend to the Regiments of Light Infantry and Fusiliers . . . After [them] if we omit the Highland Regiments (which no Englishman in his right mind can begin to comprehend) we come to the absolutely plain run of Regiments of the Line.

These social considerations are present in Colonel Farmar's musings as well. Mynors does not seem to have considered his own regiment, the Lancashire Fusiliers, for Roger; instead his first suggestion was 'the 60th', the Rifle regiment he had lacked the money to join and in which his brother Hugh had died at the age of twenty-five. Having dropped all thought of the Coldstream Guards, Mynors selected two other regiments, the 43rd (the Oxfordshire and Buckinghamshire Light Infantry) and the Northumberland Fusiliers for Roger's consideration. In February 1955 the Colonel of the 43rd, General Sir Bernard Paget, wrote saying that he would gladly put Roger on his list provided he made the 60th his second choice, 'as I only accept candidates who put my Regiment as their first choice'. Mynors sent this letter on to Mary with the comment, 'This is the answer

to be expected from any Colonel-in-Chief of the now comparatively few
first rate Regiments . . .'*

Mynors showed just as much concern for Toby as he had for Roger,
although he does not seem to have grasped the difference in character
between the two boys. Apart from arranging for Toby to join the MCC he
assumed that he, like his brother, would be interested in the army. In 1954,
when Toby was twelve Mynors wrote to Mary from his club, 'the Senior'
in Pall Mall, 'My Precious, I have been thinking of Toby and if, after consideration, you will like to talk over with him the points which come to me . . .'
This was the beginning of a six-page letter in which Mynors proposed to
use 'some personal interest now possible with the Princess Royal'.

A week later Mynors wrote again from 'the Senior', the United Service
Club being the ideal place for such research, this time suggesting that
Toby should do his National Service in the Intelligence Corps. Despite
these attentions Toby remained unresponsive, showing no interest in his
grandfather's idea of a military career. But at least there was still the family
school, Eton, and this was where his grandfather, his mother and Carol
all wanted him to go. One of the reasons why Roger had been taken out
of Summerfields was because his younger brother had been promoted
above him to the scholarship stream. Toby was duly entered for the Eton
award, but he, like his mother, could be difficult. He sat the exam in May
1954; but refused to answer any of the questions, having decided that he
would rather go to a coeducational school. When the exams were over he
returned to Summerfields and was beaten by the headmaster for letting
down the school. The following term, aged thirteen, he started at
Bryanston, the school John Platts-Mills had chosen, despite Lewis Clive's
urging, for his six sons.

In her published memoir, *Part of the Scenery*, Mary made no mention of
the three years spent at Knoll House; she never mentioned them in newspaper interviews and it was to be some time before she agreed to speak
about them. In 1990 she asked to be driven through Broughton again and

---

* Roger's family connections with the 43rd included Mynors's forebear, the
Lieutenant Girardot who in 1852 had ordered his men to remain on parade on
the deck of the *Birkenhead* while the ship was sinking (and after the ship's captain
had given the order 'Every man for himself'), in order to prevent the crowded
lifeboats from being swamped. As a result, 454 soldiers were drowned but the
women and children were saved. Lieutenant Girardot himself managed to survive.

after looking for a few moments at the front door of Knoll House she just said, 'We were happy in that place.'

She buried those years because they had represented an untypical period in her life, but it had been a time of high hopes, and she had bitter memories when she thought of how it had ended. For as long as Eric held his job at Portals their position was assured. She could look her parents and her sister in the face and know that the time when they could patronise or manipulate her was past. She could grow closer to her father because she could meet him on his own ground; his talk of a 'smart' regiment, with its echoes of outdated family values, did not jar when she was so confident of the success of her own values. For the first time since the breakdown of her first marriage in 1939 her life was an open book. When she wrote to *The Times* defending Winston Churchill against criticism – for planning to arm German soldiers against the advancing Red Army in May 1945 – she was able to use the name of Siepmann and to publish her address, in final defiance of Phyllis. And when this letter was published it emphasised and celebrated the end of her outlaw life. But the period of 'going straight' did not last long.

In April 1954 Mary had taken a holiday that lasted for nearly a month and started in Rome. It was carefully organised to fit in with a long business trip of Eric's, and the climax of it was to be their reunion in Tripoli for two weeks of sunshine and swimming in a luxury hotel. It was idleness and splendour of a sort she had not known for fifteen years since her travels with Carol before the war. In Rome she stayed with the Riccis and had such a good time that she cancelled a villa she had taken in Ischia and stayed on. She dined with Baroness Corsi, went to the races and lunched on the Via Appia at the Villarosa. Eric, meanwhile, was battling his way round Beirut, the Persian Gulf, Karachi, Baghdad, selling banknote paper. In Hong Kong he dined with 'les boys' (MI6) and wrote to tell Mary that his hosts had been Michael Handley – 'if Richmond* asks' – and Courtney Young, who was 'as slinky and sinister as usual'. Eric's trip was long and very demanding, but all went well until he got to his penultimate stop in Damascus. In his official report to the chairman of Portals, Eric played the incident down:

* Richmond Stopford, Mary's former boss. Mary continued to see him regularly in London.

I had a foolish misunderstanding with the British Council, of all
people, about some indiscreet remarks which I was alleged to have
made about Arab Nationalism, within hearing of Arabs. They took it
up with the Embassy, and I shall have to report to you privately about
this. However the Minister in Cairo, whom I consulted, said: 'I
shouldn't take it seriously!!'

When Eric met Mary in Tripoli he was more direct. He said, 'I'm going to
lose this job. I got drunk in Damascus and told people there was going
to be a war. The Foreign Office are very angry and are going to report me.'
This prospect rather spoiled the two weeks they spent together on the shores
of the Mediterranean in Libya, Tunis and Algiers. Portals could hardly
employ an overseas sales director who got drunk and caused a diplomatic
incident, and Eric was forced to resign within two weeks of his return to
England. Another reason to fire him was that during his business travels he
made frequent contacts with MI6 station officers, and on his return reported
back to Richmond Stopford. These contacts, which were probably part of
his job, demanded discretion and reliability.

His first reaction was relief. No more examination of worn banknotes,
or discussion of the merits of watermarks, or the weight of paper. Part of
his work when travelling through the Third World had been to tell clients
(that is, national banks) that the reason their banknotes were wearing out
so fast was not because Portals' paper was too thin, but because the local
population did not understand how to treat banknotes. Nonetheless, he felt
rather aggrieved by his dismissal and spent his first days of freedom in a
characteristically quixotic attempt to gain his revenge by setting up an
Anglo-German agency for the export of banknotes, printed in Germany
on German banknote paper, in direct rivalry to Portals. Surprisingly, Eric
seems to have been supported in this scheme by his brother Harry, who
had retired from the Court of the Bank of England a year previously, embit-
tered by the failure of the Chancellor of the Exchequer to appoint him
Governor and now looking for amusement. Eric wrote to three German
bankers in Hamburg and Frankfurt at the beginning of May and received
some encouraging replies. One of his contacts renounced any future association with Portals following Eric's departure, stating that his cooperation
had always been based on 'my long-lasting friendly relations with your
brother and yourself'. But nothing finally came of the Anglo-German
project and by the end of the month Eric was working unhappily in London
for a small publishing firm, Simpkins Marshall. Mary's reaction to Eric's

misfortune was to distract herself on behalf of someone who was in worse trouble than she was.

In March 1954, Toby's friend in the village, Jacko, aged fifteen, had been arrested in Andover, found guilty of stealing two pairs of socks and sent by the juvenile court magistrates to Botleys Park Hospital, Chertsey, in Surrey under the Mental Deficiency Act of 1927. This punishment was the 'ASBO' of its day, evidence of an unofficial, and illegal, policy to confine troublesome young people, without time limit, in a place where they could no longer make a nuisance of themselves. In Jacko's case it wasn't just the socks; it was all the trout he had so skilfully removed from neighbouring estates, with Toby's help. The boy's mother, Mrs Butcher, who knew that Mary had encouraged a friendship between her son and Toby, and had turned a blind eye to the poaching, appealed for help. Her husband was a road mender, neither of them had been present at the court hearing and it was two weeks before they were told that their son had been locked up in a mental hospital in the company of adults, some of whom were severely ill.

After hearing of the situation – a sane boy of fifteen confined to a locked lunatic asylum at the Superintendent's pleasure – Mary had 'a sleepless night thinking of [his] mother' and decided to devote herself to getting Jacko released. She went to Chertsey to visit him, then organised a petition that was signed by most of the neighbourhood. This petition had little effect, so Mary decided to ask for help from John Platts-Mills, whom she had not seen for years and who was by now a successful criminal barrister.* In October 1954 Mary wrote to Platts-Mills at his chambers in the Temple saying that she had been to see Jacko, 'in the bin, he is very unhappy and, apart from the pigs on the farm, is surrounded by imbeciles of all grades'. Within twenty-four hours of arriving he had organised a mass escape, but had been recaptured. He had no idea when he would be released and felt that he had been labelled as 'mental' for life.

> What meagre papers we have about the case [she wrote] would take you half-an-hour to digest, or I can come up and see you. We are low in funds at the moment so we cannot afford more than a small fee so if you

---

* Platts-Mills, having been elected to Parliament as a Labour MP, had been expelled from the Party by the Prime Minister, Clement Attlee, as being too pro-Soviet. His telephone number in the Temple was CENtral 1984.

think you can help this boy will you let me know and let me know your
fees too? I shall be most sincerely grateful. Yours ever.

John Platts-Mills replied,

> ... You shall have my opinion at any cost. The one thing that barristers
> are not allowed to do is to discuss their fees, but as I would pay to see
> you anyway we can set off the one against the other, and they will cancel
> out. You must not think from this that I would pay only a modest sum
> to see you, because my fees are enormous!

Mary went to the hairdresser's (Antoine's) before the meeting with John
– who responded to her request by drafting a petition to be sent to the
Board of Control of Asylums, and spoke to the National Council of Civil
Liberties. Platts-Mills also arranged for a friendly solicitor, Robert George,
to take over the management of the case.

Robert George commissioned an independent medical report and
contacted the Sunday newspapers. For six months nothing happened, then
Mr George wrote to the medical superintendent informing him that he
was going to mention Jacko's case in his forthcoming evidence to the Royal
Commission on Mental Deficiency. The last move was decisive. Three days
later Robert George heard that Jacko was shortly to be sent home on licence,
after spending a year locked up. Mary's diary entry for 20 April 1955 reads
'Jacko home'.

Summarising the case, Mary wrote in a memorandum, '[The Butchers
are] the kind of people who man lifeboats, join Commandos, good country-
men and poachers all.' In a final exchange of letters Robert George wrote,
'Thank-you very much for the ... statements of [Jacko's] mother and
himself regarding his treatment and her treatment in the hands of the authorities. I should very much like to give evidence at the Royal Commission of
the beating with a cricket bat ...' In April 1955 Mary replied, saying that
her involvement in the case would have to end as she was 'leaving the
district'. She was leaving because she and Eric had decided to sell Knoll
House and move back to Devon.

When Eric lost his job, Mary lost her hopes of regaining her conventional
father's conventional approval. In 1945 she had justified her decision to have
an abortion partly through fear of her parents' anger at an illegitimate grand-
child and partly through her own desire to give her new child 'the very best

start'. Nine years later, following Eric's undiplomatic behaviour at a reception in Damascus, before the long-awaited baby could even walk, the 'good start' had once again gone up in smoke. Her sister Susan, who had recently remarried a suitably wealthy man, was living close to Mynors and as their father's health declined over the following six years Susan took control of their father's life and Mary saw him less and less. Her chance of establishing the close relationship with Mynors that she had lacked even as a child, was gone. She had missed her last shot at an ordinary life.

CHAPTER TWELVE

Thornworthy

'I find what I need in the Church. And what I can't take, I simply leave.'
Mary Wesley

There are practically no references in Mary's 1954 diary to Eric after he left Portals, and no surviving correspondence for that year. This may have been because his behaviour in Damascus had caused a rift (it was still a painful subject forty-eight years later) or it may have been for another reason. In a letter to Eric dated 2 April 1945, from Boskenna, Mary had written:

> Mental fidelity seems to me desperately important, and physical, because of its effect on the mental, is the same to me. I aim at both and with your help I'm a sticken . . . For you, if you are unfaithful casually I would be 'disgusted' (too strong) and would hate it and if you are very fastiduous [sic] I would be madly jealous. I would rather have you faithful . . . Let us talk about it next time we are together. It is too long a subject to write about.

Mary said that she had always been faithful to Eric and that he had been unfaithful to her only once, while she was pregnant, 'but I expect he was drunk'. The interrupted correspondence and the silent diary of 1954 suggest that this may have been when she discovered Eric's single infidelity. At the beginning of the year he had been able to take out an insurance policy for £2,400 intended to cover Bill's education. Now they were back in the familiar situation of wondering how to keep the wolf from the door. While Mary moved back to Devon, Eric took a number of short-term jobs in London. By September 1955 he was selling advertising – and considering various other stratagems, from selling the car (which they had not yet paid for) to stopping payment of the rent on their new home, which they had only just started to pay. He described the office where he was working (Coleman, Prentice & Varley) as 'a mad house'. His boss had once been the youngest soldier in the Czech army, 'modest, blushing, shy, timid . . . [but] His real name was Stensch' and he had turned into 'a monster'. Eric decided to write to Sir Richard Livingstone, the former president of Corpus Christi College, Oxford who had once been his tutor, to ask about chances of employment in an Australian or even a British university. Failing that, Antonia White, who had come back into his life after an absence of many years, had introduced him to some 'Catholic friends' who were on their way out to Uganda and would look out for opportunities for him in the colony. To encourage Mary he added 'nice people guaranteed'. Another of his old friends, Emily Holmes Coleman,* wrote to him from Avila in Spain to say that she was 'praying for your Australian job (though I should hate you going there). Is it near Sydney? . . . I know how you must loathe what you are doing now. I had jobs. They take one's life-blood.' This was a point of view that Eric wholeheartedly shared, although, unlike Emily, he had no private income. Mary once recalled Eric as being happiest, 'when not working in some unsuitable job, and all jobs are unsuitable for him'.

Nothing came of any of these plans and Eric was soon forced to sell the school fees' insurance policy to his brother Harry. At the same time he decided to give up work and earn a living from writing, which was how he had always wanted to live anyway. It was a risk but Mary also wanted to write and together they would make it an adventure. Harry Siepmann, who had missed his knighthood in the New Year Honours List of 1954, was appalled by the decision and wrote from his City address in Throgmorton Avenue to Mary's brother Hugh, 'I prophecy penury, both sooner and later . . .'

Meanwhile Eric and Mary had chosen to return to the place where they had always been made welcome, the village of Chagford on Dartmoor. They found a large house for rent on the moor a few miles out of the village. It was called Thornworthy, formed part of a farm, and they moved in May 1955. It was such a big house that it was later converted into a hotel.

Mary revelled in the experience of living on Dartmoor. She had loved the moor for many years with its skies and rocks and streams. In the early morning

---

* American novelist, painter and poet, author of *The Shutter of Snow*. Her friends included Peggy Guggenheim, Dylan Thomas, T. S. Eliot and Mervyn Peake. Sexually adventurous in youth, she later converted to Catholicism, which she embraced with twelfth-century fervour.

and evening there were no tourists and she would swim with her dog in
pools she knew on the River Dart. Another pleasure, which she mentioned
in *Part of the Scenery*, was riding out from Thornworthy with the farmer,
Harold Wonnacott, and his dogs to round up his black-faced sheep. In winter,
when the snow blew into drifts under the hedges, she became very conscious
of the notorious prison at Princetown. She enrolled as a prison visitor (going
to see No. 383) and she got into the habit, when she left the house, of leaving
the door open, with a cold meal on the kitchen table and a change of clothes
on the washing line – always hoping, when the prison siren wailed, that some
desperate fugitive, perhaps No. 383, might find the house and gather his
strength and continue on his way. The fugitive eventually arrived, but only
in her imagination, and became a central character, a matricide on the run,
in *Jumping the Queue*.

Mary and Eric lived happily enough at Thornworthy from May 1955
until August 1960 and during those years Eric wrote down a description
of the view from his study window:

> I sit looking, through the window, at the garden and beyond the garden
> at the valleys which roll like grassy waves now the colour of grapefruit
> because it is spring. All winter there have been slopes of coloured bracken
> dividing the valleys, and this bracken which was of a reddish colour while
> it was dead is coming to life and whorls and shoots of pale green pierce
> the dead cinnamon-coloured surface . . . The geese smacking the garden
> with their feet, honk loudly. There are three geese, and I am watching
> them. They honk proudly, they are arrogant. Indeed, they have reason
> to be proud. They do more than protect their territory, they challenge
> all comers. It is an active challenge, and when I walk in the garden they
> are aggressive and rush at me with their heads down hissing and they
> frighten me. I have discovered that if you let a goose approach and seize
> it by the neck just under the head and swing it round the goose is help-
> less and it becomes humiliated and goes away when I release it. These
> geese make love to my wife.

Mary had always been fond of geese. She considered that geese were intelligent creatures, '. . . to be called a goose should be taken as a compliment'.
She also found them highly affectionate. At Boskenna the geese she kept
became her friends. She felt guilty about eating them but less guilty (for
some reason) when she ate only the ganders. The geese she kept at
Thornworthy were white Chinese and Pansy was the most affectionate of

all. 'Lying naked in the sun' was always one of Mary's 'highest most extreme pleasures' and at Thornworthy she had enough space to pursue it discreetly. Pansy would sit on her lap, twining its neck round hers '. . . making little throttling noises of affection'.

Looking back, Mary described Thornworthy as a place where they had gone to write and, sure enough, within six months of moving there, Eric unexpectedly laid an egg. While working at Portals in November 1951 he had started work on an autobiography 'to avoid going mad from boredom'. When he finished it he threw it away, as usual, but Mary, realising that this was no time for perfectionism, fished most of it out of the waste-paper basket and in February, the remains were accepted by Victor Gollancz.

Confessions of a Nihilist was greeted with mixed reviews in November 1955. Gollancz had taken a single-column advertisement in *The Times*, with plugs from Maurice Bowra, Philip Toynbee and Peter Quennell. This was, in the last case, generous since Siepmann's novel *Waterloo in Wardour Street*, a satire on the British film industry published in 1936, had contained a character called Cora Quenell [*sic*], a blonde, beautiful, unconventional, good-natured film starlet. Now Eric received an enthusiastic letter from the film producer Michael Balcon and there was a good, unsigned review in the *Times Literary Supplement*. The *Observer* described it as the story of 'a discontented young intellectual shouldering his way through the inter-war years as energetically as a strong urge to destroy himself would allow . . .' and *Punch* recalled that in the Twenties he had been 'a famous playboy'. Cyril Connolly gave him the lead review in the *Sunday Times*, but described Eric as 'a complex lightweight', wanted more of his 'Satanic past', lamented the lack of any 'creative madness' and said that it should have been entitled 'Confessions of a Nobody'. Evelyn Waugh published nothing about the book but mocked it in a letter to Nancy Mitford – 'have you seen Eric Siepmann's autobiography? I roared. He thinks Col.[*] is a jew. Is *he*? I mean Siepmann.'

The reasons for Waugh's settled hostility towards Siepmann remain obscure. They had much in common: both had joined the Royal Marines, converted to Catholicism and were friends of Nancy Mitford. Mary thought that the mutual loathing dated back to Oxford, where they were contemporaries for one year. Waugh and Siepmann shared many Oxford friends including Patrick Kinross, Douglas Woodruff, Christopher Hollis, Claud Cockburn, Graham Greene and Maurice Bowra. The most likely explanation for their

[*] Gaston Palewski – lover of Nancy Mitford.

enmity is that Siepmann was also a close friend of Basil Murray and Peter Rodd.* Waugh disliked both these young men and drew on them for his character Basil Seal. Waugh once described Murray as 'satanic', while Murray described Siepmann as 'the Devil'. Waugh's reasons for disliking Murray included the fact that the latter once 'quietly but efficiently' beat him up. Unusually, Waugh made no exception for Siepmann after Eric's conversion to Catholicism; they remained enemies. Mary remembered them glaring at each other over Caroline Cobb's open grave. In his letter to Nancy Mitford, Waugh misquotes Siepmann who had not said that Gaston Palewski was Jewish but had quoted a French source 'Maître Lemaitre', who said, 'Palewski, being a Jew, is ultra-French . . .'†

The most perceptive comment inspired by *Confessions of a Nihilist* was made in a personal letter to Eric from someone who had never met him, J. B. Priestley, the foremost 'man of letters' of the day.

> *The truth about you, I think, is that you are a writer* – not by the way a thinker – who has never spent enough time getting down to the sheer hard grind of writing. Thus, it is surprising how little there is about work in your autobiography, and I suspect much of your earlier restlessness was due to the fact that you didn't really work for a living but flitted from one fairly cushy job to another. *Your whole temperament, outlook and abilities seem to me those of a writer, and I hope you will keep on writing as hard as you can.*

In this paragraph Eric underlined in red the words italicised. But the sting, and the truth, of the comment lies in the rest.

On the whole Eric must have been disappointed by the reviews of *Confessions of a Nihilist*. As so many of the reviewers pointed out, the first half of the book was much better written and more interesting than the second. The first half remains a true confession and a fine portrait of his generation in the Twenties and Thirties. Some passages are irreplaceable;

---

* Peter Rodd – husband of Nancy Mitford.
† Another French source, the celebrated writer Pierre Drieu la Rochelle, anti-Semite and pro-Nazi, a specialist in the matter, identified Gaston Palewski as *Juif polonais* (*récemment naturalisé?*) (Polish Jew (recently naturalised?)) in his diary entry for 21 March 1940. As for the Siepmanns, the family believes today that Otto Siepmann was of partly Jewish extraction. Otto told one of his grandchildren that in Clifton his windows had been broken before the Great War because he was Jewish and during the War because he was German.

the record of the Clifton common room, the narrow, venomous colleagues who insulted Otto during and after the war, even while the military exploits and medals of his older sons were being listed in the college magazine. Eric described them as 'slight, unmeritable men, whose type is eternal, and flourishes under academic stones'.

He also remembered the way his brother Harry, thirteen years older, changed when he returned from the war and the silence that fell over him: 'The First War was a hard war, and the Peace was like a hard frost.' When Eric went to Winchester as a scholar his best friend was Anthony 'Puffin' Asquith, his fag was John Sparrow[*] and as a prefect he beat R. H. S. Crossman[†] – but not, as he himself confessed, enough. Eric had been beaten 'weekly like a gong' for several years and by the time he became a prefect he was against beating. But for Crossman he made an exception. He said that in later years whenever he read Crossman's articles in the *New Statesman* he much regretted that he had only beaten him once. 'I have one consolation,' he wrote. 'I beat him without the slightest excuse. It was the triumph of a powerful, un-reasoning indeed prophetic instinct.' The *New Statesman*'s reviewer described the author as 'an agreeable, friendly, rather naïvely egotistical person'.

In the most memorable chapter in *Confessions of a Nihilist*, Eric described his friendship with the Asquith family. As a boy, staying at the Asquith house in Sutton Courtenay, he met Keynes, Stravinsky and Marshal Joffre. When Eric met Mr Asquith, now Lord Oxford, the great Prime Minister had said to the schoolboy, 'How do you do? I've heard of you, of course.' Asquith was the last scholar to rule England; he loathed music and he never read newspapers. At Sutton Courtenay there was an aura of Double Firsts, of the Bar, the Woolsack and Downing Street. The ambience was not just ambitious, it was high-minded, even highly moral. It was essential in life to do good, but in order to achieve good it was essential to think well, in other words to be clever. Eric eventually decided that in leaving Oxford after one year he had betrayed the standards of Sutton Courtenay.

[*] In later life the brilliant but idle Warden of All Souls, sociable raconteur and voracious cruiser.
[†] Sanctimonious Socialist Cabinet minister and millionaire farmer. Noted for piercing blue eyes, 'massive thighs' (Maurice Bowra), obsessive loathing of wood-lands and economy with the truth. R. H. S. Crossman got his revenge on Eric Siepmann. In 1944, as a senior officer in the Psychological Warfare Department, Crossman blocked Eric's application to join a combat unit of the French Intelligence section and sidetracked him to Sardinia.

There was to be no second edition of *Confessions of a Nihilist* and the book soon went out of print. Eric Siepmann subsequently finished a novel, but it was rejected as 'a prestige book'. He continued to write and his flow of new ideas remained as strong as ever, but nothing more was published. Instead, he earned some money from journalism, sub-editing at *The Times* and giving occasional radio talks for the BBC; he appeared on the *Brains Trust*. He also reviewed for the *Times Literary Supplement* and Mary later said that when Eric was too busy he asked her to write these influential but underpaid and anonymous articles for him. Most of the money he earned came either from tutoring for Common Entrance or teaching English to boys from France and Germany. Here the size of Thornworthy was an advantage; there were rooms for more pupils than Eric could teach and Mary was kept busy running a one-woman boarding house for the pupils. Eric was a gifted tutor, but he found the work exhausting because it prevented him from writing. For some years he had a small private income – his share of the royalties from the sale of his father's language books – but Otto's estate was eventually bought up by an agency and this income ceased.

All his life Eric's politics remained those of an Asquithian Liberal. He was innoculated against the fashionable Communism of the Thirties by this commitment, as well as by his lifelong interest in religious belief and even by his brief experience of the Spanish Civil War. Eric had been in Andalusia in July 1936, when Franco's forces invested Seville. He had reported this for the *News Chronicle* and he returned to northern Spain in April 1937. At that time he entered a Catholic church just after the congregation had been machine-gunned by anarchists. Among the bodies he found a blood-stained prayer book that had fallen to the ground open at a litany of the Rosary; he kept this little book with his papers until he died and it may have sown the seeds of his own faith.

The fact that Mary and Eric both believed in God had always been an important link (Eric had mentioned it in the last chapter of *Confessions of a Nihilist*) and they had talked for some time about their shared interest in Catholicism. Even Eric's reflections on geese were linked to his religious speculations.

All three birds are proud, and honk as they go round our garden which they take to be their realm. Does it ever occur to them that outside and beyond their perceptions there is another universe of which they know nothing? No, it does not. They rely on us for shelter, and at night we shut them up. There they are safe from the beautiful but merciless fox. They take this for granted, and they continue to make it plain by their attitude that we are nothing or very little in their lives, and that they intend to be self-sufficiently grand. They are brave, protecting their world and each other and the gander does most of the protecting. One day the fox will have found a loose board in their shelter and snapped off the gander's head as if it had been cut off with a pair of scissors like a flower. This has not happened yet. The gander is honking and I am watching the geese through the window. I am God, and the fox is the Devil; I suppose . . .

In contrast to her husband, Mary's Catholicism was instinctive rather than intellectual. The writing of Simone Weil, Teilhard de Chardin and Graham Greene – who portrayed a 'church of sinners' that she recognised as hers – all reinforced her childhood attraction to 'the theatre of the Mass', but she was never governed by rules. In Rome with Eric in 1950, on the day when Pope Pius XII declared the bodily assumption of the Blessed Virgin into heaven as a new dogma, she suggested that they should cause a public scandal in St Peter's Square; but Eric thought that between them they had caused enough scandal already. Sister Wendy Beckett, who became a friend of Mary's many years later, considered that it was impossible to speculate very much about her religious belief because she had an instinctive privacy about 'everything deepest within her'. Eric noted a conversation he had with Mary in his *Journal* for September 1948, some years before either of them was considering a conversion to Catholicism: 'After we had read about his gambling and the martyrdom of his wife I asked M: "What do you think of Dostoyevsky?" "I think he was almost a saint." She explained that he understood what good and evil were. It is this valuation of FAITH above works which distinguishes Mary, and rejoices me in her. It is uncommon among intellectuals and every kind of "realist" nowadays.' Mary once said, 'I find what I need in the Church. And what I can't take, I simply leave.'

After resigning from Portals, while working in London, Eric had renewed his old friendship with the novelist Antonia ('Tony') White and at one point he took lodgings in her house in Ashburn Gardens, South Kensington. While he was there he complained to Mary about 'Tony's insanities'. Antonia White, who had written about her loss of faith in *Frost in May*, had since returned to the Catholic Church and she regarded it as a challenge to convert Eric, whom she had once described as 'the most dangerous of all [the men she knew] because he hates what makes him happy . . . He's a real homicidal maniac.' After one of Eric's and Mary's visits, Antonia White made a diary entry: '[Eric] can't drink moderately. He just has to go on till he gets to the truculent, bullying stage. Half-way he's the best, most stimulating companion imaginable. Mary is a wonder.' In the autumn of 1955 Tony started to insist that Eric should attend Mass. He described the experience to Mary.

> I am a poor catholic. Driven out by Tony in pelting rain to 'mass at 10.45' last Sunday, I walked noisily up the aisle at the Brompton Oratory – like a railway station: and there is a flunkey with gilt buttons to take your umbrella – . . . bumped and bobbed as near to a distant priest in green vestments as I dared, was swept out again by the crowd, only to find myself standing on the street in pelting rain at 10.44. I had arrived for the tag end of the previous mass, and escaped (feeling rather afraid of Tony, not of God) . . . Tony was dreadfully upset, until we discovered that I came in for the last collection, by nuns, which meant that I had attended mass. (but the next day she decided I hadn't).

In 1956, mainly in response to reading Dostoyevsky, Eric decided to take instruction as a Catholic. He told Mary nothing of this but she discovered where he had gone and tracked him to Farm Street, London headquarters of the Society of Jesus, indignant because the idea had originally been hers. They were instructed by Father Richard Mangan SJ, described by Mary as 'the best-looking priest she had ever seen', who made short work of his task. Their first visit was 3 August 1956 and they were received on 26 August, after only six sessions. Mary had long before decided that she wanted to convert, but, as she told Richard Mangan during their instruction, she was not prepared to join the Church without Eric. During one discussion Eric thumped the table, saying that he would not join if he could not have his dog with him in heaven. Father Mangan answered, 'You shall have him if you need him.'* In view of the apparent problems – both had been previously married at least once in church and so they were not married to each other under canon law – their Catholic friends were baffled

---

* This answer contrasts with the experience of Roald Dahl who, when his seven-year-old daughter died, sought comfort from the Archbishop of Canterbury, Dr Geoffrey Fisher. Dahl told Dr Fisher that he liked to think of his daughter in the company of the dogs that she had loved so much on earth; Dr Fisher angered him by answering that dogs could not go to heaven.

by the speed with which they were received. Their godmothers were Antonia White and a mutual friend, Phyllis Jones. The reception service, held at Farm Street, involved a conditional baptism, to remove any doubts about the Anglican sacrament, and Mary took the name 'John' while Eric took 'Peter'. Antonia White's present to them was a slim volume of *Ancient Devotions for Holy Communion* from eastern and western liturgical sources. Mary bought the *Roman Missal*, with the order of Mass in Latin and English, and Tony taught her the words of the 'Hail Mary' (a prayer new to Mary, who copied it out, inaccurately) so that she would feel less of a stranger during the 'bumping and bobbing' with which Eric had been confronted in the Brompton Oratory. Two publishers invited Eric to write a book on 'How I Became a Catholic', but he did not respond.

In 1957, a year after they had been received into the Catholic Church, Eric wrote a letter to Mary about the fact that they were committed to a relationship which the Church could never recognise as marriage: 'I am quite clear now about sex; and I hope you'll agree. With us, it's love: and I have no intention of giving it up. I *had* the intention to try, when I became a Catholic.' Just over a week later he wrote to her again from London: 'I told my confessor [at the Brompton Oratory] . . . exactly what I feel about sex and our marriage; and I told him clearly that I had no intention of living "as brother and sister", although I had recognised that as the aim when [I] joined the Church, and still recognise a spiritual life as preferable . . . He [the priest] said God would recognise our good intentions, and knew best; and not to torment ourselves . . . (And I told him, I cannot think it wrong.)' Eric's candour did not always pay off and on another occasion he was thrown out of the confessional by a French priest who had just given him a penance of three decades of the Rosary, a sequence of prayer that would have taken him about forty-five minutes to complete. He also had problems with the humdrum appearance of his local church, Our Lady's in Lisson Grove, St John's Wood.* 'Mass was in the most hideous church I've ever seen,' he wrote in June 1957. '[It] . . . made the people look like Belsen Warders and Wardresses. Very elaborate and hideous.'

On the following day he returned to the subject: 'I am reading Jane Austen, who is even more detestable than I imagined. The English ideal. Class-conscious, money-conscious, sexless and Refined. I will say that for the Catholics I saw [in church] yesterday, they all looked like murderers.' Later Eric abandoned Lisson Grove, 'the Catholic Belsen, the *Palais des*

---

* Then the parish church of the author's family.

Horreurs', and took refuge in St James's Spanish Place, 'which is old, beauti-ful, fashionable and has Mozart'. By the end of the month, looking forward to his return home, his spirits had lifted and he could write, 'Prepare your-self for mortal sin.' Mary, living close to the beauty of Buckfast Abbey during this same period of separation, was less troubled. She wrote to tell Eric, 'I really feel a Catholic now. Not a good one but I have been given the vehicle, the life belt which I needed.'

Mary made light of her conversion, regretting only that it blighted her renewed friendship with John Platts-Mills. When the latter ridiculed her beliefs and boasted that he had taken care to bring his six boys up as atheists, she turned him out of the house. Platts-Mills was not prepared to take offence and she got her own back when he eventually invited her to attend the confirmation of one of the 'atheist sons', and she was able to tell John that he had grown to look 'exactly like an Anglican prelate'. On the other hand the move may have brought Mary closer to another old friend, Father Paul Ziegler, now a monk at Quarr Abbey on the Isle of Wight. In the middle of her instruction Mary went down to Quarr to see Paul and on the day of their reception Paul Ziegler wrote to Eric,

> . . . When I left you two years ago I was thinking you over and I came to the conclusion that you were a most unlikely person ever to find your way back to a positive Christian faith. It depressed me . . . because I felt that if someone is intelligent and honest and courageous, and all the same feels quite at home in a conception of life which is without any meaning – is absurd – then what can we offer him? Modern psychology has taught man sufficient tricks to explain anything away and the facts which make up our truth are not immune against this kind of attack; if I am told that I believe because I want to believe and am given a number of excellent reasons why I do want to believe although remaining quite unconscious of any desire to do so – what am I to say? And very quickly the word 'escape' is hovering in the background – 'escapism' is one of the most efficient bad names invented in our times to hang undesired dogs.

For Mary the adoption of Paul Ziegler's faith was another attempt to reduce the compartments in her life, to maintain a link with Heinz, and this may indeed have been one of her subconscious motives for converting. The Farmars considered that she was probably just trying to inflict further pain on her anti-Catholic, anti-German mother. Inevitably, her conversion did mark another stage in the breach with her family, but she took religion too seriously to convert for frivolous reasons, as her correspondence confirms.

Eric, as always, followed a more tormented path. Long before he converted his *Journal* reveals his enduring interest in religion. In July 1947 he had likened prayer to listening to music since both were 'a kind of hypnosis based on the devotion to something outside self'. In June 1956, two months before he set off for the Jesuits in Farm Street without telling Mary, Antonia White had sent Eric a long letter about her faith in God. She warned him of the comments that would be made about his emotional 'need for a refuge' and 'intellectual dishonesty' when he converted, and said that her fifteen years outside the Church had been a long search for the truth.

Their conversion gave Mary two new friends; the first was Antonia White who admired her work and encouraged her to continue. Writing in her diary, Antonia White described one of Mary's unpublished books, entitled *The Heirs*, which has disappeared but which was probably an early version of her novel* for teenagers, *The Sixth Seal*:

> . . . An extraordinary book – the first part marvellous – the rest not up to it but with wonderful bits in it. Tremendous imagination, wonderful visual sense . . . But it goes quite wild . . . You can't begin to criticise a person like that with an amazing natural gift and no logic. She just goes on inventing and inventing . . .

In 1956 Mary was able to help at a time of crisis, when Antonia was sued for libel by a young actress called June Sylvaine. By mischance, White's novel *The Sugar House* included a character with the same name and there was a High Court hearing. Mary sat beside Antonia throughout the case. She 'was taut with terror', wrote Mary later 'when we drove to the court . . . [The actress] was very pretty; the judge liked her. But when Antonia's turn came, she twittered with terror, could hardly speak and the judge did not like her. She lost the case and damages had to be paid.' Antonia described the cross-examination (by Gerald Gardiner QC) as 'Horrible . . . like Kafka . . . Perpetually trying to trap one, to make one break down and lose one's temper.' When the judgement was given Antonia did break down and became hysterical. 'I took her home,' wrote Mary, 'and plied her with

---

* Eventually published in 1969.

whisky . . . this was the nearest I ever got to seeing what others saw –
Antonia losing control. Her fragility had been publicly exposed.'

The second friendship was with another of Eric's former girlfriends, the
American author Emily Holmes Coleman. Emily burst with enthusiasm and
was a prolific correspondent. She regarded Mary as 'one of the most amazing
women I ever met. She is capable of anything . . .' On learning of Mary's
conversion, Emily wrote to encourage her and to state that she considered it
'a living miracle' that she herself had remained in the Church. 'You do not
know, Mary, the power of my passions, nor the utter recklessness of my will.
I say this to help Eric, for I too am a monster.' Emily lived in the grounds
of Stanbrook Abbey, the Benedictine nunnery in Worcestershire. She became
a constant presence in their letter box, though rarely leaving Stanbrook in
person. She was entranced with Mary and told all her friends about her. One
of these friends, the novelist Robert Liddell,* who was living in Greece,
responded by writing directly to Mary, describing Emily as 'the most anthro-
pomorphic of believers: she told me Heaven and Hell were places. She quite
looked forward to having tea with Rose Macaulay, and almost talked as if
Dame Rose had gone on first to put the kettle on.' These women, particularly Emily and Phyllis Jones, with Felicity Corrigan, the Abbess of Stanbrook,
and other members of the community, were to provide Mary with the first
circle of women friends she had formed since leaving the finishing school in
Malvern. They were also to teach her the limits of undue reverence.

Shortly before his final decision to become a Catholic, Eric had been
rushed to hospital in what he said was a dying condition. Even Mary was
quite alarmed. The symptoms were dramatic but probably hysterical and
caused by his religious anguish. Emily Coleman turned the tables on his
dilemma when she wrote, '*Be* an agnostic. Above all don't let your brother
(who is not really the Devil, but just a weak, disappointed man), nor the
Foreign Office, nor the BBC, take precedence over realities that are everlasting. *You may have nearly died.* God may not give you such a chance
again.' Earlier on the same day Emily Coleman had written Eric a longer
letter, four pages of single-spaced quarto, typed in red, in which she had
first addressed the question of Harry Siepmann: 'I don't know exactly how
you can convince your brother that he also is inhabited by Satan – if he

---

* Bachelor and aesthete, expatriate novelist, author of *Stepsons*. Good musical ear;
in old age enjoyed company of attractive young women who were paid to read to
him aloud.

does not believe in him.' And encouraging Eric not to worry about poverty she added, 'You should know the life of George Barker. He's never had a penny . . . (His *The True Confessions of George Barker* is one of the greatest poems ever written . . . It makes *The Waste Land* look like a stubble field.) I am TERRIBLY interested in you. There isn't another like you . . . I feel awful about your money situation. I hate having an income when others haven't. Very lovingly Emily.' At the top of the letter she had noted, 'I thought Mary might become a Catholic one day – but not you . . .'

Much of Eric's real hesitation seems to have been connected with his fear of the disapproval of his 'brother the god', Harry. Eric once described his brother as 'the evil genius of our family' but he did eventually write to Harry, setting out his own views on religious belief, and in reply received a nineteen-page letter in Harry's small, neat manuscript hand explaining why Harry was right and Eric was wrong. This letter had been started in the Athenaeum and finished, a day later, in Glasgow. In philosophy, Harry counted himself 'a realist'. He suspected that man had invented God and he considered that if there are to be any gods at all, there should be 'quite a number of them, and goddesses too'. He conceded that man had a presentiment (*'Ahnung'*) or intimation of 'something that lies altogether outside and beyond immediate experience'. To people it with goblins, fairies and demons was a consequence of our 'beautiful capacity of imagination'. Harry accepted that 'the territory which the scientists painfully annex is as nothing compared with what lies – must lie – beyond the range of their vision and ours, and beyond the range, as it may be, of human reason altogether'. He had no objection at all to other people's religious convictions. He welcomed and admired

> the irrepressible human tendency to try and look beyond [humanity's] horizons; a tendency which is far from being irrational . . . I am quite certain that the ordinary man or woman is much the better for having a religion . . . I am wholly in favour of all the queer aberrations, which Ronny Knox* describes in his book *Enthusiasm* . . . Prompted by their numinous apprehensions, they are exercising their imaginations in a way which often brings out the best in them . . . Any religion, however absurd, is a respectable attempt on the part of man to discover new horizons . . .

---

* Monsignor Ronald Knox, notable Catholic polemicist, Oxford don and biblical scholar; subject of devout biography by Evelyn Waugh.

His letter ended, 'I am afraid that I disagree with you profoundly; but that is not any reason why we should be the less comprehensible to one another. Love Harry.' Some years earlier Eric had written in his *Journal*, 'Harry, who is cleverer than I am, disbelieves in God. When I feel depressed by his intellectual scorn, I console myself with the thought that Voltaire, who believed in God, was cleverer than Harry.'

While at Thornworthy Mary heard from an old friend who was in even more trouble than she was. In March 1957 Betty Paynter called to say that Boskenna was to be sold and everything in the house was going to be auctioned on site. She wanted someone with her on the day. After the war, Betty had married Solicitor Hill – Colonel Paynter's wartime partner in the black market. Pat Morris, who stayed in the house at this time, woke one night to hear Colonel Paynter's voice in the bedroom. The voice said, 'Tell Betty to be careful with the money.' Unfortunately Betty paid no attention to the phantom's message. The marriage was childless, and the combination of his management skills and her business sense had bankrupted the great estate in eight years. The auctioneers' particulars listed Boskenna's seven farms, five market gardens and 'vacant Manor House with beaches and cliffs'. Everything had to go, the furniture by Chippendale, Sheraton or Hepplewhite, the Georgian giltwood mirrors, the grand piano, the long-case clock, the family portraits, the books – including a seventeenth-century edition of Chaucer – the motor scythe, the flowerpots and two wheelbarrows with rubber tyres. In all, Betty's inheritance raised the modest sum of £30,000, which was just about enough to clear her debts to the Inland Revenue. Within the parish of St Buryan dark rumours began to circulate about the Colonel's will. It was said that there had been two wills. In the original document, witnessed by Alice Grenfell, the Colonel left the estate to Sonya, his granddaughter, through trustees, thus disinheriting Betty. He was thought to have considered his only child too flighty, and too much under the influence of Paul Hill. Then, as Alice put it, 'Miss Betty produced another will.' Under the second will, forged by Solicitor Hill, the estate passed to Betty. The sale of the entire property in 1957 was the foreseeable result. The Colonel had left a cash sum to settle death duties, but Betty blew this soon after her father's death on a disastrous redecoration of the house and a number of frocks from Dior.

At Thornworthy, Mary was staring the same sort of catastrophe in the face every week of the year. Their idea was to earn enough money by working in the summer – either tutoring or sub-editing – to pay for writing during the rest of the year. When Eric was in London working at *The Times*, Mary would take up to eight French or German boys, give them board and lodging, and teach them to speak English. The rent was £30 a month and each pupil paid £50 a month; in a bad month all debts were left unpaid and only the bank overdraft settled.

It was while working at *The Times* in 1957 that Eric had one of his more eccentric journalistic ideas, which was to undertake the rehabilitation of Dr Hjalmar Schacht, who had been tried at Nuremberg as 'Hitler's banker'. It was Eric's equivalent of helping 'Jacko'. Although Dr Schacht had been acquitted on four counts of conspiracy to wage war, he was subsequently convicted of lesser war crimes by another German tribunal. After serving a short prison sentence, Schacht staged a comeback as a freelance international adviser to central banks. (On his notepaper he continued to describe himself as 'ex-President of the Reichsbank'.) He had been a friend of Harry Siepmann's before the war, and both Schacht and his daughter came to stay with Eric and Mary at Thornworthy. For three days Eric grilled 'Hitler's financial wizard' in fluent German about guilt, his conscience, the anti-British advice he had recently been giving to the Iranian and Indonesian governments, the devaluation of sterling, the dangers of inflation and the limits of Keynesianism. Dr Schacht, who had enabled Hitler to rearm the Third Reich, was a fanatical believer in sound money, a grandfather of Thatcherism – and New Labour economics. Harry, by now retired, translated the final transcript of the conversations into English. The talks form an absorbing postscript to the Nuremberg trials and shed an interesting sidelight on pre-war Germany, but they were rejected by both the BBC and the *Daily Telegraph*, who judged that Britain was not yet ready for a sanitised Nazi banker. In correspondence with Eric, Dr Schacht said that he had never expected the sympathetic interviews to be published in England and added, 'Please remember me to your adorable Wife.'

If Violet Farmar had ever heard about this forlorn enterprise it would have confirmed her worst suspicions. Mary was told that her mother had by now started to refer to Bill Siepmann, her ten-year-old grandson, as 'the little Hun'.

In the time-consuming work of running Thornworthy as a guest house Mary had some help from her new friend and godmother, Phyllis Jones, whom she had originally met through Emily Coleman. Sometimes, when Mary was exhausted she would go to Stanbrook Abbey to stay with Emily and make a retreat. In the autumn of 1958 Eric wrote to her hostess, 'Mary should if possible sleep until nine or nine-thirty (she can speak with reasonable intelligence by eleven) but she is *not* to go without breakfast. Please be very kind and see that she has a tin of biscuits, with a pint of milk, first thing.' Later he wrote again: 'Dear Em . . . Your notion of praying for Sartre to become a Christian is like Mary's All Souls' prayers for Hitler. Only you two could be so daft, and saintly.' Later again he warned Phyllis Jones that Mary prayed the rosary 'anti-clockwise', contrary to the chart Phyllis had provided, adding, in mock anxiety, 'Is this all right?'

Phyllis Jones, 'a lean, handsome redhead', typed for both Emily Coleman and Antonia White, and in due course for both Eric and Mary. Shortly after Coleman left Rye in 1957 to live in the retreat house of Stanbrook Abbey in Worcestershire, Phyllis Jones also left the town to live for two years with Mary and Eric at Thornworthy. Henry Ziegler, nephew of Heinz and Paul, who visited them at that time remembers being taken to a Liberal Party tea party by Mary to meet the local MP, Jeremy Thorpe.[*] Another recalls Mary and Phyllis cooking and smoking and drinking and praying, and talking of Emily (still a ferocious correspondent) and of Marx, 'three castaways on a boat of their own making, affirming it all, whatever the cost'. Catholicism had become a central part of their daily life. Eric started to attend morning Mass at Buckfast Abbey and to make regular retreats there; for him Catholicism remained a cerebral adventure. He would have fitted very happily into the intellectual life of a provincial university town in France or Germany, where he would probably have found a publisher and a circle of friends. Instead, he struggled to make sense of post-war Europe, and to make his soul, in a damp, draughty barracks of a farmhouse on Dartmoor, reading Maritain, Bernanos and Camus, and spending long hours arguing with either Father Gabriel or Father Wilfred, two of the younger monks at Buckfast for whom he kept sherry – when he could afford it. Their conversations were conducted with no holds barred and with small regard for the Abbot's imprimatur. Father Gabriel remembers Mary in those days, busy in the kitchen and listening, amused, but saying little. When Father Wilfred left Buckfast to marry, and reverted to being Malcolm Upham, Eric and Mary were among the first to call on his wife,

[*] Jeremy Thorpe MP, urbane leader of the Liberal Party, member of parliament for North Devon. He resigned his seat in 1976 after being acquitted at the Old Bailey of conspiracy to murder an alleged blackmailer. The police did not prosecute the blackmailer.

Peggy, offering friendship and support. They were all the more welcome because Mary could recount her experience in the confessional at Buckfast, where she had incautiously mentioned the sudden departure of 'ex-Father Wilfred' and found herself on the receiving end of a tirade from the Abbot.* Part of this experience was to be used in her early children's novel *The Sixth Seal*. Mary set this book on the moor in the countryside around Buckfast Abbey and based one of the characters on ex-Father Wilfred. But in a characteristic touch she reversed reality by making the fictional monk the only member of the community to survive disaster, living on in the Abbey alone, while all that remained of the Abbot was his ring.

---

* There was something about the confessional box that seems to have provoked Mary's anarchic nature. Richard Mangan SJ, urging her to visit him at Farm Street when she came to London, added, 'Don't bother about Confession unless you murder much'. And Mary once told Jenny Murray's husband, also a convert, that, impatient to catch a train and trapped with a long-winded priest in a confessional in Westminster Cathedral, she had lost patience and burst out with, 'Oh for God's sake, Father, shut up and give me the bloody absolution.'

CHAPTER THIRTEEN

Hammer and Tongs

'They've been at it hammer and tongs ever since the day they first met in the nursery.'

Hugh Farmar, of his sisters Susan and Mary

On 1 September 1958 Mary Siepmann, abandoning her lodgers, went to bed early in the big house at Thornworthy with two dogs and a hot-water bottle, and started to write her memoirs. She called them *The Fruits of My Follies* and she had finished by the following March. Emily Holmes Coleman was enthusiastic, describing the first draft as 'a most extraordinary document . . . pure genius'. It was inspired by such nineteenth-century *succès de scandale* as the memoirs of Harriette Wilson, who had provoked the Duke of Wellington into saying 'Publish and be Damned'.

'I am stung into writing this,' was Mary's first sentence.

I shall be extremely libellous . . . I am forty-six and I am sick and tired of reading the biographies of famous men and women. The women will tell you what they wore at the balls . . . and who they sat next to at dinner, and who they married. They don't usually tell you how they made fools of themselves, no, they tell you how behind the scenes they influenced their important husbands and helped them in their careers. The men are worse. Secretive. You would think they sat at their desks twiddling their thumbs waiting to be offered a portfolio from Downing Street. They show us their public faces. When they are offered a peerage they say they are surprised, honoured and pleased; they don't tell you about the scramble up the ladder . . . how much they paid in humiliation . . . how they kept a mistress round the corner, who they truly loved and why they married for money and position.

The possible targets of this passage might have included Harry Siepmann, director of the Bank of England, who had many mistresses (and who married three of them), or Duff Cooper who, five years earlier, had published the very popular *Old Men Forget*, through which most of the author's numerous mistresses pass without mention. The fashion in autobiography at the time was to construct, as skilfully as possible, a gilded frame for the official portrait.

The Fruits of My Follies was a very different sort of life story; it was frank, defiant and ahead of its time. The second page starts, 'I have had two husbands, quite a lot of lovers and these three dear boys, not one of which has the same father though some of them think they have.' Later in the memoir Mary wrote that 'Counting lovers is like counting sheep to me', although she left out many of their names. She also wrote about Eric's 'occasional violent drunkenness', which 'terrified' her, and she wrote about Roger and Toby in equally affectionate terms. She described Roger as 'shrewd, discreet, loyal and . . . naturally good', whereas Toby was 'Even more selfish than me', with 'brains, humour and ideals; he was a good idea of mine'.

It is unlikely that *The Fruits of My Follies* was originally intended for publication, but apart from *The Glass Bugle*, her unpublished novel of 1948, it seems to have been the first full-length work that Mary finished. There is no evidence that Eric ever read it or even knew of it, it was never mentioned in their correspondence and her high-spirited accounts of her love affairs would have made him furiously jealous – and it was still in manuscript form in September 1962, when a friend who saw it remembers that 'it was written in pencil I think, and the punctuation wasn't there. It was notes.' Unpublished, it remained as it had started, a private memoir for her children, to tell them who their mother was and who they were, and a settling of some long-standing accounts with her own family. In the event her children never read it.

While Mary and Eric went their own way on Dartmoor, life in the Swinfen and Farmar families moved on. Carol had remarried in 1950, to Averil Knowles, and had thereby acquired two young stepchildren. He continued to work for some time as a civil servant, but then took early retirement and moved to Ireland, where he lived off his income from the Swinfen Trust. Although the boys never saw their parents together, Mary and Carol had remained on good terms. They maintained a friendly correspondence and had no problems in agreeing on how much time Roger and Toby spent in each house.

In 1953 Susan too had remarried. Her new husband was a wealthy land agent named Stephen Scammell, who sometimes acted as a freelance moneylender. He also operated as an amateur financial adviser and investor. Three members of Mary's family – her brother Hugh, a cousin known as 'Aunt Buttercup' and another Wellesley cousin – at various times entrusted Scammell with money for investment, and later regretted having done so. The Scammells lived in the village of East Knoyle in Wiltshire and steadily acquired property in the area. Stephen Scammell's hobbies included water divining and table turning.

After moving to Dartmoor, Mary saw less and less of her father, while her oldest son Roger began to see more and more of Susan. Roger would spend part of the summer holidays sailing on the Isle of Wight with his aunt, rather than going to his mother at Thornworthy. For these visits Roger remembers that he was driven to Lymington and put on the ferry. His mother did not accompany him. Roger was sixteen in 1955 when Eric and Mary moved from Hampshire to Dartmoor, and with the big house full of pupils in the summer Mary had little room and less time for her teenage sons. Roger had always hated moving house. As a child his ambition was 'to have children and live in the same house'. Roger wanted fixed points in his life, and his aunt's house at East Knoyle became one of those points. The growing influence of Susan over Roger was deeply resented by Mary.

The last of Roger's school letters that his mother kept was written from Westminster in December 1955, on his seventeenth birthday. He was by then due to leave school and go on to Sandhurst. He thanked Mary for offering to knit him a ski hat but said that he probably would not wear it as the cold did not 'worry his ears'. He ended, 'You ask me whether I am officially on the list of the Royal Scots or not, well the answer to that is that I am. Brigadier Crockett told me definitely that my name would be put on it as soon as he got in touch with the regiment. I should think that he has done that by now.' This piece of information made his mother very angry.

Susan's son by her first marriage, Robin McLaren, four years older than Roger, had followed his father into a Scottish regiment and Mary decided that at some point Susan must have suggested that Roger might do the same. Mary's anger over this decision was not due to any particular objection to the regiment; it was because she thought that, without any consultation, Susan had taken the matter out of her hands and once again cut across her own relationship with their father. Today Roger remembers that a Scottish regiment was his grandfather's idea, but Mynors's letters to Mary*

---

* Written in the previous year (1955) and already quoted in Chapter Eleven.

suggest otherwise. Mary recalled asking Roger to explain what had happened and her son saying, 'I'm going into the Royal Scots. Aunt Susan and Grandpa have arranged it.' It was the beginning of a process that Mary described as 'Susan stealing my oldest son away from me'. Mary had always been on the lookout for differences that might arise between herself and Carol over the children's upbringing, but she had not expected to be displaced by her sister. Meanwhile, as Susan's influence over Roger grew, Mary was becoming increasingly concerned about her second son, Toby.

The child she had 'always fought for, even from months before he was conceived when he was just an idea', became a serious preoccupation for his mother while he was still at Bryanston, aged sixteen. By then, September 1957, Roger's course was settled, for better or worse. He was going on to Sandhurst and he had chosen his regiment. Toby, on the other hand, was in a state of turmoil. In a series of letters written to Eric, Mary – signing herself as 'Polly', his nickname for her – described her growing uneasiness. At that time Eric was working at *The Times* in London and Mary was teaching English at Thornworthy to a procession of foreign pupils. Both Toby and Roger had joined her for the last weeks of the summer holidays.

A sleepless night. Toby came back beautiful and nervous and ranged about my room until 11.30 – so like his father . . . Then a long outpouring over Carol's futility and Averil's – '*I wish to God Eric were my father.*' Nothing ever decided or done for him except by us and terrible embarrassing uncertainty as to whether he is to go to a university or not. I must go to London and see Carol but when? My two-edged sword is overtaking me alright. 'They never read a book. Those idiotic cocktail parties! I suppose I've got to go there for Christmas.' The sharp cruel judgements of adolescence and the furious sense of not belonging, of being different from other people.

. . . Naturally I long to tell the truth. I need someone to advise me. You. Father Mangan. God. In a way I am inclined to tell him the truth, a terrible risk, and that Carol has been made use of long enough, my sin. What does Carol know? I don't know . . . Then how deep how serious is this? Begun how? Friends who have intellectual fathers? Other values than Carol's – unworldly? What is certain is that he now needs you urgently as you always said he might.

Paul [Ziegler] says never tell and I suppose he is right? I told him [Toby] that we *all* criticise our parents. That I consider myself very lucky he even speaks to me . . . That Carol, with all the negative points,

is generous and kind. That he *must never* expect people to be other
than they are, that it is waste of breath . . . I feel astride a bolting horse
and can only pray hard . . . All due to a bright idea in a Hungarian
restaurant in Soho 18½ years ago!

Your Polly.

Later on the same day she wrote to Eric again.

Toby *has* thank God gone off fishing and is doing so again tomorrow . . .
We walked together to Yeo so that more steam could be blown and he
seems happier . . . I feel it is wrong that he should dismiss my shortcom-
ings with a loving snap of the fingers as poor Carol *cannot* help being what
he is *or* what I have thrust on him and has been, whether consciously or
not, as wonderful as he can manage. Anyway now he [Toby] has unloaded
onto me he is apparently better. At Bath he was loudly greeted by a restaurant proprietor as a fellow *mittel* European and was most amused! Loud
German shouts about Prague and Vienna. What next? The Rabbi I suppose.

Eric replied on the following day.

My sweet Pol,
    Toby is (at last) growing up; and this is adolescence. It rouses all sorts
of memories and responsibilities in you, but these have nothing to do
with his problem . . . There is not the slightest point in 'telling' Toby
anything now, at this stage. But there is an inner (secret) argument for
his becoming independent as soon as possible. On the other hand, if he
can go to Oxford that is not to be despised. All you have to do is cope,
as usual. There is no end to it.

Both agreed it would be better if Toby were soon to become independent
of Carol's support. Carol had until then paid for Toby's education and had
always treated him as his youngest son. If everyone were to remain happy
about this situation, it was better to leave it as it was. But seeing so much
of Heinz in Toby, Mary could not believe that he would not be happier if
he knew about Heinz. Paul Ziegler, by now the guestmaster at Quarr Abbey,
had maintained his contacts with Warburg's Bank, and George Warburg still
consulted him on occasion. Mary thought that Toby might work at the bank.
    'What Toby needs', she wrote two days later,

is to be guided into some profession, from whence he can tilt at

Windmills. He is obsessed by Albert Schweitzer and the Negro problem at the moment and both Paul and I have separately suggested that he can be of greater use in helping whoever he wishes to help, when trained in something. He has asked whether he may borrow your typewriter to write to Paul, various queries about 'the transubstantiation of souls'. I think Paul will shoulder (he must) some of the burden. What Toby wants is *serious*. He is deeply serious. The *foux rire* [sic] is there too I am glad to say ... Of course it is a phase of adolescence but I know that family.

She ended,

Roger and Toby are curiously protective. I suppose I must get used to this change of roles now they are so large ... I won't do anything silly over Toby. It would only hurt him.

When not fishing Toby was reading '... everything at once. Plato, Dostoyevsky and has taken to *grunting*. When I complained about the grunting he said he was "agreeing with himself" and grunted agreement.' The following day Mary wrote again:

Toby reading The Bible, Plato, Cicero, Ilya Ehrenburg and two books on religion and busy writing a very boring short story. Hysterical with excitement last night on hearing the *Eroica* for the first time ... Otherwise he grunts, stalks about and is aloof ... He is obsessed with the downtrodden. Loud groans of rage at the racial segregation in America; must be in his blood. All that energy must be well-directed. I must as usual go and start on another meal. Numbers have crept up again to seven, eight on Monday ...

It was the genial contempt with which Toby regarded her in 1957 that had 'stung' Mary into writing *The Fruits of My Follies*, her irritation at his assumption that his mother was no more than the woman who cooked for lodgers and kept the house clean, was the spur. She felt the need to assert the fact that she too had once 'had a life', and rather an interesting one. But, faced with the practical dramas of adolescence, she followed Eric's advice and decided to keep this information to herself.

Though Carol had not been pleased when Toby declined to go to Eton, particularly since there would probably have been a scholarship, he paid the boy's fees at Bryanston without demur, and he talked to Toby about university. Carol told him that Oxford was 'no longer a place for people like us', but eventually suggested that Toby should apply for a place at his old college, Christ Church. This Toby once more declined to do, on the grounds that there were too many Old Etonians there. Carol then declined to pay for Toby's university education. This decision – the first time that Carol had been 'difficult' – angered Mary, who was on retreat at Stanbrook Abbey. She told Eric that she was going to consult a solicitor, to put pressure on Carol.

Eric was alarmed and wrote to Mary in September 1958,

> I doubt if it would be a good idea to disclose your hand by inviting Carol to account for his investments. I think you must try every diplomacy, up to the limit of and including (if necessary) stiffness. But lawyers are a declaration of war . . .
>
>   Rather show your skill, as you always have, in dealing with Carol! Toby will be all right, whatever happens . . . That was an important fuck, and its consequences fully reward the Life Force that guided you . . .

Mary allowed herself to be persuaded and decided to write to Maurice Bowra (friend of both Heinz and Eric) and Toby was offered a conditional place at Wadham for the autumn of 1959, provided he passed the entrance exam. In this way a measure of independence from Carol was finally achieved.

Mary usually described her first husband as a rather ineffectual, amiable man who bored her. But he seems to have noticed a lot more than he let her know. 'Carol did behave terribly well over Toby,' Mary once wrote. 'He loved him and there was never a word said, no hint dropped that Toby was not his child . . . He had rather an Edwardian philosophy; a wife, he believed, provided the heir, after which she was free to have lovers . . .' Although Mary always remained confident, as she had once told Eric, that she could 'manage' Carol, she was never certain of exactly how much he knew.

In fact, Carol seems to have been aware from an early moment that he might not have been the father of the boy he always acknowledged as his second son. His niece Venice, who had been Mary's bridesmaid, remembers that in July 1945, three months after his divorce from Mary, when he had won custody of both children, Carol had told her that Toby was not his. Venice made a guarded reference to this confidence in her diary for Sunday, 29 July. Realising that this was an important secret, she only confided it to her younger brother, Peter, and to their old nanny, who was living with them in Ovington Square. It seems unlikely that Carol Swinfen would have supplied his teenage niece with information that was not already known to older members of the family such as his friend and witness Hugh

Farmar, Mary's brother, and her widowed sister Susan – who had become one of his close confidantes during the war.

Their brother Hugh once said that his sisters had been 'at it hammer and tongs, ever since the day they first met in the nursery'. The problem may have started as a result of rivalry, or as a consequence of Susan's abnormally managing nature, or it may have had a precise cause. That Mary's resentment towards Susan deepened in response to her sister's growing influence over Roger is confirmed by an early passage in *The Fruits of my Follies*, written three years after the date when Roger chose his regiment and Mary left Broughton. On page 4 she introduces her sister Susan as a child. She was '. . . a little girl with curly hair and black eyes who grew up into the biggest Godless prig I've ever met . . .' Later, when Susan was widowed during the war, Mary wrote,

> . . . We all rushed to console her. She did not want consolation, she wanted to be left alone. She was very brave. She set about bringing up her two children and making a life for them and herself and she has been extremely successful. Endowed with money sense, common sense and horse sense, she now has calm and poise, a nice house, a nice new husband, horses, a yacht, and all the family furniture.

In conversation with me in the last year of her life Mary described her sister twelve times, and it was not a pretty picture. Sometimes Susan cropped up unexpectedly. When I asked Mary why several of her books included an incident in which one character pushed another into water, sometimes with fatal consequences, she replied, 'I've never pushed anyone into the water. I've been pushed. One day my sister pushed me off a pier in the Isle of Wight and I found that I could swim. I wasn't a very courageous child.' That memory led her unprompted to the story of not trusting her mother to take her near the edge of a cliff; it was as though she suspected that her mother had been trying to find out whether she could fly. On other occasions when she discussed Susan, Mary said that she was 'incredibly bossy, not at all sexy, sex was the last thing on her list'. Was her sister intelligent? 'In some ways. She was very clever about acquiring property and running other people's lives.' Susan 'stole my son and married that fiend who made my other son's life a misery . . . I blame my sister . . . All my life she bossed me and squashed me whenever she could . . . She was like my mother, fiercely possessive and managing . . .' At the end of her life Mary was convinced that Susan had stolen both her father and her son; she saw her sister as someone who acquired property and people, and made little distinction between the two. Throughout their relationship the sisters competed for their parents' love and in that competition Mary felt that she invariably came off second best.

The last letter Mary kept from her father was dated 15 June 1956 and bore the news that the College of Heralds had, after three years' deliberation, 'granted authentification of our Arms, Crest and Motto, based on those of Fermor of Easton Neston . . . I am so glad we keep the Gallic Cockerel (of Normandy – with Coronet).' Mary may have kept this letter because it was so characteristic of her father, and so revealing of the gulf between them.

Mynors Farmar was both kinder and more intelligent than his wife. Mary sometimes mocked his attempts to 'get himself crowned King of Burgundy'; in fact, he was a deeply spiritual man who spent much of his time working as a volunteer for Toc H and who had refused an order during the Battle of Passchendaele to move a military chaplain away from the front line. The chaplain was Anglican, and Colonel Farmar had noticed how many of his men, about to go into battle, claimed to be Catholic, merely because the RC chaplain was the only one nearby.

On two occasions following the Great War, Mynors experienced the paranormal. One night in 1921,[*] while staying at the Ismail Pasha Kiosk in Constantinople, he was attacked by 'a satanic force'. He and Violet were occupying a room that had once been part of the seraglio. He woke at night, while his wife slept peacefully beside him, and felt that 'an evil power was near' that would 'possess his soul. I prayed with all my Being and Faith.' The force gradually released him and he was able to get out of bed to find that his 'pyjama suit was soaking wet with perspiration'. The other experience had occurred six years earlier during the second day of the Battle of Gallipoli. On the first day of the landings at 'W' Beach, as the senior surviving officer, Mynors Farmar had taken command of the 86th Brigade for much of the day, while it suffered fifty per cent casualties. Early on that day, when Mynors was under Turkish fire near the Lighthouse, the Brigade Major, an officer of the Royal Dublin Fusiliers named Frankland, was killed within a few yards of him. On the following day Mynors Farmar was transferred to the neighbouring 'V' Beach at Sedd-el-Bahr to find out

[*] The year he revisited 'W' Beach at Gallipoli.

what was going on. Here he found men of the Royal Dublin Fusiliers who had just taken a hilltop position with a reckless bayonet charge. This advance had followed a period of over twenty-four hours' continuous action, during which their battalion had lost all but three of its officers. As Farmar gathered the Fusiliers together, trying to calm them and reorganise them, the Dubliners began to tell him about their bayonet charge. 'I said how well they had done. One replied, "It was Mr Frankland that led us. We would never have done it but for him" . . . and then several others chorused, "The Captain led us. It was Captain Frankland".' None of them knew that T. H. C. Frankland, whose father had commanded the battalion and who had spent most of his own professional life in it, had been killed on a neighbouring beach twenty-four hours earlier. But Mynors Farmar had no doubt that Frankland had come back to help his men when they needed him.

Accompanied by these ghosts, Colonel Farmar struggled through his last years. When his grandchildren visited him, they were instructed to make no sudden noises and to keep their voices low. He seldom spoke and suffered all his life from the wounds and gas of the Great War. At this time he became increasingly worried about Mary. She would visit him at his house in Yarmouth and they would walk together by the sea. Mary recalled only two intimate conversations with her father during the course of her life. In one, she had reminded him of how as a child during the First War she had taken a terrier for a walk on the cliffs in Devon and when the dog disappeared down a hole she had sent urgently for her father, who was at home on leave. When he came running up with a spade, it was to find the dog above ground, safe and sound, and he had cursed. Many years later Mynors said he was sorry, it had been due to the strain of his life in the trenches, something he could never discuss. Mary asked him if he had not confided in her mother and he had said emphatically not. This had taught her how much more difficult it had been for the men who had fought in the First War.

The other time they talked intimately was a few years before his death when her father had told her how concerned he was about her. He had said he was going to ask some wealthy Huguenot cousins who were spinsters if they would leave her their money. Mary had laughed and predicted that they would simply find out which member of the family was richest, and leave all their money to him. Mynors had replied, 'They couldn't be so mean.' She never received any family money, but, some years later, she noticed that her brother Hugh had acquired a number of rather good pictures.

Colonel Farmar's concern also extended to his youngest grandson, William Siepmann. He suggested that Mary should contact the French Protestant Trust 'which was endowed by two of my Mother's ancestors', and which had already treated Susan 'with such generosity'. The Trust had largely paid for the education of Susan's children when she was widowed. Mynors frequently mentioned the pressing need to help Mary but before he could organise a rescue operation he died at his house in Yarmouth on the Isle of Wight in June 1961. Mary was so upset that she fell ill but she could not stay in bed for long. Susan, who had looked after Mynors in his last weeks and repeatedly told Mary that he did not want to see anyone, arranged the funeral for Mary's birthday, which fell only two days after their father's death. Mary called Toby and asked him to accompany her to the funeral saying, 'They won't let Eric into the house.' They arrived at the crematorium just in time to meet the congregation coming away, because Mary had been given the wrong time for the service. The nurse who had been looking after Mynors told Mary that, contrary to what Susan had told her, her father in his last days had been asking for her 'all the time'. That evening Mary said to her sister-in-law Constantia, 'Susan kept me away' and Constantia replied, 'Us too.'

As Mary drove home from the funeral by herself, there was a curious incident that she always regarded as a response to prayer. She was passing through Shaftesbury when she noticed, through her tears, a sign to the Catholic church and so decided to stop and ask the priest for help. Here, in deepest Dorset, the priest turned out to be a Frenchman, Father Jeanneau. He was busy on the telephone to France, urging on a group of angry Breton *paysans* who were throwing their produce on to the road. Mary recalled him thundering down the line, 'More artichokes, throw more.' But he found time to talk to her and he insisted on knowing her father's name. Then he told her that she had come to the right place because he knew more about her family than she did – he considered himself to be the leading authority on the English Huguenots. And so they sat together in the gloom for a long time, talking, while he pulled papers from the dusty archives in his study and tried to comfort her, as Mynors might have done, by reconstructing the story of the family that had cast her out.

PART FOUR

1970–2002

CHAPTER FOURTEEN

Nothing Left to Give

'Life is like that. Things that are not on the menu keep on happening.'

Mary Wesley

As the years passed the chances of Eric writing a book that would change their fortunes began to fade. Harry Siepmann, who had no opinion at all of his younger brother's ability to earn a living and support a family, wrote of Mary's predicament, 'The only way to make literature a cottage industry is to do as a friend of mine has lately done; make and put aside £100,000 before retiring into the country ... [but] poor Mary will, no doubt, continue to march resolutely towards the stake ...' Increasingly, at Thornworthy and later, Mary lived in the shadow of Eric's struggle with his inner demons, leaving jobs, abandoning unfinished manuscripts, insulting strangers, quarrelling with his neighbours, drinking himself periodically into oblivion. His stepson, Toby, said that he had 'a genius for taking offence'. That was one side of the coin; the other was equally isolating. Jenifer Murray remembered his impatience with the human race, provoked by the fact that they were not as bright as he was: 'He was very witty but he had few friends because he was so unkind.' Mary summarised his character in the last year of her life in a deadly phrase: 'He was his own destroyer.'

But the process of self-destruction was a gradual one and much of it was almost light-hearted. Eric clawed his way up from one black depression by pointing out his own defects: 'I am of course, mentally-diseased. The job is to make my neurosis profitable.' He was always full of hope and new stratagems. 'If I can't do my Russian book ... I do not need to despair. I can write comic books which is (perhaps) my metier. Both, however involve work, which is not, yet, my habit.' This was written in 1962, ten years into his career as a full-time writer. He kept Mary alert by adroit changes of pace. 'Please don't bribe me with sex . . .' he entreated, shortly before returning home with a briefcase full of another project that was failing to get off the ground. Left alone in charge of the house, he encouraged Mary to return in view of his desperate circumstances: 'Betty [the cleaner] prays aloud that I cannot start the Raeburn.'

In one of his letters to Emily Holmes Coleman Eric described his life as 'a series of moral collapses, interspersed by light'. Eric's 'moral collapses' were invariably the result of drink. His son Bill made the point when, aged nine, he sent his father a birthday card reading 'Happy Hangover!'. Mary once told Jenifer Murray that she could never leave Eric for long because he always got into trouble while she was away. One day, when Mary was in London, Mrs Murray's telephone rang; it was Eric and she heard his voice saying, 'Mary's gone to stay in the Ritz with a Pole. Would you like a drink?' Jenifer called her husband, Patrick, to the telephone but Eric said, 'I don't want a drink with you, I was trying to get hold of Jenifer.' This call caused so much trouble in the Murray household that Jenifer reported Eric to Mary on her return and there was a temporary chill in their friendship. Apart from the mischief there were also the outbreaks of violence. The first time Mary visited St Peter's in Rome she had glass in her eye after an evening when Eric had become 'frighteningly drunk'. In order to stop him from leaving the Hotel d'Inghilterra in the middle of the night Mary had thrown all his clothes out of the window, and they had to be recovered next morning from the garden by a *valet de chambre*. Years later Mary woke Toby up one night to tell him that 'Eric has done a Marilyn Monroe'. He was in a drunken and pill-induced stupor, and together they had to carry him upstairs to bed.

Then, in 1960, after five years on Dartmoor, something occurred that was entirely 'off the menu'; Phyllis Jones bought Mary a house. At Stanbrook Abbey, Emily had made a thirty-day sequence of prayer that Eric and Mary would somehow be able to find the money to stay at Thornworthy. This prayer was answered in an unexpected way when, in Rye, Phyllis Jones's mother died. Phyllis, who was Mary's godmother, decided that she already had enough money and did not need a house in Rye. So she sold the house and gave the money to Mary – who used it to abandon Thornworthy and buy a farmhouse at Otterton, near Budleigh Salterton, in Devon. The purchase was made in a rush, so much so that Toby, who was about to start at Oxford, knew nothing of it until Eric and Mary had moved. During the move, Mary sent Eric to Buckfast for a retreat and dealt with the business without him. The diary entries are brisk: '*11th August*: Eric to Buckfast. Move out. *12 August*: Move In. *18 August*: Fetch Eric.'

It was in this house, called Basclose Farm, over the Christmas holiday in 1960 that Toby told Mary how much he liked Father Paul Ziegler; and, in response, acting on impulse, Mary told him that Paul's brother Heinz, who had died in the war, was his father.

The new house was big enough for Eric to continue coaching, but Otterton was to the east of Exeter and they did not stay there long. It was too far from her beloved Dartmoor and Basclose Farm was too close to the pub. By August 1962 they had moved again, to a rented property, Priory Cottage, Ashburton, just beneath the moor near Buckfast. It was not ideal, but it had four spare rooms for Eric's students and it would do until they found something on the moor – and there was no pub within walking distance. It had the further advantage that it was close to Dartington, the progressive school outside Totnes to which Mary and Eric had decided to send Bill, with financial assistance from Devon County Council.

Ashburton had one disadvantage: the town constable. Mary considered that this man had got his knife into her and that she was receiving too many parking tickets. She decided to ring the Chief Constable of Devonshire, at home, and warn him that if something was not done 'he would have a murder on his hands'. For some reason this call did not lead to her arrest; instead, the Chief Constable came round and they had a little talk, after which the parking tickets stopped.

It was while they were living at Priory Cottage that Lieutenant the Hon. Roger Swinfen Eady of the Royal Scots announced his engagement to Miss Patricia Blackmore, and Mary was faced with a familiar ordeal, a family wedding. The service was held at Chagford church on Dartmoor in October 1962. Two days later Mary wrote to Phyllis Jones giving an account of the occasion.

Darling Phyl,

You and Emily *should* have been there. It was the most original, prettiest and funniest wedding I have ever attended. The Bride looked lovely and behaved beautifully, Roger was magnificent . . . [and] spoke up loud and clear. Eric cried (he so loves the boys). All Chagford turned up in a body, asked or not . . . Billy crossed himself ostentatiously and boomed out several Hail Marys and Our Fathers . . . Toby made Billy drunk so that he slept laid out on a sofa at the reception. There was a splendid mixture of farmers, shopkeepers, so-called County and family and with bottles popping everyone mixed to perfection. I think Roger was very happy and Pat looked in seventh heaven and very pretty . . . I don't think Brendan Behan or any Irish Wake could have made it go with a greater swing . . . Alice got drunk and had a topping time and I was very proud of my sons, fair, dark and behaving. They all showed sweet and marked affection towards Eric, Alice and me . . . No knives (except verbal) were drawn. No smelling salts required . . . If I fell down at the end 'it was your high heels' as Alice charitably put it. Eric spent yesterday in bed but is all right now. It was a *success*. All love, Mary.

But the letter also contained darker passages showing that Mary had not forgotten her father's death and had mentally and physically divided her guests into two groups.

> . . . Roger got his way and 'put the people I love in front of everyone else'. That is Alice and Eric and Billy. The stepmother, grandmother [Violet] *and* Susan were packed away at the back . . .
> . . . My Mother, who is as mad as they come, got swept off her feet by Eric, my sister was told by Eric in clarion tones for all to hear that 'Money is a sacrament' – he had been saving this one up . . .
> . . . Susan [was] utterly and uncharitably crushed and kept penned in a corner so that [she] could do no mischief . . . The entire village came up to my mother and told her until her ears could hear no more that Eric and I and the boys are the only people they love . . .

Roger's wedding was the last time that Mary was able to put on a show of prosperity and independence in front of her family. Shortly afterwards, in January 1964, there was a more serious setback, as she later recalled:

> 'I'd gone up to London for the funeral of Biddy, the Irish cook I'd inherited from my brother when we were living in Ovington Square before the War.' That afternoon Mary returned to Devon by train, and as soon as she got to the gates of the property she knew that something was wrong. 'The drive was covered in glass and there was no car. Eric was the world's worst driver. That afternoon he had gone to fetch Bill from school and just outside the house a lorry shed its load directly onto our car. When I arrived Eric was upstairs in bed, covered in broken glass; and all he could say was "True's dead" [referring to the dog].

*   *   *

(*Above*) Colonel Paynter at Boskenna with local solicitor, Paul Hill, who became Betty's second husband in 1947.

(*Right*) Eric Siepmann – introduced to Boskenna and to Mary's children.

(*Left*) Eric Siepmann's former wife, Phyllis, arriving at the Divorce Court. *Evening Standard*, 26 July 1951. She had done all in her power to break up Mary's relationship with Eric, whom she had 'stalked' with ingenuity.

(*Above*) Eric and Mary with Roger and Toby: a new family.

(*Left*) Mary, in 1951 aged thirty-nine.

(*Above left*) Toby and Sonya, 1952. Mary treated the schoolgirl Sonya as her daughter, and had her to stay during the holidays, especially at Knoll House where she lived a more conventional life. (*Above right*) Toby holds Carol in a bear-hug. Roger, Averil's son Roderick Knowles, Carol's second wife Averil, Carol, Toby.

(*Right*) Eric with Billy, as a baby, and the dog Pebble, July 1954.

(*Left*) Mary and Roger kissing goodbye.

(*Above left*) Toby in Venice with Hans Ziegler and Hans's son, Henry (on the left).
(*Above right*) Father Paul Ziegler, a monk of the Benedictine Abbey of Quarr.

(*Above*) Cullaford Cottage, on Dartmoor, Eric and Mary's last home.

(*Right*) Mary, widowed, at Cullaford Cottage – elegance and freezing cold.

(*Right*) Mary, walking the dog on Dartmoor, at the bleakest time of her life, after Eric's death and while she was struggling to write *Jumping the Queue*. She is wearing Eric's watch.

(*Left*) Mary, the bestselling novelist. At a publication party with her long-term editor, James Hale.

(*Above*) Mary rejuvenated: with Robert Bolt, Sarah Miles and Kate Ganz. Umbertide, Italy.

(*Right*) Alice Grenfell's 90th birthday: Sonya, Bill, Toby, Alice and Mary.

(*Overleaf*) Mary Wesley, the established writer, in old age.

Following the car crash in 1965, Eric never fully recovered his health and from then on the Siepmann family income more or less ceased. Mynors had left his money to Hugh, intending that Susan and Mary should inherit their mother's money. Since Violet was still alive, this meant that Hugh was now wealthy and Susan was secure – having married a man with a talent for making money. Mary, who had the most need of money, had the least. Later she said, 'I thought your family were meant to stand by you when you were in trouble . . . My brother and sister were both rich but neither lifted a finger.'

In fact, Susan had lifted a finger. Unknown to Mary, four months after their father died Susan had written to Hugh: 'There is no doubt in my mind that something will have to be done about Mary if she is not to suffer great hardship as she grows older.' She added that 'the whole matter of Mary's life' had distressed their father very much. But Susan had sent no money and the correspondence continued for four years while Hugh and Susan's husband, Stephen Scammell, worked out a suitable scheme. The initial delay was caused by the manoeuvring between Hugh and Stephen Scammell as to who should give Mary the money she needed. This ended in 1962 when Scammell wrote to Hugh listing some of the family bequests and legacies Hugh had already received. In a letter that stopped just short of accusing Hugh of sharp practice, Scammell suggested that, in view of his wealth, Hugh should pay Mary £600 p.a.

Hugh replied in a furious note, dated 21 March 1962, 'I was astounded by [your letter's] assumption of the right to interfere in my private affairs. I do not propose to reply to your letter except to say that my Father and I understood each other perfectly, whatever you may surmise. Also I am accustomed to keep my promises, both to my Father and to other people and I have Mary's position well in mind. We had better, I think, not discuss this matter any further.' Susan had to make the peace with a further urgent plea on behalf of Mary. There was then another delay of three years as Hugh Farmar's proposals were refined by Stephen Scammell to make them less costly and more tax-efficient, and during this process Scammell, who was already – as Mynors's executor – responsible for paying some of Mary's monthly income, gradually gained the ascendancy over Hugh.

In November 1962 a letter from Scammell to Hugh Farmar shows the extent to which the former had mastered Farmar family politics. Hugh's idea was to transfer a capital sum to Mary. Scammell put him off: 'Although I do not want to manufacture difficulties, there are I think a number of reasons why your proposal would not work.' This letter was written two weeks after Roger's wedding which Scammell had not attended, but Eric's witty remark to Susan about 'Money being a sacrament' had not been forgotten. Scammell continued, 'I think Eric Siepmann may well survive Mary. One does not want therefore to hand over . . . capital which might in such case eventually accrue to him . . . [Mary] is all one is concerned for.' Another passage shows the extent to which Scammell felt he could safely interfere in Mary's family life.

It would be I suggest a great pity to make Roger a trustee [of Mary's settlement]. A few years ago Mary was running a campaign to convince him [Roger] that he should regard himself as in duty-bound financially responsible for William [his younger brother], and as he is very conscientious this idea worried him a bit at one time! I think and hope he has now rejected it entirely, but the less he is drawn back into that economic vortex the better . . . Toby of course would be quite untrustworthy as a trustee.*

After Eric's car crash in January 1964, Toby, who had just started a career in the City, asked to see Hugh and was invited to lunch with him at Lloyds. It was obvious that Mary now needed help urgently and Toby, who was then earning £750 a year, said that he proposed to give his mother £100 a year, and asked whether Hugh and Susan would do the same. After a pleasant lunch Hugh walked Toby out of Lloyds and said that he could not afford to chip in and that it was not worth approaching Susan since she 'would never agree'. Realising the urgency of the situation, Toby then wrote to Hans Ziegler, Heinz's middle brother who was living in America; Hans sent Mary $500 and continued to help her every year until he died in 1981.

Toby's visit may have nudged Hugh into action. For three years Hugh had achieved nothing apart from writing to Harry Siepmann, pointing out the seriousness of Eric's situation. Hugh had suggested that it would be better to wait until matters had reached a crisis and Harry Siepmann had agreed. 'I despair of persuading either of these hopeful refugees (i.e. from "reality") . . . It would take more than a small material inducement to deflect them,' Harry Siepmann replied. In any event, in March 1965 – by which time Mary had been fired from a part-time job as a French teacher in a

---

* An early example of Stephen Scammell's manners. Toby was twenty-one years old and still at university.

prep school when the headmaster discovered that she had no educational qualifications of any sort – Hugh finally wrote to his youngest sister offering his help. He proposed to set up a trust to pay her £300 p.a., as a gift 'in consideration of his natural love and affection for her'.

Mary expressed her gratitude in a seven-page letter written from a new home on Dartmoor, Cullaford Cottage; it started, 'Darling Hugh, Thank-you so much for your letter. Thank you too for your concern for me.' She said that she and Eric and Bill were very happy in their new cottage, and that they were able to live there far more cheaply than when they were living in Ashburton, 'and with far less strain on the nerves than when we had four or five boys living in the house'. Mary told her brother that the only family money she had been receiving at that point was £5 a week from her mother. She also said that she had never been told anything about any future bequests in her mother's will and 'I certainly have not enquired'.* She mentioned that she had not been able to afford to travel to London since Eric's accident, by then over a year earlier. 'Eric is still not recovered nor do I think he ever will be from his accident, but that is between ourselves.' She said that she had a 'quite excellent lawyer who produced the mortgage for this cottage and watches my interests like a hawk as he came to the conclusion on first meeting me that this was necessary as I was "too unversed in financial matters"'. This lawyer refused to be paid the proper amount for his work. Her bank manager had taught her how to fill in tax returns to save on fees for an accountant, and 'he charmingly sent me off to see the Tax people as he said They would never believe anyone could live on as small an income as we do but [would] suspect us of hiding cash under the bed!'. The tax people had proved helpful. They had said, '"there are too many people round here who pretend to run mink farms at a loss", so they become suspicious.'

Mary said, 'We are earning nothing until Eric gets going with a book . . . I would like to say how *enormously* I appreciate your kindness [but] I do not want you to feel that because you have planned a generosity that I feel I am entitled to it. Constantia and your boys must come first.' In this letter Mary also mentioned that she had just received a letter from Stephen Scammell in which her brother-in-law had – rather belatedly – offered to increase the money paid to her under her mother's covenant by £150 a year, an increase of fifty per cent, if she would 'like him to do so'. She was worried in case this increase meant that Hugh would not go ahead with

---

* As Violet's executor, Scammell should have volunteered this information.

the help he had offered. When combined with the tax relief which came with the covenants it meant that Mary's income for the remaining years of Eric's life amounted to £970 a year. From that she had to pay the mortgage, repair the house, bring up her son and look after her sick husband who, as a formerly self-employed man, received a minimum disability allowance. Fortunately, over the years she had become highly skilled at managing on very little.

Eric Siepmann lived for six years almost to the day after his car accident, but he never recovered his health. For months he tried different remedies and different doctors until in 1965 one abruptly said, 'There's nothing I can do for you. You've got Parkinson's.' 'Eric being Eric went home and read everything he could about the condition. Then he told his sister [Edith], "I'm not going to have Mary dealing with this ghastly disease, it would be too awful."' He was now handicapped by failing physical strength, in addition to his usual self-destructive impulses. Three months after his accident he gave up taking pupils and he wrote to Mary in exhilaration.

He described his coaching, the only way in which he had nearly earned a living, as 'the biggest mistake I ever made'. He had been rereading the reviews and letters he had received for *Confessions of a Nihilist* – and decided that he had been wrong to write the book off as a failure, they were '"brilliant" notices and tributes to my abilities" . . . As for my using you as housemistress, it was . . . "to harness a thoroughbred to a dung-cart!" *I am terribly sorry* . . . We must recapture time and happiness.' The prospect of glittering prizes beckoned him on once more. In June 1966 Eric wrote to tell Mary of a further change of direction: 'I am cannibalising all I have written – except the play – in last 18 months into one book. Thrilling . . . *On s'en tirera* . . . but I am terribly sorry it's a rough patch . . . Best, I feel sure, is to bloody well carry out our intentions and stick it out. You are a marvel and a help and I love you.' His *Journal* for November of that year contains the following note: 'I see now that a murder I committed in New York in 1928 had some influence on my life but at the time I thought nothing of it. Now that the English have become so americanised I can even see that the whole story may be of historical significance, but it didn't strike me that way at the time. I just lived with a girl at 41 west 10th and killed her . . .' (This was presumably an idea for a fiction.)

In July 1967 Eric was still at work and wrote to tell Mary that he had 'finished Part I (34,000 words)' of the work in progress. But his neat, scholarly, pencilled hand has begun to change, '. . . and having it typed helps immeasurably. Like Bill, I can't write decently and a decent size. What is this disease? When I've made money I'll get a tape recorder.' In his next letter the note of desperate optimism was replaced by rage. The local optician, faced with a customer whose eyesight was failing, had swindled Eric into paying five guineas for unnecessary new frames. And in the last letter from a correspondence started twenty-three years earlier, he wrote,

> My darling Pol – . . . We are flourishing thanks to a lovely summer . . . A little work and a little lust. The current *Stern* magazine has a photograph of a [girl] with a figure like yours, looking down and smiling as if she were being had. And I say to myself, that is how Pol laughed and looked down in the gay times. So hurry home. Don't put yourself out. The time to cash in will be when my political thriller . . . has appeared . . . I still AIM to end in September. (Secret! Tell NO ONE. New title is *Maquis International*) . . . I have all that I want in knowing that you and Bill exist. I love you both, and I am proud of you. 'You are my *raison d'être*' . . . to be sung to tune of 'You are my heart's delight'. I kiss you tenderly.

In the following month, August 1967, Eric wrote to tell Mary that Toby had decided to leave the City and go into business as a literary agent. Five years later Toby moved his business to New York. Mary found his absence very hard to bear. He fell in love with a girl called Diana and Mary was furiously jealous. She tried to break up the relationship, to no avail. It ran its course and Toby stayed on in New York, where he could lead his own life. Mary felt that from then on 'he kept away'. It was to be many years before he found a companion who was able, in the words of one of his friends, to 'slip beneath the barbed wire of his mother's disapproval'. The only good news came in 1969, when Mary – who had been writing and throwing everything away for twenty years – sold two children's books. In January she went to London to see two publishers, Faber and Macdonald. In April *The Sixth Seal*, her novel for older children about the survivors of a mysterious world catastrophe, set on Dartmoor and dedicated to Bill, was favourably reviewed in the *New Statesman* by Mary Borg. And in October *Speaking Terms*, an anti-blood sports story for young children, was published. Mary dedicated it to Phyllis Jones, who had, apart from everything else, typed it. When these books appeared Eric 'Wept with joy'.

The *Journal* that records Eric's losing battle to continue writing also logs his spiritual struggles. Emily Holmes Coleman had become very ill in 1964 and had returned to America in 1968. In London Antonia White, also in poor health, was no longer a regular correspondent. Eric continued to visit Buckfast Abbey, but he had become too solitary to feel part of any intellectual Catholic community. 'Does death make life meaningless or Absurd? (Yes!)' That was in March 1965. By December he was writing, 'I am excited by S[imone] Weil and G[eorge] Herbert. I feel as if I had come to life again. (Wrote Toni [Antonia White], Phyl [Phyllis Jones] and Gollancz.) Mary is responsible for all.' Mary appears in the *Journal* repeatedly, sometimes as reassurance or inspiration, sometimes after a row. He notes that he has to be nicer to her and Bill, now aged twelve and an increasingly assertive presence. He slaps Bill who produces two iron bars that he raps together menacingly. Mary chides Eric for shouting. Eric writes, 'I am annoyed by [Bill's] endless assumption that I "count" less than Mary, am – in fact – the weakling of the family. But I can't admit this – to them!' In March 1968 he wrote, '*I face* my life. This (today, here) is all I've got and it won't change! Loneliness? Prison? My whole life I have waited for a complete transformation to be affected by a "best-seller". Now I *must* look in the work itself for my satisfaction?' On 5 April he writes, 'Gave up! (Must make money?)' On the next page the word LOST is surrounded by the words 'June, July, August, September, October, November, December'.

Eric Siepmann's health deteriorated throughout 1969. He stopped writing and jotting down ideas, and he fell silent for long periods of time. For days he and Mary hardly spoke. He could not get out of bed for two days in succession and he found it an effort to walk. He could not concentrate when he read and he could not finish a sentence when he wrote.

In a press interview in 1990 Mary said that Eric had died after contracting pneumonia while she was away for a few days: 'By the time I got back he had gone into a coma and then he died.' In the last year of her life Mary gave a fuller account.

Eric had always been intolerant of children in the house and for that reason Bill usually spent part of his school holiday with Alice Grenfell in Cornwall. On 27 December 1969, Mary drove Bill to Penzance, then returned to Combe. Bill's term started on 6 January and on Sunday the 4th Mary went back to Penzance to spend the night with Alice and bring Bill home.

That day Eric looked so miserable. I was going to get Bill and I said, 'I'll never leave you alone again.' It was a very stupid thing to say. When we got back I saw to my horror that the cat dishes were full. If you do that the cat will leave most of it, so he must have done it the previous night so that the cat would not go hungry. He was upstairs asleep. Next morning the roads were icy. I took Bill to school and when I got back he was still asleep. I called a neighbour who was an ex-nurse. She told me to call an ambulance. The ambulance could not get down the lane to our house because of the snow. They had to take his stretcher up on a tractor. He never regained consciousness. He died in Torbay Hospital three or four days later. He had killed himself, as he had told his sister he would.

Among those who wrote to comfort Mary were Maurice Bowra and Patrick Kinross. John Betjeman's letter described Eric as 'kind, funny, brave and clever' and added, 'I often used to talk to Eric of Otto Siepmann and Clifton'. Philip Toynbee wrote an obituary for *The Times* and he and his wife invited Mary to stay. Her brother Hugh sent her £100 and arranged for the Drapers' Guild to make a grant towards Billy's education. Father Paul Ziegler obtained permission from the abbot to stay at Cullaford Cottage, but Mary told him that she did not want him. Eric's despairing death had triggered a crisis in her faith, as she confessed in a letter to Antonia White.

Inside the front cover of Eric's last bound *Journal* he placed a sheet of printed paper that he had used when he was coaching; it was a standard report form for Common Entrance candidates. On the back he pencilled his own epitaph – or suicide note. It is almost the only complete manuscript to have escaped this failed writer's waste-paper basket and it lay unread for twenty-four years following his death.

Here at my desk I mock my fate,
If help comes now it comes too late.
The valued pictures in my mind
By sheer neglect have made me blind.

My dream deserved a steady look,
I failed to put it in a book,
And now, and now I cannot see,
My dream destroyed reality . . .

No fact consoles me for my flight,
No truth can give me back my sight,
No dream can make me think I see,
No life is left, so bury me.

CHAPTER FIFTEEN

Nothing Left to Lose

'I think the main thing, don't you, is to keep the show on the road.'
                                                              Elizabeth Bowen

The years that followed Eric's death were a time of creative sterility for Mary as well as years of poverty and despair. In 1973, still deeply troubled by Eric's death, she wrote to Antonia White, her godmother, seeking guidance or comfort. Antonia White replied on 1 August.

Dearest Mary,

What can I say? Your letter moved me so much. I do understand now why you feel as you do. If only, only you would not be so hard on yourself. Of course there came a point in Eric's illness when you were so mentally and emotionally exhausted that you felt you had 'nothing more to give' and thought 'what a mercy for me if he died'. I think why you feel this awful guilt is that you did not pray for the supernatural – and it would have been supernatural – strength to bear what was more than human nature could stand. Yet, Eric himself must have reached a point where the illness and the future were too much for him and it would be a mercy for him if he died. Of course the way it happened - and perhaps you will never know – makes you blame yourself so terribly because you had those thoughts. You gave him everything you had – no woman ever gave a man more or loved him more – and, darling, you must accept his forgiveness – and God's – for what you feel you did wrong . . .

Very much love,

Tony

Her mother, Violet Farmar, had died in 1971 and Mary started to receive
a small annual allowance as her sole inheritance. She needed money even
more urgently than usual. She was worried about her youngest son, Bill.
Having abandoned Catholicism and left school, he had gone to London to
become a Trotskyite. In 1974, aged twenty, he wrote to say that he had no
work and that – having been thrown out of a London squat – he was sleeping
'under a tree in Regent's Park'. A Siepmann cousin put her in touch with
an American couple, the Dorments, who were looking for a quiet place where
the husband, Richard, could finish a book. His wife, Kate Ganz Dorment,
wrote to Mary, who replied on 14 February, 'We really ought to meet and
find out how much you can pay . . . [so that] . . . I can make a profit as I am
fearfully poor and only want to let to make some money for my "going
abroad" fund or paying the mortgage or the rates or just breathing!' They
arranged to meet at Totnes station, Mary saying that she would be wearing
'a red weskit', Kate wondering whether she would be greeted by a bag lady
draped in some sort of bedspread. The visit was a success, the Dorments
took the cottage and Kate Ganz quickly became a close friend.

Kate remembers that the cottage was incredibly cold, and that Mary was
broke. She tried to help, but Mary was too proud to cash cheques and sometimes returned cash as well. Eventually Kate devised a scheme whereby she
found work for Mary, knitting sweaters for their friends, for which Kate
paid. In response Mary wrote, 'Darling Kate, Thank you for your letter and
shower of cheques and fivers. *Too much!* I return one, we can squabble about
the rest later. You paid for your wool you know . . .' They revelled in each
other's company; Mary was delighted to have a young New York art historian as her friend. 'I wish I were a young Jew instead of an old gentile,' she
wrote on the outbreak of the Yom Kippur war (October 1973) in a strongly
pro-Israeli tone. In August 1974, following a visit from her grandchildren,
Mary told Kate that she was 'almost working again', and three months later
she could report that she had 'got 17,000 words into a book', *Jumping the
Queue*. But, between those two letters, she had written in her diary on 26
October, the anniversary of her first meeting Eric –

> 30 years –
> Hold my hand
> Stay close
> Don't leave me
> Drive carefully

– phrases that read like last words exchanged before she left Eric on a winter's night to drive to Cornwall to fetch their son.

The following April she wrote to Kate to say that she was stuck halfway through *Jumping the Queue* and could 'only look at it sourly'. Lack of money had forced her to abandon her usual programme of Christmas family visits, and isolated in the cottage she had become 'bored and suicidal'. This mood was to last for several more years. In January 1978, she first wrote '<u>Please</u> do NOT Resuscitate' in the front of her diary. In February 1979, she wrote to Kate again. 'I am surviving. It takes up all my time and energy and I have long since passed the point of wondering what am I bothering to survive for, for God's sake?' And she was still struggling with the same book twelve months later.

In February 1977 Mary had written to Carol for the last time. She knew that he was very ill.* She told him that she had been working in an antique shop for two years and 'though it barely paid for my petrol to get there . . . I really enjoyed it'. She did not mention the book she had finished which was about a widow contemplating suicide. Instead, following the death of Carol, she seems to have made a serious attempt to find a publisher for *The Fruits of My Follies*. The agency, David Higham Associates, sent it out as 'by Mary Siepmann'; she subsequently scribbled out that name and changed it to 'by M.S.'. This made no difference and the typescript joined the small pile of unpublished material she bothered to keep. The fact that she was prepared to publish the memoir shows how little she thought of the trouble it could cause. Mary's sole achievement as a writer during these years was when Virago republished *The Shutter of Snow* in 1981 and the publisher Carmen Callil (who had just rejected *Jumping the Queue*) asked her to contribute a brief portrait of Emily Holmes Coleman to the Introduction.

Among his cousins it was thought that Roger was neglected by his mother and treated with less affection than Toby, that Mary, in other words, had never really managed to carry out the promise she had made in 1951 'to defend and fight for him'. Mary was aware of this criticism; as she wrote in old age '. . . Roger has been stuffed by my family with the idea that I deserted him and have been a thoroughly rotten mother . . .' At other times Mary felt guilty about her role as a mother and considered that she had failed all three of her sons. A pattern of family preference and exclusion

* He was to die four weeks later.

can be traced through three generations. Hyacinthe Wellesley and William Dalby were supposed to have preferred Violet to her sisters; Violet certainly preferred Susan and excluded Mary; Mary herself was accused of preferring Toby and excluding Roger; rivalry between the children grew with each generation. This rivalry was to have destructive consequences and was further enflamed by the circumstances of Eric's death.

By January 1970, when Eric Siepmann was dying, Roger had left the army and qualified as a chartered surveyor. He and his wife Patricia were expecting their fourth child, and were living in a large country house near Canterbury, in Kent. When Eric was taken to hospital in a coma, Toby was in Toronto. Mary arranged for Bill to stay at school as a temporary boarder and a neighbour telephoned Roger to give him the news. He decided to drive down to Devon to be with his mother. In her anguish over Eric, Mary needed to reconnect, to gather her family round her. She told me,

'When Eric killed himself it was awful, mid-winter. I had this idea of getting all my family close, and so – trying to get close to Roger again – I told him about Toby's father. I was feeling so desperate. Never in my wildest dreams did I think it had anything to do with money. Some time later Roger needed tax advice. I warned against but he went to see Stephen Scammell, and Scammell turned the affectionate brothers against each other. He started plotting how to stop Toby inheriting from Carol.'

In June 1971, Violet Farmar died. Mary had seen very little of her mother in the ten years since Mynors's death. When she did go to Yarmouth, she generally took the opportunity to visit Father Paul Ziegler in nearby Quarr Abbey. Mary considered that, in her life, she had four close relationships that failed; the one that troubled her the most was the one with her mother. She knew that her father had loved her, even though his love could never be expressed. Her sister she frankly loathed. And although she greatly regretted the destruction of her relationship with her oldest son, she was confident that the offence had not been hers. But with her mother, Mary remained wary and respectful, almost plaintive, even in her final dislike.

The immediate consequence of Violet's death was that the influence of Stephen Scammell over Mary's financial affairs increased. He became solely responsible for managing her very small income from the Farmar family trusts. Despite knowing how poor she was, Scammell repeatedly failed to pay Mary's monthly allowance on time. She resented both this and his growing hold over her son, Roger.

During the early 1970s Roger Eady got into financial difficulties and
borrowed money from Scammell. He also approached the Swinfen Trust
for an advance against his eventual entitlement. Both Roger and Toby were,
at various times, advanced money from the Trust, with Carol's approval,
but in November 1976, five months before his death, Carol Swinfen wrote
to his fellow trustee as follows. 'Dear Derrick, I am concerned at Roger's
(latest) request. I am sure that in the past I have been seriously over-
generous in acceding to these requests . . . I have had no personal news
from him for many months . . . These advances put me in the embarrassing
position of feeling that what I do for him I ought always to feel prepared
to do for my younger boy Toby as well.' By then Roger had become critical of his father's use of Trust funds, objecting in particular to money being
spent on Averil Swinfen's donkey stud in the west of Ireland. As Roger
Eady's financial difficulties grew, he fell increasingly under the influence
of Stephen Scammell. He attacked his father for misusing the Trust and
diminishing his inheritance, and he told Carol that Mary had told him that
Toby was not Carol's son. Soon, Carol and Roger were barely on speaking
terms.

In view of this rift with Roger, Carol asked Toby to look after his widow,
Averil. By then, Carol himself had told Toby that he had always loved him
and considered him as his son, and that he continued to recognise him as
such, despite anything that may have happened during the war.

Carol Swinfen died in March 1977. For as long as he was alive, his wish
– part of his long understanding with Mary, to treat Roger and Toby equally
– prevailed. But following his death the initiative in settling his estate passed
to Stephen Scammell. Between 1977 and 1982 Scammell, in his capacity as
adviser to Roger Eady, now Lord Swinfen, and therefore to the trustees, waged
an energetic campaign to gain control of the Trust and to disinherit Toby,
using tactics that were as subtle or as brutal as he judged most effective.

It was at this time that Mary apparently started to think of suicide. An
appeal she had made to Toby in January 1979 to spend more time with her,
had failed. Any comfort or guidance she or Eric might have received from
their Catholicism seems to have waned after the Vatican Council's decision
to abandon the Tridentine Rite in 1965. To a large extent they were both
victims of the Council. It had been the beauty and certainty supplied by
the old Mass that had originally attracted Mary to the Church and that
nourished her faith. The monks at Buckfast no longer sang the Daily Office
in Latin, and so, on the advice of a Catholic friend, the publisher Nigel
Hollis, she started to attend Sunday Mass at Syon Abbey, a small convent

outside Totnes where the New Rite was celebrated with the minimum of change. Alarmed by the worsening situation between Roger, Toby and the Swinfen trustees she tried to make the peace for the last time in April 1978 when she invited 'Susan and Stephen' to spend two days with her at Cullaford Cottage. It was shortly after this visit that she abandoned any thoughts of peace-making when Scammell hired a private detective and sent the man down to Cornwall to interview Alice Grenfell, by then aged eighty. He wanted to discover as much as possible about Mary's life during the war. Scammell also wrote to Carol's widow, Averil Swinfen, whose inheritance was frozen by the dispute; he was trying to win her round to give evidence in favour of Roger, and against Toby and Mary. In order to put pressure on Averil he hinted at social disgrace, knowing that other problems in Averil's family made her vulnerable and easily alarmed.

By this time Scammell effectively owned Roger's family home. On inheriting the title Roger had demanded compensation from the Trust for the money he claimed his father had misspent. He had also moved to have Toby barred as a trustee. Scammell now advised him that he must go further.

In 1978, one year after his father's death, Roger Swinfen informed the family trustees that he had been told by his mother that his middle brother was illegitimate; this meant that Toby could not be a beneficiary of the trust and that Carol's Will was therefore invalid. When taking this step, Roger was assured by the trustees that a letter from Mary denying the suggestion would settle the matter. In fact, behind Roger's back, Scammell raised the stakes. The professional trustees had complained to Roger that Scammell's activities were causing unnecessary expense to the Trust; Scammell now retaliated by threatening them with a court action for mismanagement on the grounds that they had ignored Roger's information. The Swinfen trustees, a legal firm based in Jersey, then decided that they were obliged to seek a direction from the High Court. In June 1980, Roger received a writ, and in reply he formally requested that his brother be legally disinherited and declared illegitimate. Mary's diary entry for 29 June 1980 was 'Roger's body blow at Toby'.

It was during the following winter that Mary, alone in the cottage on Dartmoor, fell seriously ill and was forced to sell her house. She was not only worried about Toby, she was also disturbed by Scammell's influence over Roger. She felt responsible for the whole situation and she felt guilty about the problems caused for Carol's widow and for his nephew and niece,[*] the other beneficiaries of the Trust – none of whom could draw on their

---

[*] Venice, once her bridesmaid, and Venice's brother, Peter Myers.

capital or income until the matter was settled. On 16 March 1981, the day
of her recovery from double pneumonia, Mary wrote a six-page letter to
Averil, pouring her heart out.

> I am so sad and ashamed of what Roger [is] doing. He has not been near
> me for over a year and never tells me anyway, but they seem to be ma-
> nipulated by my brother-in-law and that too is awful . . . Carol would have
> hated it . . . I feel unhappy and responsible and angry that something
> which was decided by Carol forty years ago should now be questioned.
> He was an extraordinarily good and fair man as you know even better
> than I and to have this happen after his death is monstrous . . . It does
> seem sad when Carol loved Toby and Toby Carol and I feel sad and
> responsible and I must say ashamed of Roger . . . [Do] try, as I must, to
> forgive Roger. He is obstinate and weak . . . and now being manipulated
> by a very clever man. I wish I could stop it but I don't see how I can.
> All I can do is be uncooperative, I am quite good at that. Affectionately,
> Mary.

Mary also wrote to Roger warning him that he was being manipulated and
asking him to drop his attack on Toby, but Roger merely passed his mother's
letter to Scammell, who replied on 7 April 1981 in his most ingratiating
and sinister manner.

> Dear Mary,
>   Roger has told me of your letter, and I write because evidently you
> have been misinformed of the position. (I would be very interested to
> know by whom!) The Channel Islands solicitors have as I know made
> mischief by giving a wholly false account of the position, so perhaps you
> had it from them, if not direct then perhaps via Toby. I am not
> 'Manipulating' Roger. Roger was on the edge of bankruptcy following
> the folding up of his job, and I am trying to sort out his difficulties . . .
> I suppose eventually you will be asked for an affidavit, and you should
> I think then take legal advice as to whether to give it or to decline to
> give it. As far as I know the court could not then compel you to give it,
> but I suppose they would draw conclusions from the refusal.

Scammell's objective was plain. While apparently aiding Roger to overcome
his 'difficulties' he was in fact attempting to increase Roger's share of the
Trust Fund (and thereby his own). By putting the trustees on notice of
legal action he was freezing the distribution of Carol's estate and of all Trust

monies, so exerting pressure on the beneficiaries to cooperate. And he now started to bully Mary, whose precarious way of life he knew well.

A comparison of Scammell's letters to different correspondents clarifies his tactics. To Roger he is a concerned ally; to the professional trustees he is a threatening presence. To Mary he blames the Trust's solicitors, while issuing a veiled threat about her being forced to give evidence. In another part of the letter he blames the whole business on Carol for making a mess of his Will and suggests that it is Averil who now owes Toby money in compensation. He declares that there must have been 'misunderstandings' and laments the whole 'wretched' business (which is in fact largely of his own making). When writing to lawyers he uses a competent typist, when muddying the family waters and issuing threats in private correspondence he types the letters himself.

Meanwhile the case of *Swinfen Trustees v. Baron Swinfen and others** moved forward. The High Court was to be asked to rule on Toby Eady's status as Carol Swinfen's legitimate son. The evidence would have to come mainly from Mary and Roger – Alice Grenfell having seen off the private detective with a flea in his ear. In September 1981 Roger duly swore a nine-page affidavit recounting the conversation he remembered having with Mary at the time of Eric's death and asserting that his mother had installed a 'live-in lover' during the war while she was still at Ovington Square. This was a reference to the hapless baronet, Derry Bethune, who had once wanted to marry Mary. The only source for the information was his aunt, Mary's sister Susan Scammell. Under this joint barrage, Mary was faced with a dilemma; her stated policy of non-cooperation was not going to be enough. At this point, with a strong hand and in his element, Stephen Scammell took a step too far: in a letter to Averil Swinfen he resorted to open blackmail.

'Dear Lady Swinfen,' he wrote on 6 January 1982, with an air of courteous menace. 'We have never met, and since we live so far apart I suppose we are unlikely to do so. It is a pity, since a conversation can usually get things clear more easily than correspondence. This wretched business of the Settlement has been forced on all of us not by Roger (as I fear Mary and Toby both assume) but by his cotrustees . . .' Scammell then told Averil about an (entirely imaginary) offer he had made to buy Toby out of the Trust, sending her a copy of this, presumably so that she would urge Toby to accept his proposed exclusion. Scammell pointed out that if the offer

* Not its exact name.

was accepted it 'would save Mary from a continuation of these wretched enquiries', a reference to the private detective he himself had set on her. He then made his mistake:

> There is also something else that worries me. And makes me wish very much to see a settlement by agreement. I have not yet seen Mary's . . . affidavit but from what I hear the Court if it decided against (her) would inevitably be saying that (she) had been guilty of perjury. One does sometimes hear of a Court passing the papers in such case to the Public Prosecutor: probably it is unusual: I am making enquiries. But if such a Prosecution did happen it would be appalling. Quite apart from anything else the publicity that is safely avoided in the present case by a private hearing would fall full blast on any perjury proceedings. If on consideration you think the proposal a good one I hope that perhaps you might be able to persuade Toby to agree? . . .

Scammell knew that Averil would probably pass this letter to Toby. She did, but the blackmail backfired. Instead of accepting an offer to abandon his claim Toby decided to sue Scammell for libel.

Counsel's opinion, given in March 1982, was that Scammell's letter amounted to 'a gross and offensive libel . . . as insulting as it is distressing'. The fact that Scammell had not even seen Mary's affidavit when he wrote the letter to Lady Swinfen rendered 'his conduct all the more deplorable'. Even if the court decided against Mary's evidence, there was no question of perjury. 'Mr Scammell is evidently motivated by some personal animosity towards our clients' and 'by a determination to deprive Mr Eady of his interest in the trust . . . We are of course aware that [Mr Scammell] has a personal interest in achieving this result,' counsel concluded.

Some time after Mary Siepmann told Toby of her belief that Heinz Ziegler was his father he asked her why Carol had always recognised him as his son, and she replied that because he had been conceived before her final separation from Carol it was theoretically possible. In law, Toby was the acknowledged and legitimate son of Carol Swinfen and there was no certain evidence to support his mother's private conviction to the contrary. Toby had the strongest possible objection to being declared illegitimate on his brother's allegation, following the self-interested meddling of Stephen Scammell. Mary, who was appalled by Roger's behaviour, agreed to support Toby in any way she could. She realised that she would need a very good solicitor and went to see David Freeman, of D.J. Freeman. In the ensuing case Roger Swinfen and Toby Eady were parties, as was Stephen Scammell, and Mary Siepmann was subpoenaed as a witness. Despite its dramatic nature – the plot straight from Anthony Trollope – the case of the Swinfen Trust went unreported as it was held *in camera*, in the Chancery Division of the High Court.

Mary swore an affidavit on 17 November 1981. In her evidence she said that she was responding to the allegations made by her son, Lord Swinfen. She had met her first husband, Carol Swinfen, the second baron, at a dinner party in London in 1932. 'He was then a practising barrister and the son of the former Master of the Rolls.' She said that they had lived on the income produced by Carol Swinfen's share in his late father's Trust and that they had started out with three domestic servants, reduced to one on the outbreak of war. They had divorced, she had remarried and in January 1970, when her second husband Eric lay dying in hospital, Roger and his wife had come to stay with her, against her wishes. She was heavily-sedated, taking three times the normal dose 'of sleeping tablets and tran-quillisers', but still unable to sleep. Bill, her youngest son aged sixteen, was grief-stricken. Eric had been diagnosed with Parkinson's Disease five years earlier, 'and for two years we had known that he would die. I believed that he had . . . taken an overdose of drugs as he did not want to become a vegetable. He in fact died as the result of a blood clot.' The weather was icy cold. Eric, in a coma and strapped to a stretcher, had been carried on the back of a tractor up the lane to the ambulance, which could not get down the hill to the cottage. 'I had been spending days and nights at the hospital with my husband without sleep . . . I can recollect little of the conversation that I had with [Roger] . . . but I suppose it is possible in my fuddled state that I told him as he alleges, that [Toby] was not the child of his father.'

Mary then admitted that at the time when she conceived her second son in May 1940, she had been having an affair with Heinz Ziegler. He was a Czech and a Lutheran by religion, and a professor of economics, who was working for Lord Vansittart in October 1939, when they met, and who had subsequently obtained a commission in the RAF and talked himself on to active duty. She said that when she had intercourse with Heinz she used a female contraceptive but that when she had intercourse with her husband she used no form of contraception. Following the birth of her second son, Toby, she parted from her husband and drifted apart from Heinz Ziegler. She broke with Ziegler in 1942 and learned later that he was killed in action

in May 1944. 'I only knew of this as I had been informed that he named
me as his next-of-kin in his Service book.' She added, 'To the best of my
information and belief my husband, the father of my son [Roger] was also
the father of my son [Toby].'

It may be that in order to protect her younger son from his older brother,
Mary *was* prepared to swear a false affidavit. Shortly before the case she
told a friend, 'This disgraceful case fills me with shame, to have mothered
such an ass!' But if she was ready to lie she took a reckless gamble. She
expected to be cross-examined on her evidence and she had seen what cross-
examination could do. She had watched Melford Stevenson break Phyllis,
her stalker (who had been lying); and she had sat with Antonia White while
the novelist (who was telling the truth) was reduced to a nervous wreck by
Gerald Gardiner. In following this desperate course of action Mary was not
just protecting Toby; she was also defending the civilised – if unspoken –
agreement she had reached with Roger's father. Carol Swinfen had followed
the Edwardian convention, set out by Ford Madox Ford in *Parade's End*:
'. . . A child born in wedlock is by law the father's, and if a man who's a
gentleman suffers the begetting of his child he must, in decency, take the
consequences: the woman and the child must come before the man, be he
who he may.'

Mary's signature at the foot of her nine-page statement, sworn at Totnes
on 17 November 1981, was a lot wobblier than her diary entries for that
week.

In the event Mary was never cross-examined on her affidavit, though
Scammell kept up the pressure to the last moment. He had inserted himself
into the case as 'the agent of Lord Swinfen'; he had twice overruled his
own counsel's advice to accept that Toby Eady was Carol's legitimate son;
he had repeatedly provided supplementary information intended to support
the allegation and was still refusing to settle two weeks before the case was
due to be heard.

But the Swinfen Trust case was finally settled, after three years, virtu-
ally at the doors of the court. Stephen Scammell had decided that he did
not want to be cross-examined in public before a libel jury on the threatening letter he had written to Averil Swinfen. His bluff had been called.
A Chancery master accepted Mary's evidence, endorsed the validity of
Carol Swinfen's Will and directed the trustees to distribute the Trust Fund
on its original basis. Mary's costs were directed to be paid by the Swinfen
Trust, but were finally settled by Toby. On the front of the letter from her

solicitors confirming the victorious settlement, dated 8 July, 1982 Mary wrote in a firm hand, 'Black cloud lifted'. She was seventy years old and she told Averil Swinfen 'this last two years have aged me twenty'.

The final consequence of the Swinfen Trustees case was noted by Venice in a letter to Mary dated 13 June 1995. She said that she had just heard from Toby that he would be 'bequeathing the Trust share he will inherit from Averil to Roger's children', an intention he had first declared in a letter sent to Mary after the case. Isobel MacLeod thinks that the case was not really about Toby. 'Scammell was about power.' It was a battle between Scammell and Mary.

CHAPTER SIXTEEN

Euphoria

'He's the sort of husband one could borrow for the afternoon.'
Mary Wesley, replying to an enquiry about the husband
of a new friend.

When Mary Wesley looked back on the transformation in her life that had occurred between 10 and 27 July 1982 she said, 'Overnight despair became euphoria.' The fate which had dogged her since Eric's drunken indiscretion in Damascus, twenty-eight years earlier, relinquished its hold. A curse had been lifted. In a strange sequence of events her enemy, Stephen Scammell, was defeated and she no longer had to fear the ordeal of cross-examination in the High Court on her dubious affidavit. Two days later on a Monday morning, she heard that *Haphazard House* had at last been accepted and she was back in business as a children's author. And then, two weeks after that, she was told that Macmillan had offered to buy *Jumping the Queue*. At the age of seventy, she was to be a published novelist. For these two books she received advances of £1,600 – not an enormous sum, but one which tripled her previous annual income. To a woman who had become an expert in scraping by on next to nothing, it was a small fortune. Her accountant greeted the news with the gloomy reflection, 'We shall lose our rebate.'

At some time in 1978 or 1979 Mary reached her lowest point and started to struggle back towards the surface. Completing *Jumping the Queue* was part of the process and her work for the Samaritans, which began at this time,* may also have helped. She managed her recovery without help from her friends – few of whom realised the extent of her despair. Among those who failed to notice was the publisher James MacGibbon, who was a neighbour

---

* She became 'a listener' in August 1979.

in Devon. MacGibbon was a throwback to her pre-war friends, a charming, very good-looking man who had been a member of the Communist Party in the 1930s and had worked for Military Intelligence throughout the war. He was a dedicated philanderer whose relationship with Mary was regarded by some as being closer than friendship. She knew nothing of his work for the KGB. During the war he had passed secret information to the Soviet embassy in London, and he had acted as a Soviet agent, out of ideological conviction, after the war as well.

One morning, standing in the fish queue in Totnes Market, Mary was accosted by Sarah Hollis, wife of the publisher Nigel Hollis, who recognised her from the cover picture of *Jumping the Queue*. They became close friends and after Nigel died at the age of forty-five in 1988 Sarah Hollis wrote to Mary to thank her for her help: '. . . The boys and I regard you as someone really special in our lives – you've been such a loving, encouraging and strengthening friend, part of our family . . . your generosity in every way has truly sustained us – especially me. Giving me strength to grow and be myself.' Sarah remembered Mary in Totnes at this time as a stylish figure in a donkey jacket and a French beret, who no longer had to do dozens of little jobs to keep solvent. She made young friends easily, possibly because she was chronically anxious about Bill and she wanted to understand his generation.

Mary had always had friends in the antiques trade; she appreciated the louche ambience and she had 'the eye' for beautiful objects; through her part-time work in antique shops she was introduced to the mysteries of the trade and was always on the lookout for a bargain that she could sell on at a profit. Asked about one of her friends she said, 'Seems quite respectable. In fact he's an antique dealer and smuggler' and he became the inspiration for one of the characters in *Jumping the Queue*. Another dealer she met in Totnes, Tony Grey, had a shop in the High Street and through him she met a farmer, John Tuckey, described by his friends as 'off-the-wall' and by his daughter Anthea as 'a bit of an old queen who liked dabbling in pictures and antiques'. John Tuckey was at that time in the process of starting an affair that was to end in tears; Mary became his confidante and was eventually to use him and some of the events in his life in her books. Another friend was David Salmon, who with his wife Sara lived near Cullaford Cottage on the moor. David Salmon travelled regularly to Nepal and traded in Tibetan art. He offered Mary marijuana, since alcohol made her feel increasingly ill. It was the Salmons who introduced Mary to another new friend who was the main reason for her overcoming the lassitude and *accidie* that had prevented her for ten years from breaking out of her depression; this was the playwright Robert Bolt.

When Mary first met Robert Bolt – there is a reference to him in her diary in June 1977 but it may have been a year earlier – he was divorced from his second wife, the actress Sarah Miles, and living near Totnes in a manor house 'alone . . . with a large woolly dog . . . riding a veritable monster of a black Japanese motorbike. The first time he rode up to my cottage I was quite alarmed, not knowing who this giant in black leathers and menacing helmet could be.' He soon became one of her knitting customers. In 1979 Bolt left Devon and went into tax exile in Hollywood, where he suffered the stroke that ended his motorcycle career. On his return to England in 1980 he married an old friend, the actress Ann Zane; but the marriage ended almost at once and he asked Mary to find him a good solicitor. She sent him to David Freeman. After Mary moved to Totnes in 1981 Bolt became a regular house guest and came to stay with her over Christmas in 1982. 'We will force our way onto the Salmons for a sumptuous Christmas lunch and maybe even supper,' he wrote when accepting her invitation. He continued to order enormous knitted sweaters. Then he fell in love with Mary and asked her to marry him.

Mary, then aged seventy, was very fond of Bolt, who was twelve years younger than her. Their affair started at the Salmons' beautiful but rather under-heated house on the Moor. Mary had been too well entertained to drive home after supper so she stayed the night, and because the house was so cold she and Robert shared a bed. To the astonishment of her friends she was prepared to cook for him and even to watch Westerns on television with him. But that was as far as it went. 'Bloody woman won't marry me,' Bolt grumbled to Toby. When this was reported to Mary she said, 'There are men you want in your bed, but you don't want them in your head.' Bolt had given her the confidence to concentrate on writing; she was free of Eric's jealousy and she did not want to start a second career as another writer's loving supporter. To comfort Bolt for his disappointment she introduced him to a younger friend who was just divorced. 'He was on the rampage and very angry with me, but responded like a pointer seeing a snipe,' she remembered. However Bolt's relationship with Mary's beautiful young friend did not end in marriage. Instead, he went back to Sarah Miles and they remarried in 1988. But he remained more than a little in love with Mary, as his letters over the following years show. At first he complained to her about his marital complications. ('Goodness, they are a nuisance these ex-wives . . . my third ex-wife is playing up . . . I cannot wait to see you.') She sent him a copy of the proofs of *The Camomile Lawn* and he wrote to thank her. 'Darling Mary, I finished the novel in the early hours of this morning . . . really marvellous. Every unnecessary word honed down . . . I now see what Macmillan's are doing when they plan to make it one of their big sales for next year.' Bolt's writing career was drawing to a close just as Mary's was starting. In 1985 he wrote to commiserate over the inefficient book distribution system. 'You have exactly the same problem over your sales of *The Camomile Lawn* as I have with my plays. I shall ask my booksellers to get it for me, and then I'll let you know what happens. I think there are secret service agents knocking about in the publishers to see which one can sell the least number of books. So far Heinemann is the clear winner . . .'

Following his remarriage to Sarah Miles, Bolt continued to maintain his affectionate friendship with Mary by correspondence. He read her books as soon as they came out. In 1987, referring to *Not That Sort of Girl*, he said, '. . . Far and away the best you have written . . . funny, wise, witty and above all surprising . . . it was so frank about such things as coming, what to do in bed and so on . . .' And in reference to Eric he wrote, '. . . Your man was a very much loved man. I wonder if you know how lucky you have been . . .' In 1988 she dedicated *Second Fiddle*, a novel set in Totnes, to Robert Bolt and in 1989 she wrote a whole page about him in a magazine series, 'My Hero'. His reply came a week later.

Darling Mary, . . . Thank you for writing that adulatory piece in the *Independent*. Here I am offering incredible thanks. I do hope you think that of me. Such a gay, thumbs-in-the-air sort of chap he seems, and so attractive, debonaire. I don't know what to say, except a thousand felications [*sic*] – oh God the spelling, I suppose it will never reach the lofty heights of my previous incompetence . . . I anticipate that the pounds must be rolling into your account in a steady stream now, your name is one to conjure with, your books are discussed, so surely you can get a house with a garden for the dog to take its ease in? I often think of you. I envy you the war years when you seem to have had such a stunning time . . . You have your husband to keep you warm, even when the days and nights are chilly. I suppose you know that all your books are a hymn to him and yourself? Or so at least it seems to me. Extreme thanks for the article, Love, Robert.

In one of his last letters Robert Bolt, who was a firm atheist, remembered the 'Methodist dogmas' which had surrounded his childhood. Now, 'God seems to be a clerical figure, dressed in black, always in black, questioning me on Maths and Latin, on and on . . . My pleasure now is P. G. Wodehouse. It lulls me to sleep after the ten o'clock news . . .' He last wrote to Mary on 18 February 1995: 'Darling Mary, This is a begging letter . . .' He was asking her to plug a forthcoming book in which he was interested. She received the letter on the day he died.

Mary's friendship with Robert Bolt had begun when she was at the low point of her life and it ended, with his death, at the height of her success. He watched her change from a widow, taking in knitting, into a celebrated novelist, but it was a gradual process and her new wealth took several years to arrive. When *Haphazard House* was sold in July 1982, she wrote to her agent, Tessa Sayle, to tell her the good news adding, 'this will give me the *oomph* necessary to get on with the book I am at present writing so slowly . . . I hope to meet you before too long.' The next day she went out to have her hair cut, a reckless piece of extravagance that brought her total visits to the hairdresser that year to four. She also had her horoscope cast. But two months later she was still waiting for the Macmillan advance.

That August, Mary went to Venice on a holiday first suggested by Kate Ganz, and paid for by Kate and Toby. They went shopping and in a small hat shop Mary found what she had always desired, 'a curé's' wide-brimmed black felt fedora that she wore when Kate took her photograph in profile overlooking a canal.* She later described this as her 'lucky hat'.

On Mary's return her daily routine was dominated, as it was for much of the following fourteen years, by 'Work'. *The Camomile Lawn*, which she had been struggling to bring to life since 1980, was restarted. The new version was written on folded sheets of A4 lined paper, without margins, in black ink, and its working title was 'Period Piece'. On page 58 the A4 runs out and the Ms continues on quarto typing paper on the back of part of the typescript of *Haphazard House*. Page 111 breaks up in disorder and turns into a telephone message, or a shopping list or a cry of despair. Written at right angles to the text are the words,

> She's tone deaf
> That's why I love her
> She's a freak,

---

* See book jacket.

then 'Rewrite it', then 'Stanhope Hotel 24th November' and something about 'Mr Paine Logs 1 Belmont Terrace'. Page 112 continues with a conversation between Hamish and Helena about Monika throwing herself over a cliff. The manuscript has words, sentences and half-paragraphs crossed out, and ends two and a half pages short of the published ending. This is an author writing in a tearing hurry, seizing whatever paper comes to hand, heedless of posterity or her typist, liberated from two years of dejected inactivity by an incredible stroke of fortune, a carpenter shoring up an unlooked-for opportunity before it is swept away by the passing seconds. And that was more or less the pace at which she wrote to the end.

Mary started *Harnessing Peacocks* on 12 May 1983, which was two months after finishing *The Camomile Lawn*. The first title, *Jumping the Queue*, had just been published. She wrote no more children's books, despite the fact that *Haphazard House* was shortlisted for the Carnegie Medal, but she published a novel every year for six years and four more novels in the following nine years, a very unusual and possibly unique achievement for a writer whose first adult fiction appeared when she was seventy. An early sign of future success came with *The Times* review of *The Camomile Lawn* by Nicholas Shakespeare. Mary was delighted and said to James MacGibbon, 'I've had this wonderful review. Do you think I could write and thank this Nicholas Shakespeare? He must be such a nice old man.' He turned out to be what Mary called 'An absolute baby. Younger than Bill.' He became a close friend whom she 'saw through several love affairs'. Mary continued to work voluntarily for the Samaritans until 1992, though she gave up knitting for money and working in shops. When she was not writing she spent time with her friends in Totnes and started to make new friends, sometimes because she was able not just to admire their work but to buy it. She asked the sculptor Jilly Sutton to do her head. She ordered her coffin from a local craftswoman, Annie Long, and asked that it be finished in red Chinese lacquer, and she kept it as a coffee table for some time in her sitting room. Her own suggestion that she be photographed sitting up in it for a feature in the magazine *Country Living* was politely declined.

For the first time for many years, Mary started to make female friends. They included novelists such as Barbara Trapido, who tempted her to stay in Oxford with promises of not one but 'two lurchers. (They could both come and wake you up.)' The writer Julia Blackburn first met Mary when her stepmother, one of Mary's neighbours, died and she came to clear out the house. Mary put her straight about how to do this: 'You take everything that means something to you. And then you take anything else you like the look of,' possibly a familiar line in the antiques trade. When Julia Blackburn's marriage was breaking up Mary was worried and used to call her frequently. Rather than disguising her concern in some tactful conversation about the issues of the day, she would say, 'Just checking, just checking.'

Janet Day first came to work for Mary after the publication of *Jumping the Queue*. 'I hate housework,' Mary said. 'You're my touch of luxury.' To start with Mary could afford two hours a fortnight.

We were always Mrs Siepmann and Mrs Day, we were old school. But she wasn't a snob. When people came to the house she would say, 'Do you know Mrs Day? She's my friend, she comes to help me.' She was always up early, she had her bath at seven in the morning. The afternoon was her writing time. A lot of people who get rich and famous seem to lose touch with reality but when I had a bad back she would jump in the car and drive me down to the chiropractor. And she paid my daughter's poll tax when her husband went bankrupt. If it hadn't been for her I don't think I'd be here. Because I could talk to her. She was very understanding. I never knew she worked for the Samaritans. We used to talk about our mothers. She had awful hang-ups about her childhood. She felt she wasn't wanted and she *hated* her sister, but she never talked about her father or her brother. What she put on her plate wouldn't feed a sparrow. Whenever she was ill she was unbearable, but when she got grumpy I just used to ask what side of the bed she got out of that morning. I never recognised that 'Mary Wesley' at all. She hated her voice on the radio and said that she sounded 'a pompous prig'. She was terrible for keeping things to herself. She had cataracts but she never had an operation for them. When she got the shakes I used to say that she could start a new profession as a cocktail shaker. It's obvious she was very troubled about things. Maybe she was too shameful. Because in those days she may have felt ashamed of some of the things she did. Maybe her mother and sister made her feel shame? I think she spent a lot of long, lonely hours. I used to drop in sometimes in the evenings and she was always pleased to see me. But quite often she used to fight off her grandchildren coming. Her granddaughter Katherine was the one she was most comfortable with.

Mary's preference for Katherine Eady, Roger's second child, had started at an early age. The four grandchildren would come to stay with her on Dartmoor during the summer holidays, to be bumped around at speed in the back of the Mini. Her grandchildren remember her as 'always writing'; during their visits, she wrote at her desk every day, even in the 1970s, in the years immediately following Eric's death.

When Katherine was about eight, Mary said, 'Katherine is beautiful. She will be a bolter, like me.' Mary would sometimes stay with Roger and his family in Kent. Roger and Pat began to dread her visits because, they said, she would start them arguing with each other within half-an-hour of her arrival, and they thought that she was unkind to their children, with the exception of Katherine. Roger was also angered by his mother's attentiveness to her favourite. Many years later when Katherine was living with her boyfriend – later her husband – Mary marked her approval of Katherine's choice by welcoming Captain Gareth Davies of the Royal Tank Regiment with the words, 'What beautiful feet. You *must* be good in bed.' She then caused Roger further offence by presenting the young unmarried couple with a splendid double bed. She was unable to attend Katherine's wedding in 1993 because of the breach with Roger and she was very upset on the day, which she spent in a small town in Tuscany walking around the streets in the heat of the afternoon. Mary always identified with Katherine, who was clever and whose looks may have reminded her of her own grandmother, Hyacinthe Wellesley, and who confided in her. By this means Mary maintained a long-distance relationship with Roger, just as her affection for Sally McLaren, Susan's daughter, kept Mary in remote contact with her older sister.

All her life, even up to her ninetieth year, Mary Wesley possessed a warmth and physical magnetism that left a strong impression on her friends. In 1989 Beryl Bainbridge, who was about to go to the Hay-on-Wye Literary Festival, received a scrawled note from someone she did not know whom she described as 'the mysterious Fred', which she forwarded to Mary. Part of the note read,

> I see that there's life even after the latest novel and that you may well live to be in Hay-on-Wye for yet another bun-fight. Darling friend will you do a last favour for me? Also there will be a lovely woman, now about 76, who long ago (1960 to be precise) did me a most extraordinary kindness. She writes under the name of Mary Wesley but only since she was 70. She is really Mrs Eric Siepmann . . . Tell her I've never forgotten her *then*, when *she* thought she'd nothing more to give or *shine* with. You'll do that, won't you, my darling pal?

(On the back of this note Mary pencilled in 'Wolsey'.)

In 1992 Mary received a letter from a distant Wellesley cousin: 'It is difficult to think of you being 80 today . . . God – or Providence – has given you all that is precious, with both hands, beauty, wealth, talent, and Love of men who worshipped you and who enriched your life . . . Your loving, most ancient, 99-years old friend, Valerie.' Another friend who regained contact with her was Bill Armstrong, who had been Paddy Green's radio observer, flying Beaufighters in North Africa. He wrote to her from his home in France in January 1989, 'Boskenna needs a book . . . the path through the hydrangeas to the sea, the haunted wood . . . and that attractive Czech pilot, and drinking in "The First and Last" at Land's End at Christmas – *Que de souvenirs! Que de regrets!* I am coming to England this summer . . . I am looking forward to seeing you again. Your photograph in the *Literary Review* brings you back – that kind but caustic poise I remember. And the laughter lurking. My love, Bill.'

There had been a last grim echo of Boskenna with the departure of Betty, who had gone out with a bang in July 1980 a few weeks after calling on Mary for lunch. In December 1979 Betty's husband, Paul Hill, had been tried for the murder of her lover, a thirty-six-year-old, eighteen-stone Penzance antique dealer who had been trying to break down Betty's front door in order to renew their relationship. Betty was then aged seventy-three. She told Mary that her antique dealer had been a violent drunk and a wonderful lover, the only man who had ever given her an orgasm. Solicitor Hill was acquitted of murder by a Bodmin jury, and left the court with no further stain on his character. His body was found floating in Penzance Harbour in March 1985. Toby remembers him as 'a very fine shot. He shot woodcock and snipe. He was a very big man with small hands who was brilliant at plucking small birds. His main problem was that he was not interested in making money honestly.'

As Mary's royalties started to accumulate she upgraded her wardrobe, her one extravagance being cashmere. Julia Blackburn described her appearance at this time: 'You have to imagine her; tiny, delicate and very ethereal, with a mane of silver hair, silver slippers, dressed in cashmere or silk, trembling with age or perhaps it was simply the effort of concentration, a wonderful jewelled ring glittering on her finger. And then, just as you grew accustomed to this very quiet, dignified presence, she would roar with laughter and say something irreverent and laced with obscenities.' Mary, she said, had 'beauty like a gazelle, you get it in animals and children'. Jilly Sutton remembered Mary's anarchic sense of humour, the improbable story she told of her sister leaning over a balcony and falling into a chip pan, and the way she once wrecked a lunch party by flirting with the husband of another eighty-year-old woman guest, who was twenty years younger than his wife. 'She did it because she was furiously jealous. She wanted a younger husband too. It was a sudden revelation of a different side to my dignified, demure, beautiful old lady friend.' On another occasion they went to Plymouth to visit an art show that Mary had spotted. It turned out to be mostly larger than life-size male nudes. The Plymouth public tended to view from a safe distance. Mary went right up to have a good look and called out in a loud voice, 'Look, Jilly, what do you think of this one?' She caused further clucking in the Ladies when, made impatient by the long queue, she decided that when her turn came they should save time and go in together.

Her granddaughter Katherine remembered visiting Mary and going for a summer picnic to a favourite pool on Dartmoor, when she was about eighteen. Her grandmother assured her that it was completely private so Katherine took off her clothes and jumped in. A party of German tourists then approached, whereupon Mary sat on Katherine's clothes, preventing her granddaughter from getting dressed. 'Don't worry, darling,' Mary shouted, as the tourists lined up to admire the glade. 'They've seen it all before.' Some years later, when Mary was in her eighties, the lavatory at Bogan Cottage in Totnes became blocked just after she had moved in. A plumber was called and Katherine's grandmother watched from close range while the plumber set to work. The blockage turned out to be a bundle of rubber johnnies. 'Nothing to do with you, Mrs Siepmann,' spluttered the embarrassed plumber. When he had gone Mary exploded with anger. 'Fucking cheek!' she said. 'How dare he assume that?'

Her son Toby remembered Mary's high spirits when, following her affair with Robert Bolt, she had a new man in her sights. Her old friend, Adrian Gale, the architect with whom Mary openly flirted during her last public appearance at the Dartington Festival in June 2002, was startled to be assured at one dinner party that he could slide his slippers under her bed at any time. Toby asked her about a new acquaintance she had mentioned and what the husband was like. 'He's the sort of husband one could borrow for the afternoon,' his mother replied. On another occasion Toby discovered that Mary was about to set off for a week in the sun with a man whom she had known in the Thirties and who had long since married, and voiced his disapproval. 'It doesn't matter, darling,' said Mary. 'His wife's a lesbian.'

The long years of managing on very little and dealing with Eric's impracticalities had given Mary an acute sense of the value of money and she proved to be a competent manager of her own business. The US rights to *The Camomile Lawn* were sold for $10,000 in 1983, a year before British publication. This cleared her advance and ensured that she soon started to receive residual royalties. This success increased Mary's self-confidence but nearly led to a breach with Tessa Sayle. One month after the US sale Mary wrote to her agent saying, 'Do you not feel since the sale of *The Camomile Lawn* was made by James Hale and not your New York agent, that Macmillans should be rewarded for it? Then they will have a bit more money for the promotion of my book. This would help them with their tiny budget.' This letter must have caused Tessa Sayle to splutter over her breakfast coffee, since Macmillan had not purchased US rights in the first place. Her note on the bottom of Mary's letter reads: 'Ring to explain why agents must have their 10% and a few other facts of life.' Mary was not taking this rebuff lying down. One month later she wrote to Tessa Sayle suggesting that in future Tessa should cut her commission on US sales from twenty to fifteen per cent. Realising when it would be wise to concede a point Tessa Sayle, after a silence of two months, agreed to this change.

Mary's close relationship with her editor, James Hale, who had been responsible for accepting *Jumping the Queue*, lasted for the rest of her writing career. He thought that her first novel was notable for its dialogue and its original style: 'it had enchanting sentences, a sense of fun and she was not afraid of dealing with intimate issues.' But it was not until he met its author that he realised he might have a winner. 'She was wonderful and I thought we just have to get her to meet reviewers and literary editors.' Hale also thought that, because of her age, there might not be a follow-up. He knew that *Jumping the Queue* had been written some years before he saw it, so was encouraged to hear that she had returned home to get on with another book. Mary finished *The Camomile Lawn* on 5 March 1983, then put it in a drawer for six weeks. When Hale asked her why she had done that Mary said that she wanted to look at it again to decide whether it was any good. He pointed out that that was his job, but it stayed in the drawer and she only handed it over when she came up to London to have lunch with him the week before publication of *Jumping the Queue*. He read it in twenty-four hours and telephoned as he was leaving for a business trip to New York to tell her that he wanted it. 'It looked a mess,' he recalled. 'It was a continuous narrative that needed breaks and chapters.' She was extremely worried about it and let James know. On his return from New York he wrote to reassure her.

> Dear Mary,
> Either my mouth isn't working properly or you're not hearing me . . . It's wonderful; it's complex; it's very moving; accomplished, witty, sexy; you have a large cast of characters who are entirely and immediately real and sympathetic; you give them lives your readers are going to wish they had lived themselves; special as *Jumping the Queue* is, you have stepped forward, in literary terms, roughly a mile from there; I haven't *enjoyed* reading a novel so much in years; I am more delighted than you can imagine to be publishing you; and Walter is an excellent name.

This one-paragraph sentence would have intrigued Mary, particularly for its dedicated use of the semicolon.* Hale ended his letter – 'There is a great deal more to be said about the book – and it will – but I don't want to turn your head . . . As ever, James.'

Kate Parkin worked for James Hale and was the line editor for Mary's first two books. She remembered the curious mixture of 'distance and warmth' that marked their relations. Parkin was in her early twenties and found Mary

> patient, and courteous, inclined to be amused by my queries. She was very tolerant and slightly intimidating. I would call her and she'd say, 'Darling, I'm much too tired and much too old to deal with that now. Ring me back when I've had a drink.' That characterised our relationship. She used to listen to what one said. She was new to the process but there was never any hesitation or doubt about what she wanted. She was not at all arrogant. *The Camomile Lawn* has quite a complicated structure, moving through time. It was an extraordinary achievement and very cleverly put together. She didn't suffer fools gladly and her readers were expected to keep up.

Mary took steps to ensure that her plots were comprehensible to younger readers. When Katherine Davies was at university, she received a call from her grandmother who wanted an update on anal intercourse. 'Tell me, darling, is it still popular? During the Thirties it was the only way to avoid

---

* It was to be several novels before Hale wrote to congratulate her on her own discovery of the semicolon.

pregnancy so we all did it.' Her next novel, *A Sensible Life*, included a conversation between two mothers chatting and knitting in a hotel lobby in the 1930s in which one says to the other, quoting her husband, 'Angus says a bit of healthy buggery never hurt anyone . . .'

Although Mary was diffident about the merit of her work she became increasingly confident about the business of being a successful author and, as her early clash with Tessa Sayle showed, she was a good judge of how far she could push her point. Unlike many less successful authors, she did not resent being involved with publicity; in fact, she made her publicity tours one of the main planks in her success. James Hale recalled that she turned out to be 'brilliant' at being interviewed and she enjoyed the company of sales reps and booksellers. Major publicity started when Black Swan bought her paperback rights. In 1985 she was objecting to being photographed – 'I loathe photo-sessions . . . such a fearful time-waster' – but as the great citadels of celebrity fell one after another – *Woman's Hour*, *Wogan*, *Desert Island Discs*, *Kaleidoscope*, lunch with Iris Murdoch – she began to enjoy herself. Mary started her publicity work for *The Camomile Lawn* in 1984 and soon got into the swing of radio interviews. 'I am going to . . . do local radio, Plymouth Sound, on Friday,' she wrote to Tessa Sayle. 'I must remember not to say "fuck" this time.'* After one broadcast Sarah Miles reported, 'Your deep, mellow, classy voice was vibrating all around my bathroom.' In December 1989 Tessa Sayle noted, 'Mary has asked for her Bantam publicity girl to be changed as the original talks too much.' She became particularly interested in the question of illustrated book jackets. In December 1986 Transworld complained that she had 'gone through four of our most distinguished Black Swan artists'. She was holding out for Susan Moxley – who illustrated Anita Brookner's 1984 Booker Prize winner *Hotel du Lac* – and her publishers could afford to be accommodating; swelling sales eventually won Black Swan its first number one position on the best-seller lists. Despite this success Mary remained a stern critic of jacket design. A memo written in 1993 concerning *Harnessing Peacocks* read: 'The idea of hands holding a pear is not bad – a bit arty – but it should be an *apple* (see Eve in Genesis) and please ask the photographer to find someone who does not bite her nails.' Despite the waspishness, she remained modest about her success. Paul Scherer, the chairman

---

* On a previous occasion the producer had cut Mary's entire contribution, saying he could not broadcast 'fuck' since the next item was an interview with the Duke of Edinburgh.

of her second publishers, Transworld, particularly appreciated 'her talent for self-deprecation, the last thing you expect in a popular author'.

Her sales grew steadily throughout the second part of the 1980s. *The Vacillations of Poppy Carew* went to No. 1 on the *Sunday Times* hardback list in August 1986, two months after publication. In August 1988, by which time there were five titles in paperback, Patrick Janson-Smith, then of Transworld, could report that 'the success of *Not That Sort of Girl* has led to an upsurge of sales in all your previous novels'. This success was supplemented by Tessa Sayle's skill in negotiating television and film rights.

In December 1988 James Hale left Macmillan at short notice and informed his authors, about sixty of them, over the weekend. 'When I rang and told her,' Hale remembered, 'she was the only one to ask about me. The rest quite rightly worried about themselves. But she said, "Darling, are you all right? Do you need any money?"' Mary decided to leave with James. After the break with Macmillan, Tessa Sayle negotiated an unusual deal with Transworld allowing them to publish Mary in hardback as well as paperback as long as Hale remained her editor. Macmillan's advances had risen in six steps over six years from £1,000 in 1983 for *Jumping the Queue* to a maximum of £30,000 for *Second Fiddle* in 1988. Transworld offered much more, but James Hale considered that the move to Transworld was significant for a different reason, because it made 'Mary Wesley' the first serious writer to be sold as though she were 'Catherine Cookson' in a full-blooded, commercial way. In May 1989 Transworld ordered reprints of four titles amounting to 120,000 copies and in August Janson-Smith wrote to her again: 'I thought that you'd like to know that we've just put in hand reprints for *Not That Sort of Girl*, *The Camomile Lawn* and *Jumping the Queue* of 30,000 copies each! The sales rate for the latter two titles is quite extraordinary: over 10,000 copies each this month alone. We will, of course, and at long last, be using the Susan Moxley cover for *Jumping the Queue*.' When Bantam published its first Wesley hardback, *A Sensible Life*, in March 1990, the 50,000 print run was sold out by Christmas and *The Bookseller* placed it at No. 2 in the list of best-selling novels of the year. Her advance payment had been £100,000, to be improved to £135,000 for the next title, *A Dubious Legacy*.*

---

* The typescript of *A Dubious Legacy* was delivered by hand to James Hale in Peckham Rye, by a street cleaner who had found it in a litter bin on the South Bank. It had fallen out of a Post Office van. Parcel Force refunded the Datapost fee of £15.70 on 3 April 1991.

Mary's ambition during her first seven years as an author had been to make 'enough money to move house and have once more a tiny garden and a cat or dog', and she achieved this goal in July 1989, six years after the publication of *Jumping the Queue*, when she moved, for the last time, to a house round the corner in Totnes, Bogan Cottage. She was very happy here, although her writing arrangements were quite eccentric. She placed her kneehole, leather-topped desk on a small landing with her back to the spare bedroom door, facing a window that was hard against an outside flight of stairs leading to shops. Shoppers mounted and descended these stairs, children shrieked, just outside the window, within a few feet of her head, while she started and finished three more novels. The entrance to the cottage – up an alley, off a back street – made it hard to find, which was one of its chief attractions. Mary planted an acacia tree in the stone-flagged garden, just outside her bedroom window, and commissioned not one but two good-looking architects to construct a sumptuous outside lavatory for the use of visitors. 'There's nothing worse than wanting the loo,' she said, 'knowing that the man who won't come out is lolling in the bath reading *The Times*.' She never locked the front door until the day a burglar walked in while she was writing upstairs and stole a precious ring made from stones that Eric had brought back from Siam. After that she left the door keys in a pot outside, a secret known only to the several hundred people she trusted in Totnes. On the wall outside the door she fixed a ceramic relief of the Virgin and Child.

The entrance led into the kitchen where she kept a stuffed fighting cock in a glass case that had once belonged to Alice Grenfell's father when he was the publican of St Buryan. On the opposite wall was a large coloured print of the 1st Duke of Wellington riding past the statue of Achilles in Hyde Park. Beside it was a framed drawing, ink on paper, entitled *Abraham's Sacrifice*. Abraham, his knife raised above the child on the altar, is looking up to heaven, and she had tucked the palm crosses from three successive Palm Sundays into the frame. Other pictures included a profile of a hare's head by Katharine Swinfen Eady, a *Country View* by Francis Farmar, and a print of the battle between *HMS Quebec* and *Surveillante*, that took place in the English Channel on 6 October 1779, in which Captain George Farmar died. Both ships are dismasted and the *Quebec* is in flames.

Her bedroom window looked north towards the Moor. On the wall was a curious drawing by Emily Holmes Coleman entitled, *The Blessed Trinity Drinking Tea, in a Pavilion by a Lake in Heaven*. By her bed were photographs of Eric, Heinz, Bill and Toby and her grandmother, Hyacinthe

Dalby, in a silver frame. The books included the Authorised Version and a copy of *Hymns Ancient and Modern* inscribed to her by her grandmother on her twelfth birthday, St John the Baptist's Day, with a marker in 'Oh God Our Help in Ages Past'; 'Jeremiah 45-5' was scribbled on the front endpaper in her handwriting. Among the books she frequently re-read were *Our Man in Havana* and *Travels with My Aunt*.

With the switch to Transworld the money started to pile up even faster. In May 1992 her accountant, Joe Reevy, wrote to her in mild alarm pointing out that there was £440,000 'approximately' in her bank and building society accounts, and that even after paying a tax instalment of £31,000 she would be well advised to pay off her mortgage. He added, 'Thank-you for the excellent lunch the other day. I wish we could get *baguettes* of that quality in Bovey Tracey . . . I enclose *The Periodic Table*. I hope you enjoy it as much as I did.' Since her days of extreme poverty Mary had relied on her accountant to manage her money. Two years earlier she had, however, rejected a tax savings scheme he had drawn up which depended on her firstly living to the age of eighty-six and secondly residing in the Channel Isles. Tessa Sayle noted, 'Mary cross with her accountant . . . Could I countermand his instructions not to pay her any more money. I think she gave Mr Reevy a hard time.' After her death, Joe Reevy said that he had had other poor clients who had become unexpectedly rich but that she was the only one who had never shown any interest in reducing her tax bill.

By the time of her eightieth birthday, in June 1992, Mary was beginning to flag. Audrey Gale, a friend who had started her career at the Bar in the chambers headed by John Platts-Mills, gave her a present of '80 hopeful pencils', to spur her on, and she put them in a vase on her desk where they reminded her of '80 good resolutions, pointing heavenwards, like weapons of war'. In March 1993, with *A Dubious Legacy* about to appear in paperback and total sales heading for the two million mark, Mary was asking for fewer press interviews feeling that she was getting 'over-exposed'. But her attention to detail remained unrelenting. After a tour of Holland she received a letter from her Dutch publicist thanking her for the flowers, 'You are the first author who has done this.'

By then it had all proved too much for the novelist Anita Brookner, who (while reviewing *A Dubious Legacy*) delivered a bucket of vitriol to the readers of the *Spectator* in February, 1992. Brookner compared Mary Wesley with Agatha Christie and Catherine Cookson: she described her writing as 'stereotyped, nostalgic, reassuring, romantic, tasteful, well-bred, very slight, very unreal and very tedious', and noted in addition that the author had 'a basilisk

profile'. Mary Wesley was shaken by this personal attack, delivered out of
the blue – an adverse review in the *Sunday Times* six years earlier had
plunged her into 'a cloud of depression' for ten days – but she brushed it
aside in public. 'When you're very successful people want you to be slapped
down,' she said. 'It's a very human thing to do.' Brookner's article had been
published shortly after a long article in the *Telegraph Magazine* that was
pegged to the forthcoming TV serialisation of *The Camomile Lawn*, directed
by Peter Hall. A friend, John Bowen, later wrote to Mary to reassure her:
'I have been thinking about what you said to me about your own insecurity
and fear as a writer . . . Don't ever allow yourself more than the natural fear
we all have of the irrational malice of reviewers and the envy of the Anita
Bruckners [*sic*], forever doomed to rework the same material: she is the
Sisyphus of the Fulham Road . . .'

Mary Wesley's critical reputation grew with her fame. Novelists such
as Susan Hill, Marghanita Laski and David Hughes were among the first
to praise her work which, as it developed, was popularly described as 'Jane
Austen plus sex', a description she herself thought ridiculous. More percep-
tively, Allan Massie placed her in 'a school of light novelists which one had
thought extinct: E. F. Benson, Rose Macauley, Barbara Pym . . .' This
summarised the wit and style of her writing, it overlooked the depths which
another critic in *The Times* traced to 'her true literary antecedents . . . the
brothers Grimm . . . [she] . . . returns again and again to the classic themes
of fairy tale: the Evil Parent, the Abandoned Heroine, the Hero searching
for his lost love'. *A Sensible Life* (1990) was praised in the *New Statesman*
for presenting 'one of the most powerful images of childhood suffering I
have ever read'. Mary Hope, on the other hand, remembered the book in
The Listener for its depiction of moments of happiness: 'Perfectly to convey
the unpredictable, unexpected, unlikely quality of happiness is a very great
gift indeed.' In the *Times Literary Supplement*, *A Dubious Legacy* (1992)
was described as 'a very funny book. It stretches Larkin's warnings about
man handing on misery to man into a black comedy of English manners.'

A contributor to the *New York Times* reconciled all these views: she
creates 'an idiosyncratic, fictional world, a middle-class English world,
whose bright comic surface belies a dark subtext of sin, incest, murder and
betrayal. Cuckoldry and sexual gamesmanship thrive in her novels, and a
chilly air of malice . . . that's reminiscent of Muriel Spark.' Reviewing
Wesley's last novel, *Part of the Furniture*, in 1997 the critic Lisa Jardine
summarised her achievement:

[It] is grounded in a peculiar emotional intensity of life in England during the Second World War . . . Once again her story hinges on a haunting quality of neediness in young women who were neglected and unloved as children – a quality which profoundly colours their attitudes towards men and their later sexual relations with them . . . Her writing reminds me of the work of one of my between-the-wars writers, Elizabeth Bowen, both in style and emotional reach. [Mary Wesley] is also a writer much read and loved by women – as well as her perceptiveness about girlhood, she is at her very best writing with humour about older women, their vanities and fears of ageing, and their sexual desires beyond the age of reproduction. She is a devastatingly accurate observer of lonely women in marriages where the partners have grown so used to each other that they stay together, and in particular tensions within childless marriages. Above all, she is entirely unsentimental about the relations between parents and children.

As Mary became richer, she gave away more and more money. The Mary Wesley Collection at Boston University provides ample evidence of this, as did the letters received by her family after her death. One of the pleasures she took in her success was being able to help other people who were in trouble. Her own experience of this situation had lasted too long to be quickly forgotten. In January 2003, 'Prisoners of Conscience' wrote to her family to say that she had been a very generous donor, as well as a patron and recruiter, giving a lot of her time to help persecuted people. Speaking of her work for 'Prisoners of Conscience' in 1993, Mary had said, 'There's a lovely man I talk to called Blumenthal. He and I plot to strangle the Home Secretary* at least once a week.' Asked in 1993 what would be the perfect end to her perfect weekend, she replied: '. . . press reports that Baroness Thatcher had been pushed over a cliff.' She seldom intervened in public issues but in 1997, appalled by the 'Princess Di' hysteria, she came down firmly on the side of the mistress and wrote an encouraging letter to Camilla Parker Bowles. She received a fan letter in reply: 'My book-shelves are full of all your novels and my children and I are your greatest fans', the future Duchess of Cornwall declared.

One of Mary's causes became the private life of a forester called Eric Bealing, who lived on the Stourhead estate in Wiltshire. Bealing was an elderly man who was dying and at the same time nursing a sick wife. He had been

* Michael Howard.

in love with a married woman for most of his life, but had not seen her for many years. He wrote to Mary asking for advice. She told him to invite this woman out to lunch, and sent him the money for the taxi fare to the woman's house and the lunch. He later returned most of the money and described the visit.

> I went to see Joan [not her real name] as arranged . . . to my eye at least very beautiful . . . Her face is very thin . . . something seriously wrong with her health . . . She took my face in [her] hands as she did years ago and gave me a good look into my eyes . . . we sat on the settee my arm round her and her head on my shoulder . . . I felt I was about 20 years-old . . . To a French restaurant for lunch. Then back to her house. We talked quite a lot about our liaison . . . we both agreed that there was no future in it . . . I told her about my cancer . . . I feel that at last I have reached the tape . . . I have held her in my arms and kissed the woman I have loved for so many years . . . I thank you most sincerely for your kind help and advice . . . I used your cheque, but for taxi fares only. Thank-you . . . How much I appreciate your friendship . . . You are a very wonderful woman . . . Much of the awful pain has disappeared . . .

Mary answered readers' letters promptly, because that was how she had been brought up. Strangers who wrote to her with a hard luck story often received a cheque in reply. She paid for private hospital operations for two people in Totnes and for the critic and playwright Peter Myers, who had been page at her wedding in 1937 and about whom she was worried because his payments from the Swinten Trust remained frozen by Stephen Scammell. A struggling writer she had never met received a cheque for two thousand pounds. A young playwright who asked for help in funding her MA received 'a substantial' amount and subsequently won a nomination for Playwright of the Year. She took great trouble to send money to Uganda to pay the school fees of an orphan pupil, and when she realised that she had been caught in a scam by an African confidence trickster she just laughed. She also paid thousands of pounds every year to keep Alice Grenfell in a private nursing home in Truro, which she visited regularly. Alice was well looked-after and in due course outlived Mary and celebrated her 101st birthday. In 1995 the novelist Nicholas Shakespeare, who was an old friend of Mary's and among her first literary patrons, wrote to thank her: 'I opened your cheque on the road and gave such a whoop of delight that I very nearly accelerated into the ditch . . . it will make all the difference, both to my life in the months ahead and to the novel.' She also supported her youngest son, Bill, who was working as a train driver for London Transport, and gave her favourite granddaughter, Katherine Davies, who was struggling to establish herself as a painter, enough money to buy a house. When Sonya, Betty Paynter's daughter, was fighting, unsuccessfully, against cancer Mary sent her money and received a letter thanking her 'for all this fortune . . . You have made me feel very much less frightened of many things.'

The television adaptations of *Harnessing Peacocks*, *Jumping the Queue* and *The Camomile Lawn* brought further celebrity, and public honours followed. She received honorary doctorates from Exeter and the Open University, and was made an honorary fellow of the LSE. She accepted the CBE from John Major in the 1995 New Year Honours List. In March of that year she received a letter from the office of the Lord-Lieutenant of Devon. 'Lieut-Col. The Earl of Morley has been asked to present your award at a local ceremony in Exeter at the Guildhall . . . There will be press photographs taken after the ceremony . . .' Mary telephoned a brisk reply and another letter followed: 'The Lord-Lieutenant will be very pleased to present your award at your home on 2 June at 11.00. He will not be in uniform and will not be accompanied by the Clerk to the Lieutenancy. As we agreed on the telephone, I will not arrange any publicity. Lord Morley will be delighted to have coffee with you that morning.' The days of three curtseys with ostrich feathers were well and truly buried. Instead, there was dinner at Buckingham Palace, with two fans, her pre-war friend 'Popsie' Pakenham*, and Mary's distant cousin, the Queen.

* Better known as Elizabeth Countess of Longford

CHAPTER SEVENTEEN

The Terror Run

'Your characters are almost familiar . . . I think they could easily and
dangerously walk off the page and wander through the real world.'

Reader's letter, 1994.

When journalists called on Mary Wesley in Totnes they were put through
a ritual ordeal. They took the train from Paddington, she very kindly met
them at the station and drove them to the house where they arrived, several
minutes later, in a state of collapse. In Toby's words, 'She drove like a
snipe.' Others were less complimentary. Katherine Davies said that the
only way to get her to slow down was to remind her that if she lost her
licence she was too old to get it back. The biographer Jane Dunn, who
came to talk to her about Antonia White, said, 'She drove so aggressively,
I felt she was making a point.' One of her interviewers claimed to have
kissed the platform at Totnes Station when she made it back alive. Another
said that Mary reassured her, 'Don't worry, I have never had an accident.'
In fact, a succession of motoring accidents punctuate her diary entries over
the years: 'Killed dog', 'crash car', 'small accident on the way to Ashburton'
and so on. In Cordoba in 1971 she drove her host's new car over a low
cliff, wrecked a friendship and spent a miserable week in hospital. With
her interviewers she was not just making a point, she was throwing them
the gauntlet and instinctively using a softening-up technique that would
have met with the approval of her MI5 mentors, Richmond Stopford and
John Bolitho. Alarming journalists was a first line of defence, the parrying
of questions that had not yet been asked.

Mary Siepmann was sensitive about her privacy. After her first national
press interview, given to *The Times* in March 1984, she wrote to Tessa Sayle,
'I shall be busy closing the stable door on Caroline Moorehead's indiscre-

tions – oh well. I shall know better in future.' Exactly what was revealed was important to her, she wanted to help her publishers by publicising her existence without violating her privacy. For an unknown septuagenarian with no experience of public relations or the problems of dealing with an intrusive press it was a virtuoso performance, and she accomplished it by drawing a line between Mary Wesley and Mrs Siepmann. The former was the eloquent original of the beautiful, adventurous, laconic Calypso. It was Mary, not Calypso, who said 'War is very erotic', 'I have never been to bed with anyone I didn't love, or at least didn't find attractive', 'One could not think of my mother in terms of having an orgasm' – this last for an Irish magazine that had introduced her as a Catholic writer. But Mrs Siepmann was a different matter. On several occasions she was asked if she would either write an autobiography or collaborate with a biographer and she always refused. Autobiographies never told the truth she said, 'it all comes out washed in Persil.' As for biographers, 'there are parts of my life I don't talk about and publishing would cause pain to living people, or worse, embarrassment . . .' But in agreeing to be interviewed, and in provoking questions about her past, she was taking a chance, stepping closer to the edge of Bolt Head.

In guarding her privacy Mrs Siepmann was protecting something important within herself, but she was also guarding a writer's enlarged need for an extensive interior space where her demons could roam. The reason why there were men in her bed whom she did not want in her head was that there was quite enough going on in her head already and she was impatient to pay attention to it. From her childhood until the week before her first novel was accepted, Mary was living the material she was to use in her novels. From then, in her life, she was tying up the loose ends, whereas in her writing she was fighting old battles, suffering or inflicting each of those historical wounds again.

The nine years of 'Mary Wesley's' greatest productivity were from September 1982 to March 1991, when she wrote and delivered seven novels. These took between nine and eighteen months to complete, and she relaxed for breaks varying from two weeks to two months between finishing one and starting the next. While her age moved from seventy to seventy-nine she showed the focus and drive of a young person, somewhere finding the concentration and energy to fire up an untested creative engine and keep it running at speed.

In 1977 she had two unwanted typescripts and she was writing nothing. She seemed to be finished as a writer. In 1981, in near chronic depression, she was forced to sell the cottage that was the only remaining link with the dead husband she still missed every day; then she conveniently contracted double pneumonia. Her diary was firmly marked 'Please do NOT Resuscitate', she was alone, she had the Beaujolais and the Brie. And yet she did not die. Two further diary entries provide an explanation. At the end of the previous June she had written 'Roger's body blow at Toby'. Then, in September, another entry reads, 'Toby lunchtime lateish – walk on moor – talk talk talk.' The 'body blow' had been preceded by Stephen Scammell's arrival on the scene in the spring of 1980 when he had paid off Roger Swinfen's debts. In November of that year legal proceedings by the trustees had reached the point of a writ that required a defence. Mary's evidence in defending Toby against his brother's attack was crucial. What kept her going through her illness was the need to defend her son. Even before she was out of bed she had managed to write a six-page letter to Averil Swinfen in which she apologised to Carol's widow for the damage being caused by Scammell's activities. The forthcoming legal battle seems to have been central to her survival. She moved house and laid Eric's ghost. 'Do NOT Resuscitate' disappeared from her diary. She worked out what she could say in her affidavit. Then, quite unexpectedly, she became an author who needed to develop her material.

She sat down at her desk in the corner of the sitting room in Castle Street and started to write. She had moved into Castle Street in April 1981 and had written nothing in her new house that year. Instead, she started to paint shelves and hang pictures. She had fallen in love with Robert Bolt and started an affair. He came to stay with her in January 1982 and the first record of her return to work is two weeks after his visit. She was sixty-nine years old and she started a new book. She called it 'Period Piece'. When she sat in Castle Street she could hear the church bells from St Mary's in the High Street; and there was another new sound which she had not been able to hear from her cottage on the moor: the double note of the horn on the passing trains. Totnes is on the main line from Paddington to Penzance. She had passed that way hundreds of times, particularly during the war. 'Period Piece' became *The Camomile Lawn*. Chapter Two opens, 'Helena met the London train . . .' which had 'snaked into Penzance'. Helena is there to meet Calypso. Later that same day Calypso drives back into Penzance to meet Oliver off the midnight train. Oliver is back from Spain where he has been wounded serving with the International Brigade.

The train from London to the West Country played a significant role in six of her ten novels; it was frequently the point of entry into her imaginary landscape. *The Camomile Lawn*, her second book, was a classic first novel. Whereas *Jumping the Queue*, with its mood of quiet desperation, widowhood and suicide was a novel of bitter experience, *The Camomile Lawn*, written in Totnes, was funnier, more optimistic and had the faint hint of a happy ending. It was about high-spirited irresponsibility in the face of danger, and it introduced nine themes that were to recur in her writing time and again, among them the idea of the everlasting house – the idyllic refuge – and the set-piece social occasion – usually a funeral or wedding, the snobbish racist parents, the elderly male seducer (always male – in her fiction), and the association of twins with uncertain paternity. In both books there are references to her own life. *Jumping the Queue* recalls her time with Eric, living in a remote country cottage. It opens with Gus, a gander in love with Matilda. Their communion is interrupted by a telephone call from 'John' who has changed his name to 'Piers'. He has done this because he is a senior civil servant who is expecting a knighthood and would rather be 'Sir Piers' than 'Sir John'. This is a reference to a Siepmann family joke; Eric's brother-in-law, Percy Waterfield, married to his sister Doris, was a senior figure at the Treasury. Long before his knighthood arrived, Percy Waterfield insisted on being called 'Percival'. The honour was conferred, to Eric's mischievous delight, in 1944. The gander dated back to Thornworthy and another friend of Mary's, reading of Matilda's decision to harbour a suspected murderer, was at once reminded 'of how you used to leave Thornworthy House unlocked with a change of clothes on a kitchen chair for the odd Dartmoor escapee'.

Of *Jumping the Queue* James Hale said, 'Mary was, I swear, slightly mad when she wrote that book.' Hale remembered that when she first came to see him 'and said, "I suppose you want hundreds of changes" and I replied "Not one word" how her whole face changed and she became completely open'. Hale was never quite sure why he bought *Jumping the Queue*. 'Because it's not a book,' he contended two months after Mary's death.

It's a *Play for Today* of twenty years earlier. It either had to be rewritten from the beginning, or taken just as it was. But she never asked me why I hadn't wanted to change anything in it. Because to her it was so much part of her context, her world: surreal, Catholic, bohemian *and* conventional. A strange world that was truly hers. She had a conjunction of things that other people recognise, that was coherent to her.

Mary remembered that when James Hale answered 'Not one word' he was holding the typescript, and he tapped it as he spoke. 'I loved him from then on. He asked if I had another book and I said "yes" and he told me to go home and finish it. I never realised people planned their books. *I lived my books day by day.* I used to get stuck and go to sleep and wake in the morning and think "Oh, that's what happens". I *lived* with the characters.' Once, during Mass, at the Elevation of the Host, she found herself 'praying like hell for a man who was very ill', only to realise that he was one of the characters from her latest unfinished book.

The character of Calypso, her most celebrated heroine, may have been suggested by the title of a very bad novel by Humphrey Slater, published in 1953, which Mary read when she was living at Broughton. The Calypso of this book, 'a fantastic beauty', is about to marry the wrong, conventional, husband until she is seduced by an older man who runs off with her, first to the south of France and then to Florence. The plot degenerates into melodrama but something about the character seems to have caught Mary's attention. There is a slightly stronger connection with a very distant cousin by marriage called Calypso Baring, a famous beauty of the 1930s who married Guy Liddell, director of B Division of MI5 in 1940. His wife left him to live with her half-brother in America, a move that caused a considerable scandal at the time. When she left, she temporarily abandoned four children, one of whom was called Juno. Juno Liddell, who may have been known to Mary, worked at MI5 after the war, and died young. Calypso, who returned to England when her daughter was dying, lived to a great age. Several of the Liddell family names – Calypso, Juno, Guy and Florence (or Flora) – occur in Wesley's fiction.

As a young woman Mary resembled Polly, in *The Camomile Lawn* rather than Calypso; but Calypso appears in several more of the novels, growing old faithfully, and then – as a widow to whom the young turn for advice, and who is regarded with wary respect because of her sharp tongue. In December 1981 Mary wrote a long letter to a friend who was at the end of a love affair. 'When I was in your position I used to make it a point of honour with myself to be or at least appear to be the one who ended the affair. At the very first whiff I left. This at least saved my pride . . .' That is the authentic voice of Calypso and recalls the tactics used to such effect with Peter Hope, Norman Pearson, Heinz – whose trousers were rarely up, Raymond Lee, Robert d'Alsace and Simon Harcourt-Smith. Even in old age with Robert Bolt, she remained in charge.

Many of the characters she created and lived with were strong-minded women, trapped by adverse circumstances who find the strength to break out and redirect their lives. Her plots were both surrealistic and polemical. When Matilda pisses into the young hoorays' salad bowl, while they chorus 'super', many of her older readers would have taken it as a bugle call in the generation war. As a woman who was liberated before her time Mary Wesley challenged social assumptions about the old, confessed to bad behaviour, recommended sex. In doing so she smashed the stereotype of the disapproving, judgmental, past-it, old person. This delighted the old and intrigued the young. It was 'the generation gap from the other side', as one reviewer put it. More than that, it was deeply subversive. Matilda's steady determination on suicide is presented as a rational solution to despair.

Wesley made the faults of the bourgeois family – materialism, snobbery and hypocrisy – a recurring target, and her sympathies lay with the exile and the outlaw, the persons beyond the pale. In her third book, *Harnessing Peacocks*, she introduced another recurring theme, the affirmation of illegitimacy.* The unmarried heroine Hebe resists her grandparents' bullying and refuses to terminate her pregnancy. Hebe's decision would be supported today by both pro-choice and pro-life lobbies, but in offering Hebe salvation or independence through cordon bleu cookery and part-time prostitution Mary Wesley was echoing the paradoxes of Greeneland; if this was Catholicism it was against the grain. Graham Greene remained her favourite novelist and, as her interviews showed, she was, like him, attracted to 'the dangerous edge'. In *The Camomile Lawn*, with the invention of the Terror Run, she went back to that night at the end of the war when the coastguard disappeared over the edge of the cliff at Boskenna, and she combined it with her childhood fear of Bolt Head, and her mother urging her forward to look down and her fear of her mother; in the first draft of the book the title† of Chapter One, blue biro on unlined typing paper, was 'Who's for the Terror Run?' like a horror version of 'The Famous Five'.

Sex became her trademark though she wrote about what went on in the head rather than a user's manual. She once said that her mother's motto had been 'Duty before orgasm' and, although she never reversed these priorities,

---

* The four major themes in her ten novels were ambiguity in personal identity, the dysfunctional family, marital rape and the affirmation of illegitimacy. Among other themes that appear repeatedly are incest, revenge, suicide by drowning, parental interference, the everlasting or ideal house, parental snobbery or racism, and the elderly seducer.

† The published version had no chapter titles.

there was a time during the war when she conflated them. Her descriptions were at their best when sex was in view, and were frequently humorous. On the opening page of chapter two of *The Camomile Lawn* she introduces Polly, alighting from the London train in Penzance. She has '. . . a square jaw and startling green eyes . . . Her teeth slightly out of kilter, like a false step in a chorus line gave her smile a particular gaiety. At nineteen there was already beauty.' Poppy, on the other hand, in *The Vacillations of Poppy Carew*, is in bed, sipping tea. 'The sheets slipped back as she lifted the cup, showing biscuit coloured breasts with nipples (her) grandmother would have called Old Rose.' What had been so important in her life became equally important in her fiction and she had a powerful memory to set to work; she could summon details of the turn of a staircase, or firelight flickering on a man's face or a tree fallen in the park, from forty years past. Among her memories Mary would have had the knowledge she had gained from loving Paul and Heinz Ziegler. Paul Ziegler, who became a Benedictine monk in 1945, had never understood how anyone could become a monk unless they had first known physical love. Once, placed in charge of a party of Bavarian novices, he took his charges to a brothel in Frankfurt, believing that they would never be able to hear confessions if they had never experienced sin.* As a young man Paul had 'found a daunting greatness in Eros that went far beyond the unique pleasure lovers' bodies give to each other . . . [and that healed] . . . for a while at least the inner conflicts and unresolved tensions from which' he suffered.

Later, when Mary fell in love with Eric, it happened while they were in bed, an experience that gave him at least a considerable shock. For many years Eric Siepmann had associated sex with pleasure and, since he had a puritan conscience, with sin. He had taken comfort by quoting Masefield: 'Sexual sin is the least of the sins in Dante. It is allied to love. It is an image of regeneration. No sin is so common, none is more glibly blamed. It is so easy to cry "treacherous", "base" and "immoral". But who, while the heart beats, can call himself safe from the temptation of this sin?' For Mary and Eric the love which they had found in the hotel bedroom overlooking the Broad Walk while she read him *The Georgics* and the *Four Quartets* was based on sexual passion and seems to have remained so.

---

* As punishment for this misjudgement, Father Ziegler was sent for six months as chaplain to a convent of Belgian nuns. He described this as the worst experience of his life; to hear the nuns' confessions, he said, was to be 'pecked to death by ducks'.

As her working routine developed Mary Siepmann became fiercely protective of her solitude. Her friends knew better than to telephone during the day, she frequently worked during the mornings as well as the afternoons. She was always in a hurry, making up for lost time. There is no clear biographical thread in Mary Wesley's fiction. Asked by the writer Victoria Glendinning about this, she said: 'You can only imagine from what you already know, and I don't know all that much.' In her case certain patterns recurred; the same elements were reshaped and fitted into different puzzles. She wrote about what she knew but she changed it all in her imagination into a more fantastic version of everyday reality. Sex was more likely to be violent or comical than uplifting; one recurring character is the elderly seducer, running rings round the hidebound assumptions of his younger rivals, exerting a good-humoured charm to which conventional females respond while their conventional husbands fail to notice. After the publication of *An Imaginative Experience* the novelist Peter Benson wrote to thank her. 'You have created your own territory, a fresh and beautiful landscape; no one comes close. There's always a feeling of unease in your work, a tension you feel but cannot see. Your characters are almost familiar, like people you vaguely remember meeting; I think they would easily and dangerously walk off the page and wander through the real world.'

She developed the extreme case of the dysfunctional family in *A Dubious Legacy* where the ideal house, in this case named Cotteshaw, is haunted by a mad wife not in the attic but in what an estate agent would call 'the master bedroom', from which the master has long since retreated. That Cotteshaw is not to be an ideal house like Slepe is evident from Chapter One when Henry Tillotson brings his bride home and she, displeased by the travel arrangements, gives him a black eye. A child looking on says, '. . . that lady hit you, why didn't you hit her back?', quoting Roger's remembered words when Phyllis Siepmann hit Mary in the hotel dining room in Devon. At Cotteshaw, Margaret, the mad bride, retreats into her bedroom, and this was what in life Mrs Maitland-Heriot had done at Timsbury before the war when she had taken exception to her husband Chico's bigamy. But Mrs Maitland-Heriot had been a perfectly nice, if somewhat affronted, woman. Margaret is not nice; she's beautiful but mad; she has the character of Phyllis Siepmann – possessing a malign, all-seeing intelligence that is a real danger to the happiness of anyone who wanders into range.

Margaret Tillotson is the great monster of Wesley's imagination; the author lived with her for the nineteen months that it took to write *A Dubious*

Legacy, which was the longest time any of her books (apart from the first) had taken; she eventually despatched Mrs Tillotson by drowning her in Cotteshaw's lake, but only after Margaret had wrecked a family celebration by ripping the head off the house cockatoo. Margaret's funeral is described by Henry's friends as 'a celebration'. In the mysterious relationship of Henry Tillotson, elderly seducer and English gentleman of the old school, and Margaret his wife, a violent and undiagnosed psychopath, there is an echo of Phyllis Siepmann's effortless victory over two hard-bitten old Etonian journalists, Ian Fleming and David Astor. The book's working title was 'The Tillotson Legacy', which Hale asked her to change. She agreed, on condition that the word 'Legacy' remained.

James Hale noted that she used a recurring situation in which one character pushes another into the water and suggested that this could be worth pursuing. When asked, Mrs Siepmann's dry comment was, 'Very observant of James.' Hopes of discovering that she had once murdered someone by pushing them (probably 'her') into the Serpentine were not fulfilled. But a 'Serpentine murder' occurs in *Jumping the Queue*, and in *Not That Sort of Girl* the ashes of an interfering mother are dispatched into the same waters, a symbolic murder, post-mortem. The Serpentine murders may have been inspired by nothing more sinister than the childhood incident when Susan pushed Mary into deep water off a pier in the Isle of Wight. The Serpentine lake is also sometimes associated with a violent reaction to the discovery of infidelity.

Another recurring situation is the swim out to sea from a remote beach. In Wesley's fiction the English Channel is given an unfamiliar personality; peaceful, welcoming, a comfort, even a luxury, and associated with an easy departure. This seems to have been one fantasy she shared with her mother. Following her father's death, Mary's mother said, 'I'm not going to let that lingering death happen to me. When the time comes I'm going to crawl to the Solent and swim out.' And Mary had replied with feeling, 'I'll help you.'

Incest plays its part in no fewer than five of Mary Wesley's ten novels, but the author made no mention of this being a feature of her own life. Asked about incest in one interview, Mary Siepmann said that it was a great deal commoner than people realised, an insight she may have gained from her twelve years working as a Samaritan. She added that it had played a greatly reduced role in village life since the introduction of the rural bus service, country people now being able to get out more. In her own family both the Girardots and the Dashwoods followed the French Huguenot tradition of intermarriage among cousins, so overcoming the British tradition of primogeniture and enabling family wealth to be shared out more equally. Since it was Huguenot money that Mary had been deprived of when she was cut out of her aunts' wills, it may have amused her to make a private reference to this sombre method of retaining inherited wealth.

Another family tease was her comment to Eric at the time of her brother Hugh's wedding that the bride and groom looked 'exactly alike', a not uncommon occurrence but in this case a reference to the fact that Mynors Farmar, Hugh's father, had been a friend of Etheldreda Fane, the bride's mother, before either was married, and that Mynors had greatly admired his 'lovely friend'. From this old friendship of her father's it was but a step in Mary's imagination before her brother and his bride were brother and sister. But she realised the destructive power of the real thing and used the revelation of incest as the punchline in her last novel, *Part of the Furniture*, which must rank among the angriest, most devastating and vengeful exit lines in literature.

Incest or not, paternity is a consistently uncertain business in Wesley's fictional world. In *The Camomile Lawn* Polly decides to have children by twin brothers and in due course bears a boy and a girl. But nobody, not even she, is quite sure which twin fathered which child (apart from anything else, Polly has on occasion spent the night with both at once). This situation combines several recurring themes; the cheerful assumption of illegitimacy, sex as bawdy comedy, the uncertainty inherent in fatherhood, incest – and the tension between identity and ambiguity that is present in each of her ten novels. This last was a tension Mary Siepmann knew from long experience and one which never left her through all her years of fame.

In April, 1990, Mary travelled to Prague and paid her only visit to Loyovitz; the walls were still standing, but the iron gates were chained shut and the spirit of the house was dead; it had become a Czech government training college. Then, with Toby and his first wife, the painter Isobel MacLeod, Mary went on to Budapest to visit Heinz's grave. He had been buried with the rest of his crew in the Budapest War Cemetery under his nom de guerre – "Zetland, Henry Osbert, Flying Officer 87294, died 5 May 1944, age unknown, RAF Volunteer Reserve – UK Nationality". Isobel remembers that 'Mary howled when she saw it'. Later Mary told Toby, 'You never really believe it until you see the grave'.

In the letters written by Flying Officer Henry Zetland to his brother,

Paul Ziegler, from the wartime air bases of 104 Squadron, there was one phrase that seemed out of place. It was in a letter dated 28 November 1943 and sent from the North African desert to Great Missenden, forwarded to the Lansdowne Club, in Berkeley Square. It came at the end of a long affectionate passage in which Heinz recalled all that he owed to his younger brother's brilliance and authority. Next he wrote, ' . . .All I found to send home (for Christmas) were fruit parcels – I sent one to Gerda, one to Pam, and one to Mary, *Pour les enfants*'. In a family, those words usually mean, in French as in English, 'for *our* children'. Written from one brother to another they may well have meant, literally, 'for the children'. But why should Heinz have told Paul that he was sending fruit to 'the children' in the nursery at Boskenna. If the words 'les enfants' referred specifically to a second child, it could only have been to Sonya.

After the war when Sonya was old enough to ask her mother about her father – legally Olaf Poulsen, who had died during the war in Belgium – Betty was never able to give her daughter a clear account of the matter. For 35 years, until Betty died in 1980, Sonya continued to ask her mother the same question; once by way of reply Betty gave her a list of possible candidates, among the names on the list was that of Maurice Bowra. This may have been a joke. Mary said that Betty was 'the world's worst ever mother. She could have written a How Not to Do It book'. Frustrated by Betty's response, Sonya turned to Mary*, who said nothing while Betty was alive. Sonya died in 1998, after a long struggle against cancer. About two years earlier, Mary told her the story of Serge, the White Russian ski instructor, as recounted above, in Chapter Six. Sonya accepted this, and it may be correct, but there several aspects that, on closer consideration, do not ring true.

In the first place, if Sonya's father was a White Russian refugee, the fact that he fought with the Germans against the Red Army does not seem sufficient reason for hiding his identity. Nor does it explain why, when the war ended and Sonya was aged five, she was never introduced to the parents of Serge, her putative grandparents, who were living in Paris. Betty was always looking for somewhere to dump Sonya; grandparents would have been very useful, if they were grandparents. On the other hand, they may have had no relationship to Sonya, because their son was not actually her father. He

---

* Mary always looked on Sonya as a daughter. In a note about an unwritten novel dating from the 1950s she linked four teenage characters to Roger, Toby, Bill, and Sonya.

was just the perfect alibi, having been in Paris when Betty, unable to get to Belgium, had been able to get to Paris, officially to meet her husband. Serge remained the perfect alibi because, missing believed killed, he was in no position to dispute the matter. By the time Sonya knew his name everyone she might have asked about him had died.

Mary told Sonya that Betty, having decided that she must see Serge, a ski instructor she had met in Megève two years earlier, was determined to get a visa to travel to Paris in time of war. She made such a fuss so persistently in the Passport Office that Mary, working in the office of MI5 on the floor above, heard her 'unmistakeable voice', intervened and got her a visa. Betty returned from Paris to find that she was pregnant. This cannot be entirely correct, for – as Mary Watkins recalls – there was no staircase between MI5 and the Passport Office. There were separate entrances and to reach Mary's office you had to pass an armed guard and take a lift.

A more plausible version of those events would be that in February, 1940, when Mary was already in love with Heinz, Betty was on the loose in wartime London; at that point, with a string of admirers stretching all the way from Paul Ziegler to Maurice Bowra, Betty became pregnant. With her husband still in Belgium, living just behind the BEF's front line, and with travel to allied countries awaiting German attack all but impossible, Betty either had to have an abortion or find some means of regularising her pregnancy. She had no principled objection to abortion, she had one later during the war, but on this occasion she decided to keep the baby, probably because she had some hopes of eventually marrying the doubtless wealthy man she had selected as the child's eventual father. Meanwhile, one month pregnant, she needed to get to Paris so that she could pretend to have met her Belgian husband and so avoid a West Cornish scandal. Olaf Poulsen was a busted flush, no money as she had already discovered, and they were newly separated. But he would do, to keep up appearances and to give her child a legitimate identity, until the war was over and she could arrange a divorce. When she returned from Paris she could announce her pregnancy, and this is what she did. Mary was probably in on the secret from the start. Betty knew that Mary had some hush-hush job and so asked her friend to use her connections to arrange the visa. This seems far less improbable than the story of 'overhearing Betty's voice on the floor above' the Passport Office, as does the idea of Betty – who was obsessed as ever with money – deciding to bear the unplanned child of a penniless ex-ski instructor turned night club bouncer.

But, if Betty was pregnant before she went to Paris, why did she refuse to tell Sonya the truth about her father, and why did Mary produce the story of Serge? The most likely explanation is that Sonya's real father survived the war, but was unable to marry Betty.

In the 1970's, 30 years after he had entered the monastery and 10 years before he died, Father Paul Ziegler started to write a personal *apologia*. He wrote briefly about his happy childhood with his parents in Loyovitz, which he did not name, and of his decision to leave a country where he would 'always be in a minority'. He wrote of his love of England, its culture, history and character, his enduring love of women, his life of prayer, and his attempt to make sense of all this in one lifetime. He never mentioned how his parents had died, or that his father had been Jewish, or anything of his close friendship with Sigmund Warburg, or of how his brother had died. The importance of these omissions suggests that from the time he heard of Heinz's death – that news coming so soon after his father's death, when he was still uncertain of his mother's fate – Paul Ziegler was in a state of shock that lasted in some deep part of him for the rest of his life.

Before the war, Paul had been in love with Betty. He was supposed to marry a Warburg, but he embraced the doctrines of the Trinity, the Incarnation, the Virgin Birth and the Resurrection instead. As his friend Sigmund Warburg said, 'he swallowed the whole bag of tricks'. Paul's career as a monk was unorthodox, even unruly. Although a deeply spiritual man he wrestled with the limits imposed by his vocation and wrote of 'the failure' of his life of prayer. He never 'strangled Eros', and he approached mysticism as a continuation of the same intuition that led to a love of both women and God.* When Mary told Toby about Heinz she wrote to Paul and he replied on January 19th, 1961. In this letter he does not mention Toby at all.

"Mary dear, You say that we grow old. *Cherie*, I am. But I rather love it. The faith does give me the promised one hundredfold on earth already. The wonders of life and love change but retain their glory and freshness, quite undisturbed by all one's (disappointments)....Why should this happen to me? . . . For I am a sinful man. As if the Lord hadn't known that all the time. But it is so overwhelmingly wonderful – just think of it: to be able to please God by simply being in love with love . . . Bless you, Paul."

* In the 1950s, he was given permission to leave the monastery and live in a hermitage near Rome. Paul was not a hermit for long. He said that the Italian hermits were far too gregarious and received large family parties bearing food parcels at the weekend.

After Toby had been told about Heinz he started to visit Father Paul regularly and when *The Camomile Lawn* was published, he took a copy of his mother's book to Quarr Abbey. Father Ziegler was furious; he read it overnight and returned the book to Toby in the morning saying that he could not possibly put it in the monastery library. He was worried that the Abbot would notice that one of the characters was based on him. Father Ziegler did not identify the character in question, but Max Erstweiler, the agile Austrian Jewish violinist who took advantage of the Blitz to score a full house (Calypso, Polly, Sophy and their Aunt Helena – to say nothing of his true love, Monika Erstweiler, his devoted wife), may have rung a few ex-cloistral bells.

When Paul Ziegler died in January, 1986, Mary refused to go to his funeral, but Toby went. So many women turned up on the night before he died that he had to be carried out of the infirmary and put into a room in the guest house, so that they could say goodbye to him in turn. One of these women, the wife of Karl Schmidt, a director of Warburg's, looked at Toby and said, 'Was he your father?' And Toby replied, 'I'm not sure.'

None of the events in Mary's life really explains her repeated pre-occupation with incest and dual lovers. But somewhere in the story of her complex relationship with the Ziegler brothers and her friendship with Betty Paynter and her fascination with Boskenna, there may be a link to the most important of her fictional themes, the conflict between ambiguity and identity. Illegitimacy is at the heart of this conflict; it was a state that she found both empowering and intriguing. It is sometimes treated playfully, as in *Not That Sort of Girl*, where it is half-heartedly denied. In *Second Fiddle* it becomes a threat. In *A Sensible Life* the probable illegitimacy of the heroine, Flora Trevelyan, troubles her conventional father, whose conventional wife has enjoyed an undisclosed adventure. In Mary's most baroque novel *A Dubious Legacy* there is a fiesta of illegitimacy that turns into a comfort and a triumph. And in her darkest last novel, *Part of the Furniture,* illegitimacy, following a rape, becomes the occasion of a savage revenge.

Mary's family were not on the whole enthusiastic about her books. After the publication of *The Camomile Lawn* she received a long letter from Eric's nephew, John Waterfield, reminiscing about the war.

I remember calling on Patience —— when I came back in October '45. She was the wife of an Etonian regular soldier, fellow officer of mine in the 1st Battalion . . . and heir to —— in Norfolk . . . He was attractive and in the end adequate at fighting, and very clever and professional, he was fundamentally a crook, a real crook. Anyway in 1940 Patience had thrown her infant at me to make me embarrassed (at 19) and then taken a photo of me holding it. She was attractive but wild. When I called on her (her husband still in Italy) she showed little interest in him or me and gave me gin. She then asked, 'How many people have you been to bed with since I saw you last? I have been to bed, I think, with 100 different men.' I was horrified . . . She ended up in gaol having robbed her sister of her jewels in her large house in K——. Perhaps if Calypso hadn't had Hector she would have become like that?

This barbed anecdote (Waterfield identified Mary with Calypso) may have been a delayed response to the 'Sir Piers' joke in her first novel.

Mary's brother Hugh was more direct; he asked her how she could write such 'filth' and pretended to have noticed only one of her books. Susan, with whom she was no longer on speaking terms, strongly objected to *The Camomile Lawn*, claiming that the elderly couple, the Cuthbertsons – he a wounded soldier, she an impoverished wife – were based on their parents* and refusing to read any more of Mary Wesley's books. On Christmas Eve 1985, Susan dropped dead. A sudden death had always been the one Mary had wanted for herself and she seems to have regarded even Susan's death as a final affront, or act of theft. Mary's laconic diary entry for that day read 'Buttercup *and* Susan died'. Buttercup Wellesley was the elderly and distant cousin who had dropped dead a few hours before Susan.

Mary did not attend her sister's funeral but she went to the memorial service two months later. This was the first major rite of passage Mary had attended since Roger's wedding, and she made the most of it. Summoning her daughter-in-law, Isobel, to her side she said: 'Dress up, darling. Mink and black stockings.' Mary chose a wide-brimmed black hat with a black veil, and they were placed in a pew of their own. Leaving the church in East Knoyle after the service, Mary pronounced a cryptic valediction: 'I feel so sorry for poor Susan. She never knew the joys of *soixante-neuf*.'

---

* Mary herself identified the grandparents in *Harnessing Peacocks*, who persecute the pregnant Hebe, as the nearest she came to a portrait of her own parents in old age.

When Susan died, Mary had just finished *The Vacillations of Poppy Carew*, where the plot follows the fortunes of a 'fun' funeral parlour, and this was published a few months after Susan's memorial service. From then on the focus of Mary Wesley's work shifted and the tone hardened. With Susan's disappearance the last inhibition was gone; there was only Scammell.

There is no character in Mary Wesley's fiction who could be identified as a portrait of her tormentor, Stephen Scammell. But in *Not That Sort of Girl*, the first novel Wesley worked on following Susan's death, the plot turned on a set-piece occasion, a wedding, and she introduced a repulsive man called Nicholas Thornby. 'Nicholas Thornby peered needle-eyed into the delicatessen' are the first words of Chapter One. Thornby is living with his twin sister and they are, as it later emerges, more or less married. He spies on the heroine, Rose, and uses his long acquaintanceship to enter the bathroom while she is in the bath. Rose is a more developed version of the girls in *The Camomile Lawn*; she lives through the war as the chatelaine of a ramshackle country house with the inspired name of 'Slepe' where she is visited by her lover. Boskenna, the everlasting house, is the inspiration for Slepe. Rose's happiness is threatened throughout by the malicious curiosity and insufferable bossiness of the Thornbys, the infernal twins. It is when Rose defeats their curiosity that she achieves happiness.

In the next book, *Second Fiddle*, the Thornby twins – brother Nicholas and sister Emily – are back. This time we see them through the eyes of Emily's illegitimate daughter, almost certainly *their* daughter, Laura. Laura is a sympathetic, solitary character, doomed by her appalling parents to unhappiness but showing courage and great independence of habit to survive. The book ends with Nicholas Thornby convicted of a paternal rape. So much for Thornby – he does not appear again. He was no longer needed. As Mary Wesley's fame and wealth increased, every new title was an imaginary pirouette on Scammell's front lawn.

Stephen Scammell died in January 2002, mourned by his stepchildren, Susan's children, though not by their Aunt Mary. A month earlier Mary had suffered 'a night of nightmares, the kind which linger and nag. I realised they were to do with Stephen Scammell. Hatred and resentment is debilitating so I set about trying to remember something <u>nice</u> about him and at once a memory came into my mind of him planting fritillaries in Susan's orchard in the hope that they would . . . spread. This did the trick.' But the forgiving mood did not last. In a subsequent letter she referred to his 'death which we are celebrating this week' and she said that she would not be going to 'Stephen's party' (memorial service) as it would have felt too much like dancing on the grave. 'I hope he has met his match in the afterlife,' she wrote to a friend 'and being sorted out when I get there, which can't be very long now, I look forward to finding out . . .'

EPILOGUE

Night and Day

'As the years go by the truth becomes more and more agitated . . . the guns must be manned night and day . . .'
Diana Petre, *The Secret Orchard of Roger Ackerley*

Almost everyone who remembered Mary Siepmann agreed on one thing; she lived her life in separate compartments. In love and friendship she was happiest with one-to-one relationships, and when she loved her love grew from a response to the distinct, separate personality that confronted her own. She had three sons but in the last twenty-five years of her life she never invited them to her house at the same time. Her sons, with three different fathers, also had three different mothers – since she could be a different person to each when she saw each alone; and she never shared a child with its father. Neither Toby nor Sonya – her 'adopted' daughter – knew his or her father; Roger cannot remember seeing his father and mother together once, though they continued to see each other in a friendly way after their divorce for many years. And Bill – who grew up with both his parents – recalls that when he was alone with Mary and Eric they frequently spoke to each other in French, a language he did not understand; the children of lovers, in R. L. Stevenson's phrase, 'are orphans'. Her granddaughter Katherine, who probably spent more time with Mary in her last years than any other family member, was sometimes summarily dismissed from the room if a friend turned up unexpectedly. As she grew older Mary tried to dismantle some of these compartments, but the habit was too strong for her and even as one partition was taken down another would spring up.

She had developed her talent for dissimulation early, for practical reasons, to protect herself from her parents' interference and to enable her to spend time with Peter Hope and John Montagu-Pollock. Her father had once warned her against going anywhere near Waterloo Station, not knowing that she was working at the time in a soup kitchen under the Waterloo arches. With the conception of her second child this habit of secrecy became instinctive and with it came a growing sense of ambiguity. As time passed the skills that were essential for wartime afternoons in the Ritz could be refined and deployed with almost everyone she knew. Her gulls included her husband Carol and all her lovers with the exception of Eric. She was loyal in friendship, particularly towards the friends she found late in life – but they were still kept apart. She said of some of the first of her last friends, 'They are *friends* but we've never been intimate. Neither of them really know me. They know nothing about my life.' If you live your life in separate compartments you never have to defend a consistent personality, you can play different roles in different worlds and you never really confront the question with which Mary Siepmann opened her last attempt at autobiography – 'Who am I?'

In her own account of her life, in conversation and in writing, Mary was both consistent and partial. If the account changed it was always because she added something to it, never because she contradicted something she had said before. Where it was possible to check her story the documents, letters, diaries or other records almost always confirmed it. She *was* more or less uneducated, she *was* both cleverer and more sensual than her 'incredibly bossy' sister, her family *had* cut her out of their wills in 1945, the Stalker – Phyllis Siepmann – *had* been a very frightening woman. Mary held very little back; but there were still unanswered questions. Why, in her newspaper interviews, did she show such public contempt for Carol Swinfen after he had died and she had become celebrated? Did she withhold her love from Roger, just as her own mother's love had been withheld from her, and so leave her oldest son walled up behind her aversion for his father? And why, when she was urged to write her autobiography, did she say, 'I can't. I'm too ashamed'?

Two months before Mary died her granddaughter Katherine walked into her bedroom and told her that Roger was downstairs.

Mary recalled the experience: 'Katherine said Roger desperately wanted to see me. It was such a shock to see him suddenly like that, after nearly 30 years. I took care not to say anything difficult. But it was such a terrible shock that I did something I've never done before. I sleepwalked and fell in the night and hit my head on a radiator . . .' That was Mary's account of her last meeting with her oldest son. At the same time she twice told one of her friends – who was also a friend of Katherine's – that she had been very pleased by Roger's visit.

There were by this time parallel accounts; a division in her view of her own life had opened up, the strain of manning the guns was beginning to tell. Before recounting the shock of Roger's last visit to me, Mary made a subconscious link between the legal case involving Roger and Toby, the fact that her sister was responsible for it, the memory of her mother once telling her that she had never wanted a third child but that if she had one she had wanted a boy, the way she herself had felt utterly alone when her grandmother died, the way her family had always tried to stop her doing what she wanted, the way her mother had brushed aside her grief when her first love died because she was preoccupied with Susan's wedding, the final result being that 'I led as secret a life from my parents as I possibly could'. She then talked of Susan's interest in owning everything and running everything in the village of East Knoyle, of the fact that Susan had always spoiled Roger, and of her memory of the time when she had travelled to see her mother before she died and knocked on the door to be greeted by Violet saying, 'God. I thought it was my darling Roger.'

Mary then returned to the case between Roger and Toby, and finally talked about Roger's visit. For her, there was nothing undirected about this chaotic succession of thoughts; these were not randomly remembered grievances, they were among the deepest wounds in her life, the connection between them was self-evident and it compensated her for the guilt she felt about her warring sons.

James Hale saw similarities in the lives of Mary Wesley and her godmother and friend Antonia White, in that both blamed their mothers for not loving them and became neglectful mothers in their turn. But the similarities did not end there. Both said they were frightened of their mothers, both found comfort in the unconditional love of their grandmothers, both lived adventurous, liberated lives, both married more than once; Antonia White had a destructive affair with her lover's younger brother, Mary Siepmann loved both Paul and Heinz Ziegler; both women suffered from low self-esteem when young, Antonia White had a nervous breakdown, Mary Siepmann considered suicide; both were strongly attracted to a self-destructive man, Eric Siepmann; and for two such perceptive women both at times showed a surprisingly limited degree of self-knowledge. But Mary did achieve self-knowledge towards the end of her life. In contrast with the defiant note of *The Fruits of My Follies*, the second draft, *Who am I?* was written in a more self-critical spirit. 'Now, looking forward to Death,' she wrote in the latter, 'I look back on my unpreparedness for Life and marvel that I did not make an even greater mess than I have.' But even here she blamed her parents.

Faced with this insoluble problem, of feeling guilty but not feeling responsible, she retreated behind the ramparts of ambiguity, the ambiguity of separate friendships and successive personalities, the same ambiguity that she recreated time and again in her books. The elusiveness of Laura Thornby (*Second Fiddle*) or Hebe (*Harnessing Peacocks*), fleeing from their admirers, the secret life of Poppy Carew's gigolo father, the long double life of Rose Peel (*Not That Sort of Girl*) – forty years a mistress – the uneasy suspicions of Flora Trevelyan's putative father (*A Sensible Life*), all echoed arrangements Mary had made or observed in her own life up to the end of the war. The critical point was not reached on the day she met Eric in 1944 but on the day he died in 1970. By then she had learned to trust, she had lived in loyalty, she had acquired enough courage to break down the strongest partition of all. She could attempt to become the central anchor of a united family. And so, 'trying to get close', she told Roger about his brother and made her biggest mistake. When the storm broke she realised that ambiguity would serve her once again. In her affidavit Heinz Ziegler remained her lover and died fighting with the RAF, but he died childless. She was, after all, uniquely well placed to know.

In the last ten years of her life Mary became a friend of Sister Wendy Beckett, the Catholic nun, author and art historian, whom she accompanied on research trips to such places as Rome. After her first meeting with Mary Siepmann Sister Wendy said, 'I've always wanted to meet one, and now I have.' Meet what? 'A *femme fatale*.' Their friendship echoed an earlier group of Mary's Catholic friends, the friends of Stanbrook Abbey, Emily Holmes Colman, Phyllis Jones and Dame Felicity Corrigan. Wendy Beckett felt immediately at ease with Mary, they shared a relationship that embraced brandy and prayer. In July 1999, Sister Wendy wrote to her about the problems of forgiving one's enemies.

> . . . I've been thinking about anger, and how much quicker to anger I have become in my old age! And, struggling with my anger, trying to put it on the altar for God to transform, I thought of what you'd said to me in Rome about the difficulty of forgiveness . . . Jesus . . . on the cross did *not* say 'I forgive' but 'Father forgive them'. Isn't it always *God*

who forgives, not we, and isn't our response meant to be that we align ourselves with God's response? He forgives, and . . . we affirm this. And he forgives not what was done – which remains hateful – but the one who did it . . . These insights have clarified my intransigence to me, Mary, and enabled me to give my hardness of heart to God without anxiety – so I pass them on, in case . . .

But though Mary could never find it in her heart to forgive either her sister or her brother-in-law she did agree to see her oldest son. She could not forgive his actions – she cut him out of her will – but she was able eventually to tell him that she had always loved him. Part of her rage against Susan and Scammell, even after the case against Toby was defeated, was that the victory of one son could never be her victory, since it involved the defeat of the other. The destruction of Roger Swinfen's relationship with his mother was the main fruit of Stephen Scammell's activities on his nephew's behalf.

In April 1949 Mary and Eric had seen Laurence Olivier's production of Anouilh's *Antigone* at the New Theatre, with Vivien Leigh in the title role. According to the legend, when the twin brothers Eteocles and Polynices fought and killed each other in single combat because the first would not share the throne with the second, their uncle Creon inherited the kingdom of Thebes from Eteocles, his protégé. Creon ordered the citizens to leave the body of Polynices unburied on pain of death, and Antigone, sister to the twins, died for defying this order and protecting her brother from shame. In the case of the Swinfen Trustees, which bears no small resemblance to the plot of *Antigone*, Mary Siepmann risked execution (cross-examination on a dubious affidavit) to help her son; but in an unexpected twist Uncle Creon (Scammell) did not inherit Thebes ('the peerage fund') but was banished to the edge of the stage, where he had to roll his eyes and pluck his beard in impotent rage.

Unfortunately, that did not mean that Antigone lived happily ever after. Mary felt a heavy responsibility for 'the mess I made' and on the occasion of her eightieth birthday in a letter to Toby she wrote, 'I have been a selfish and bad mother in so many ways . . .' Seven years later, in another letter to Toby she wrote: 'I often wonder when I die which of the two, Eric or Heinz, will be there to meet me, help me across? Eric was never jealous of Heinz, he respected our love. I behaved very badly to Heinz and he very well to me though when he was killed we were close. I have, too, failed you as a mother. I am *always aware of that*. That I left Carol, putting my need to escape before your needs and Roger's was terribly selfish and inexcusable so I apologise now just in case I have a stroke and cannot speak.' She often wondered about death and was sometimes comforted by thoughts of heaven; in the last year of her life she 'dreamed vividly of Pebble and True [two favourite dogs] leaping beside my bed and woke so pleased. I have always hoped the pack will be waiting, cats too.' She had been saying her goodbyes for some time. One friend, Caromy Hoare, received a letter in March thanking her and her husband, Henry 'for all the friendship and kindnesses you give and have given over the years to my child.' This followed Toby's remarriage – he and Isobel were divorced in 2002 – to the writer Xinran. Mary recorded her delight at 'this wonderful addition to our lives'. She was in good health until the last three months of her life; then, as she grew weaker, she became reluctant, in conversation, to break new ground and she stopped eating, hoping to hurry things along. Although still a Catholic, she declined to see a priest, saying that she had 'another priest'.

She had certainly made her confession, including the matter which had always troubled her the most, the matter that went back to the night before Eric's death. She recalled that night again, one month before she died.

After I met Eric I never looked at anybody else again. We lived tremendous ups and downs but life was never boring. He was wonderful to the children. One moment he was in a very important job and the next we had nothing. I remember the brutality with which the doctor told him about having Parkinson's. So, Eric being Eric, went home and read all about it. He wrote to his sister and said, 'I'm not going to let Mary go through this.' He said to me, 'When the time comes I'm going to kill myself.' He said, 'Promise not to stop me.' He made me promise. And he did kill himself.

That day he looked so ill. He'd got so that it was an effort to walk. And he couldn't concentrate when he read and he said, 'I can't finish a sentence when I write.' I was going to get Bill and I said, 'I'm never going to leave you again.' It was a very stupid thing to say. When I got back the cat dishes were full and he was upstairs asleep. There were two notes on the table. The one addressed to Bill contained a £10 note and it read, 'Buy your mother a shawl.' *I lay awake all night not knowing what to do.* In the morning Bill said, 'He's breathing strangely.' I said, 'No, he's not.' The roads were icy, I took Bill to school. When I got back he was still asleep. My nerve gave, I called the doctor and sent for an ambulance. The ambulance could not get down the lane outside the cottage.

They had to carry the stretcher up on the back of a tractor. He never regained consciousness. He couldn't have borne not being able to read or write. He was always trying to write and bubbling with ideas. He was never one to make it come to anything much. From his point of view he was doing the right thing.

The events of that night left Mary with a burden of guilt that required reassurance thirty-two years later. Leaving her husband to die took all the courage and devotion she had, and even then her nerve finally failed. It was following that night that in her anguish she revealed Toby's identity to Roger and so enabled her brother-in-law in due course to meddle in her affairs. It was her consequent anger at this betrayal of trust that provided the energy that drove her writing.

Mary Siepmann died of cancer 'in her own bed' on 30 December 2002 at 8.30 in the morning. She had become impatient with the process for some time but remained cheerful when friends rang to enquire. She had made a joke of death in *Jumping the Queue* and in *The Vacillations of Poppy Carew*, and her own death was accompanied by jokes. Julia Blackburn was told, 'I'm not eating anything any more but I'm drinking warm water. It's absolutely delicious.' When Sarah Miles called to ask if there was anything she could do Mary said, 'Yes. Go down to your shrine in the garden [where Robert Bolt is buried] and pray that it happens today and that I pass safely through. Any messages?' She was cared for at first by her granddaughter Katherine, then at the end by her sons Bill and Toby, and by Toby's wife the writer Xinran. She told Xinran that she expected to die on Christmas Day and she held in her hands on that day an icon of Christ the Healer that Sister Wendy had given her. But the following morning she was still alive. When Janet Day came round to tidy her room Mary said, 'Mrs Day. Why is it taking me so long to die?'

'Because you're not top of the Good Lord's list yet, dear,' Janet Day replied. 'He's still trying to figure out what He's going to do with you.'

And Mary's last words to Mrs Day were 'Oh, bugger'.

Survivors, and others

Roger Eady, 3rd Baron Swinfen, started a charity that provides advanced medical treatment in the Third World. He sits in the House of Lords as one of the ninety-two remaining hereditary peers.

Toby Eady founded the literary agency Toby Eady Associates. He has four stepchildren and continues to look after Averil Swinfen, the widow of his stepfather Carol Swinfen.

Bill Siepmann remained close to Alice Grenfell until her death in 2005 at the age of 101.

———————————

Tessa Sayle died in 1993. Her agency continues under the direction of Rachel Calder.

James Hale died in 2003. He was the first person I went to see after meeting Mary.

Author's Note

This book was written at Mary Siepmann's invitation, as an authorised biography. When I first met her, she said that I could write what I wished but it must not be published before her death. In the event she died nine months later, aged ninety. She told me that I would have to rely on her memory as she had always destroyed all her papers, except for a few professional records that she had sent to 'Comrade Gotlieb'* at Boston University. She did not think it would be worth going to Boston to read through those. She agreed it was a pity that she had kept no diaries and no letters and explained that she had been obliged to destroy them because her second husband had been a jealous man. Then, just as I was leaving the house at the end of my first visit, she handed me a large carrier bag containing two shoeboxes and a battered green ring file. On arriving home I found that these contained a correspondence she had kept up with Eric Siepmann, starting on the day after their first meeting in 1944 and continuing until 1968, which was shortly before his death. Both shoeboxes were marked size 5. The newer one carried a price tag of £300, the other – dated 1973 – was priced at £4.50.

Almost the first thing Mary talked about was the death of her husband, Eric Siepmann, an extraordinary act of faith. When she chose to speak, she held nothing back, but there were other areas of her life about which she grew slightly impatient if they were raised a second time. She was evasive about MI5, and only mildly impressed when after her rather muddled recollections of a drunken wartime evening with an SOE agent, Raymond Lee, I was able to dig out the full story (and the name) of the Austrian *gestapiste*, Alfred Kraus. She was less impressed when she

---

* The late Dr Howard Gotlieb, legendary director of the university's Mugar Memorial Library.

suggested a drive on the moor one sunny spring morning and I enquired what all those yellow flowers were. 'Do you mean the gorse?' she asked. 'Yes.' The timing and emphasis of her response, 'Not a *country* boy then', were to professional standards.

Over the course of that summer we met and talked about thirty times. While she remained in good health and high spirits, she was in charge: watchful, mischievous and blunt. But it became clear that – behind the story she was happy to repeat – there were other stories that she simply refused to discuss. Unwilling to press her, I began to feel a bit like the Matricide in *Jumping the Queue*. One night, unable to sleep, I looked through the bookcase in the spare bedroom and found a copy of Diana Petre's *The Secret Orchard of Roger Ackerley* which Mary had read in 1974 and kept, unusually, because she kept few of the books she read after Eric died. Sometime early in the morning, perhaps around the time of Mary's beloved dawn chorus, the insomniac's friend, I reached the lines that became the epigram for this book.

After Mary's death, I went to Boston and was surprised to find that the 'few professional records' ran to seven sturdy archive boxes that took ten days to work through. The last item in Box No. 7 was listed as *Personal Memorabilia, Shopping Bag marked N. Peal*. She had used it to pack up some of the papers. It turned out to be a shiny, red, cardboard carrier bag with white cord strings marked 'N. Peal Cashmere of the Burlington Arcade' – a symbol of the transformation that had overtaken her life after thirty years of grinding poverty – and perhaps a posthumous 'bat squeak of contempt' for her biographer.

On returning to England, I was given access to the contents of her desk, which included family correspondence from her childhood, some love letters, her engagement diaries over a period of nearly sixty years, her second husband's diary and notebooks and the official records of two traumatic court cases, as well as other personal papers of great importance. All these, which she could easily have destroyed, she had chosen to show me, but after her death, as if, not wishing to talk about them but wanting me to have some confirmation of what she had said. The posthumous material also contained clues about the life she had refused to enlarge on: details of her family history, of the turbulent side of her second marriage, and of the depths of her despair after her second husband's death. She knew that I would eventually be presented with contradictory versions of her life, and she wanted her side of the story to be clearly set out.

An authorised biography raises questions of trust, but if the arrangement works well the biographer can hope to be both partisan and disinterested. In almost every instance where I looked for corroboration, I found it. No biographer could have asked for more freedom than I have been offered.

Patrick Marnham,
Oxfordshire,
April 2006

Acknowledgements

My thanks are due to the Estate of Mary Wesley for permission to quote from her private papers and correspondence and from her published works of fiction and non-fiction, and to the Estate of Eric Siepmann for permission to quote from his published and unpublished work and correspondence. I also gratefully acknowledge the help of Boston University, which granted me permission to read and quote from the Mary Wesley Collection in Special Collections at Boston University. I am grateful to the following for granting me the following permissions: To Rachel Calder, proprietor of The Sayle Literary Agency, who authorised me to quote from the agency's archives; to Averil, Lady Swinfen for the letters of Carol Swinfen; to Roger Swinfen for his letters as well as for the diaries and letters of Blanche, Lady Swinfen; to Edward Clive for the letters of Lewis Clive; to Kate Ganz for her correspondence; to Sarah Miles for the letters of Robert Bolt; to Julia Blackburn for her memoir of Mary Wesley; to the Estate of Antonia White for her letters and diaries; to Sister Wendy Beckett for her correspondence; to Sarah Orme for her letters; to Francis Farmar for the letters and memoirs of Colonel H.M. Farmar and the letters and published works of Hugh Farmar; to Sally Webster for the letters of Susan Scammell; to Faber & Faber for the lines by T.S. Eliot.

My grateful thanks are also due to the following for the assistance they generously gave me in interviews and letters, in many cases repeatedly. Among family members, firstly Toby Eady, who is my agent as well as being among the principal characters in this story, and his brothers, Roger Swinfen and Bill Siepmann, for seeing me when I asked and for answering all my questions about their sometimes problematic relationship with their mother. Also to Katherine Davies, Pat Swinfen, Venice Molivadas, Averil Swinfen, Xinran Eady, Sally Webster, Francis Farmar, Valerie and Roy Redgrave, Roger Bankes-Jones, Isobel MacLeod, George Menzies and Henry Ziegler.

Among those who knew Mary Siepmann personally, Venice Molivadas in Washington, Averil Swinfen in Ireland, Sarah and the late Charles Orme in Devon and Pat Morris in Cornwall, were kind enough both to guide my research and have me to stay. I am also particularly grateful to the following for their invaluable help: the late James Hale, Sister Wendy Beckett, Rachel Calder, the late Janet Day, David Freeman, Kate Ganz and the late Alice Grenfell.

I would also like to thank the Abbess of Syon Abbey, Father Gabriel Arnold, the late Mark Barty-King, Julia Blackburn, Roddy Bloomfield, Peter Buckman, Nuala Butt, Edward Clive, Pam Dorman, Richard Dorment, Jane Dunn, Kay Fitzherbert, Adrian Gale, the late Howard Gotlieb, Hilary Hale, Sister Chiara Hatton Hall, Pat Hancock, Rachel Harding, Pam Hatherley, Nicky Henderson, Charley Hurt, Kate Jones, Patrick Leigh Fermor, Wylmay Le Grice, James Long, Lindsay Masters, Sarah Miles, Jenifer Murray, Kate Parkin, Joe Reevy, Margaret Ricketts, Georgie Rowse, David and Sara Salmon, Paul Scherer, Nicholas Shakespeare, Nicky Strauss, Jilly Sutton, Elizabeth Taylor, Barbara Trapido, Anthea Tuckey, Judy Turner, Malcolm and Peggy Upham, Mary Watkins, Jean West, and Paul Williams.

Several people were kind enough to read the manuscript including Simon King, Jessica Woollard, Polly Coles, Laetitia Rutherford and William Fisher. Dan Frank in New York made a number of thoughtful suggestions and Diane Gallagher in Boston made my work in the Mugar Memorial Library even more of a pleasure. I would like to acknowledge, once again, the professionalism of Mildred Marney of Rowan Script.

At my publishers, I am particularly grateful for the timely intervention of Gail Rebuck and Alison Samuel, to David Parrish, and to my editor Penelope Hoare for her tactful advice and exemplary patience. I alone remain entirely responsible for any errors or other failings that this account may contain.

Source Notes

Mary Wesley lived a conventional childhood and first marriage, a turbulent war, a passionate second marriage and a late period of fame. Her life therefore falls neatly into four chronological periods, each presenting different problems for a biographer. My research started with the conversations that took place between March and November 2002, usually at her house in Totnes. On those occasions, she confirmed the broad outlines of the account on which she had insisted in interviews published over the previous twenty years, but she amplified it and revealed a story that she had previously hidden.

After her death in December 2002, I began to look for independent or documentary confirmation of what she had said. Her personal papers included her library, inscribed and dated, the family photograph albums that started with her infancy and continued up to the time of her second husband's last illness, transcripts and other records of three High Court cases, and other miscellaneous family records, letters and personal papers. Her engagement diaries from 1944, and from 1947 to 2002, with one year missing, have survived. The long correspondence with her second husband (they were in the habit of writing if they were parted for more than a day) lasted from 1944 to 1968.

She left two unpublished memoirs. *The Fruits of My Folly* – which was conceived as a private family record but quickly became a project for publication – covers the years from 1912 to 1958. A later untitled attempt was started in 1997 in response to requests from her agent and various publishers that she should authorise a biography. She abandoned it two years before she died. It covers her life from 1912 to 1954 and I have called this, after its opening words, *Who Am I ?* I have used both these accounts for events which only they describe, reading them critically and supplementing the information (mainly missing names) where possible.

The only published biographical sources apart from newspaper interviews and television and radio broadcasts were an outstanding televised profile, 'Not That Sort of Girl', made by Alan Scales and Nigel Roberts in 1989, and one book, *Part of the Scenery* (2001), with photographs by Kim Sayer, edited by Sally Gaminara. This is 'a celebration of life in the West Country' and a tribute to her long affection for some of the people and landscapes she knew, but as autobiography it conceals far more than it discloses. I have relied on the hundreds of additional media interviews for direct quotations only.

At the Special Collections archive, at Boston University, I was able to consult papers in the Mary Wesley Collection that included holographs and typescripts of her fiction and translations, both published and otherwise, and professional records and correspondence dating back to the 1940s. There were also letters from Bill Armstrong, Geoffrey Bailey, Beryl Bainbridge, Hugh Bannerman, Sister Wendy Beckett, Peter Benson, Thora Bernstorff, Julia Blackburn, Robert Bolt, John Bowen, Camilla Parker Bowles, Joan Brady, Carmen Callil, Dorothy Carrington, Jung Chang, Emily Holmes Coleman, John Coleman, Gwenda David, Katherine Davies, Jane Dunn, Toby Eady, Maggie Ferguson, Valerie Forman, Margaret Forster, Adrian Gale, Audrey Gale, Kate Ganz, Martha Gellhorn, Wylmay Le Grice, James Hale, Peter Hall, Pat Hancock, Sheila Hancock, Rachel Harding, Lyndall Passerini Hopkinson, Tim Jeal, James Clellan Jones, Verdell Kelvey, James MacGibbon, Sonya Menzies, Venice Molivadas, Mavis Nicholson, Sarah Orme, Dennis Peck, Christine Pevitt, Rosamunde Pilcher, the Prince of Wales, Valerie Redgrave, Tessa Sayle, Paul Scherer, Nicholas Shakespeare, Anthony Steen, Barbara Trapido, Noel Virtue, John Waterfield, Antonia White, Andrew Wilson, Susannah York and Sasha Young.

Sources used in each part of the book:

PART I: 1912 TO 1939

Unpublished family records and reference books show that the picaresque story of the Farmars is far more interesting than Mary publicly conceded. I have consulted *Some Notes and Experiences of Harold Mynors Farmar*, as well as the Dalby family story compiled by David Dalby, *The Girardot Family* by Michael Bray, the diaries of Blanche, Lady Swinfen and legal papers relating to the setting up of the Swinfen Trust.

Mary's neglected childhood, her escapades in India and several of her close relationships are confirmed by surviving documents, including letters from Harold Mynors Farmar, Hyacinthe Dalby, John Montagu-Pollock and Lewis Clive. There are also letters of or about this period from Michael Carver, Violet Farmar, Susan Farmar, Hugh Farmar, Cynthia Hurt and Roger Mynors.

Interviews and correspondence: Rachel Harding, Alice Grenfell and Venice Molivadas knew Mary in the 1930s. I also consulted Valerie Redgrave, Toby Eady, Katherine Davies, Roger Swinfen, Pat Morris, Francis Farmar and Sally Webster.

Select bibliography: *A Regency Elopement* by Hugh Farmar, *The Elder Brother* by Iris Butler, *The Young Melbourne* by David Cecil, *Letters of a Victorian Army Officer: Edward Wellesley 1840-1854* by Michael Carver, *A History of the Regiments and Uniforms of the British Army* by R.M. Barnes, *Kitchener* by Philip Magnus, *Farewell the Trumpets* by James Morris, *Gallipoli* by Alan Moorehead, *John Monash* by Geoffrey Serle, *Figure of Eight* by Patricia Cockburn, *Muck, Silk and Socialism* by John Platts-Mills, *Boskenna and the Paynters* by Jim Hosking, *Confessions of a Cornishman* by Claud Morris. *Dictionary of National Biography*, *Who's Who*, *Burke's Peerage*, *Burke's Landed Gentry*.

PART II: 1939 TO 1945

Relatively few records of her chaotic personal life during the wartime period survive. There is an account of the Ziegler family's background and values in an unpublished fragment, *The Adventure of Peace* by Paul Ziegler. The most important unpublished written sources are the correspondence between Heinz and Paul Ziegler in 1943 and 1944, and Mary's engagement diary for 1944.

There are also letters from Simon Harcourt-Smith, Jan Masaryk, John Montagu-Pollock, Blanche, Lady Swinfen, Hugh Farmar and Sir Walter Monckton, as well as communications from the wartime Ministry of Information and from the Brigadier Commanding the Plymouth Division, Royal Marines. The childhood diary of Venice Molivadas, the diary of Blanche, Lady Swinfen, and the papers of Carol Swinfen, including a transcript of the Swinfen divorce hearing, were also consulted as were the squadron records of RAF 104 Squadron Association.

Interviews and correspondence: Alice Grenfell, Wylmay Le Grice, Pat Hancock, Venice Molivadas, Margaret Ricketts, Mary Watkins, Sally Webster, Toby Eady, Nicky Strauss and Roger Swinfen remembered Mary during the war. I also consulted Roger Bankes-Jones, Nuala Butt, Philip

Dawson, Patrick Leigh Fermor, Kay Fitzherbert, Pat Morris, Jenifer Murray, Valerie Redgrave, Barbara Trapido and Henry Ziegler.

Select bibliography: *A Time of Gifts* by Patrick Leigh Fermor, *The Masaryk I Knew* by R.H. Bruce Lockhart, *The Life of Graham Greene: Vol. III* by Norman Sherry, *The Dons* by Noel Annan, *The Cornishman*, *Les Memoires du Colonel Passy*, *The Knox Brothers* by Penelope Fitzgerald, *Intelligence in War* by John Keegan, *Wartime Britain* by Juliet Gardiner, *Journey of No Return* by Richard Dove, *Diaries of the War Years* by Joan Wyndham, *Tears Before Bedtime* by Barbara Skelton, *What Did You Do in the War, Mummy?* ed. Mavis Nicholson.

PART III: 1945 TO 1970

There are many more written records for this period. The most important are the surviving diaries of Mary Siepmann, which start in 1947 and continue up to a week before her death in December 2002, and the correspondence with Eric Siepmann. Other unpublished documents consulted include transcripts of the divorce proceedings of Swinfen versus Swinfen (1945) and Siepmann versus Siepmann (1952). The manuscripts of poems, short stories and translations by Mary Wesley are in Special Collections of Boston University, and among the papers of Eric Siepmann there were notes or manuscripts of stories, essays, poems and other writing projects, as well as notebooks and diaries. Among Mary's papers was a file containing correspondence and press cuttings about the case of Godfrey Butcher. Also consulted: Westminster Diocesan Archives (1956), an account of the Siepmann family history compiled by Gisela Siepmann in 1936, *The Girardot Family* by Michael Bray, *The Cliftonian* and *A Roll and Record for Old Wykehamists* (1967).

There are letters from Emily Holmes Coleman, Roger Eady, Toby Eady, Harold Mynors Farmar, Hugh Farmar, Violet Farmar, Emma Grant, Phyllis Jones, Prof. Verdell Kelvey, Robert Liddell, the Manager of Lloyd's Bank, Ashburton, Devon, Father Richard Mangan, Roger Mynors, Claud Morris, General Sir Bernard Paget, John Platts-Mills, John Montagu-Pollock, J.B. Priestley, Hilary Rubinstein, Susan Scammell, Dr Hjalmar Schacht, Bill Siepmann, Harry Siepmann, Janey Siepmann, Averil Swinfen, Carol Swinfen, Philip Toynbee and Antonia White.

Interviews and correspondence: Roger Bankes-Jones, Katherine Davies, Roger Eady, Toby Eady, Francis Farmar, Alice Grenfell, George Menzies, Venice Molivadas, Valerie Redgrave, Sally Webster and Henry Ziegler all knew Mary during this period. Pat Morris and Georgie Rowse were also consulted.

Select bibliography: *The Letters of Evelyn Waugh* ed. Mark Amory, *The*

Letters of Nancy Mitford and Evelyn Waugh ed. Charlotte Mosley (1996), *Old Men Forget* by Duff Cooper, Introduction by Carmen Callil and Mary Siepmann to Emily Holmes Coleman's *The Shutter of Snow*, *Confessions of a Nihilist* by Eric Siepmann, *The Establishment* ed. Hugh Thomas, *Journal* by Pierre Drieu de la Rochelle, *Now to My Mother* by Susan Chitty, *Antonia White* by Jane Dunn, *Nothing to Forgive* by Lyndall Passerini Hopkinson, *The Diaries of Duff Cooper* ed. John Julius Norwich.

PART IV: 1970 TO 2002

The most important unpublished written sources were the archives of the Sayle Literary Agency and the records of the Swinfen Trustees litigation, including the affidavit of Mary Wesley, the letters of Stephen Scammell and other professional papers relating to this case. There were letters from Carol Swinfen, and Mary's professional correspondence with Transworld Publishing Ltd.

There were also letters from Father Gabriel Arnold, John Betjeman, Julia Blackburn, Robert Bolt, Maurice Bowra, Peter Buckman, Emily Holmes Coleman, John Coleman, Bernard Cornwell, Katherine Davies, Jane Dunn, Toby Eady, Hugh Farmar, Kay Fitzherbert, Kate Ganz, James Hale, Caromy Hoare, Lyndall Passerini Hopkinson, Cynthia Hurt, Patrick Kinross, Angela Lambert, Jean MacGibbon, George Menzies, Sonya Menzies, Sarah Miles, Venice Molivadas, Claud Morris, Sarah Orme, Margaret Ricketts, Tessa Sayle, Stephen Scammell, Nicholas Shakespeare, Averil Swinfen, Clare Szöllösy, Philip Toynbee, Barbara Trapido, Timberlake Wertenbaker, Antonia White and Sasha Young.

Interviews and correspondence: Roger Bankes-Jones, Sister Wendy Beckett, Peter Buckman, Rachel Calder, Katherine Davies, Janet Day, Richard Dorment, Jane Dunn, Toby Eady, Xinran Eady, Francis Farmar, Kay Fitzherbert, David Freeman, Kate Ganz, James Hale, Hilary Hale, Pat Hancock, Rachel Harding, Pam Hatherley, Wylmay Le Grice, James Long, Isobel MacLeod, Sarah Miles, Venice Molivadas, Pat Morris, Joe Reevy, Margaret Ricketts, David and Sara Salmon, Bill Siepmann, Janey Siepmann, Nicky Strauss, Jilly Sutton, Averil Swinfen, Anthea Tuckey, Malcolm and Peggy Upham, Sally Webster and Jean West all knew Mary during this period. I also consulted Charley Hurt, Lindsay Masters, the Abbess of Syon and Paul Williams

Select bibliography: *The Diaries of Antonia White* ed. Susan Chitty, *Part of the Scenery* by Mary Wesley with photographs by Kim Sayer, *Writers Writing* eds. J. Brown and S. Munro.

Index

www.vintage-books.co.uk